Well-Being: The Artfully Lived Life

Donna R. Rogers, Ph.D.
Kim R. Rogers, Ph.D.

Publishers Note

It is the intention of these authors to provide accurate and authoritative information in regard to the subject of this workbook. The workbook is available for purchase with the understanding that neither the authors nor the publisher are engaged in offering psychological, legal, or any other type of professional services. If professional assistance or counseling is required, the services of a capable professional should be engaged.

Printed in the United States of America

Book Artwork by Jeanine Downing

Copyright © 2024 by Donna R. B. Rogers and Kim R. Rogers

All rights reserved.

Dedicated to

Harmony, Autumn-Rose, Christian, JennyKay, and Ginger.
Thank you for your inspiration, love, support,
and for the joy you bring to our lives.

Contents

Acknowledgments — 08

Foreword — 09

Introduction — 11

Chapter 1 - Getting Started — 21

Chapter 2 - Tools for Uncovering Inner Wellness — 37

Chapter 3 - Understanding Well-Being and Shaping a New MindView — 53

Chapter 4 - Where We Get Stuck and How We Move On — 63

Chapter 5 - Mapping My Journey — 81

Chapter 6 - Exploring Your Inner Artist: What is an Identity? — 105

Chapter 7 - Life Strategies and Enhancing Boundaries for the Brain and Body — 125

Chapter 8 - Life Strategies for Well-being ~ Emotional MindView Skills — 149

Chapter 9 - Life Strategies for Well-being ~ Thinking MindView Skills — 167

Chapter 10 - Life Strategies for Well-Being ~ Social MindView Skills — 185

Chapter 11 - Life Strategies for Well-being ~ Spiritual MindView Skills — 207

Chapter 12 - Understanding the Journey toward Resilience and Healing — 223

Chapter 13 - Cultivating Inner Well-Being and Equanimity — 241

References — 258

Journal Pages — 262

About the Authors — 268

About the Author of Foreword — 269

About the Artist — 270

Acknowledgments

We would like to acknowledge the many authors, researchers, and educators who have contributed to and influenced the approach to wellness we share in this workbook series. We thank our colleagues and the students who have contributed to the research that forms its basis and demonstrates the efficacy of the Guided Meditation process. These talented professionals include Dr. Sue Ei, Dr. Nicole Cavenaugh, Dr. Nikki Weber, Dr. Coby Lyons, the late Dr. Mary Roehrig, Dr. Ines Acevedo, Dr. Chad Cross, Dr. Katherine Hertlein, Dr. Maya McNeilly, Laurina Uribe, and Michelle Tackabery.

We extend our greatest appreciation to Mr. Dorian Bowen, the owner of Biopulsonics. Our research, clinical techniques, and applications have been inspired by his inventive work. As the creator of the vibroacoustic sound therapy chairs used in our clinic for many years, he has made this program possible. Our clients have benefited in countless ways from his genius.

Our appreciation goes to the many staff members who have supported us as we have completed this workbook: Pam Huebner, Mark Fernandez, and Laura Haggett. We also extend our appreciation to our fantastic editors Barbara McNichol and her assistant Peggy Henrikson, as well as Ginger Forsyth and the many professionals who have supported this work. Their valuable comments have added to and quality and exciting journey of this workbook.

We also want to thank our clients, process group participants, and study participants for helping us select the most effective exercises and formats and for their meaningful ideas that have enriched this workbook. We would especially like to thank our families – extended and otherwise. Their love, wisdom, support, and faith in us have been deeply appreciated and have constantly inspired us to keep going. Finally, our hearts go to our children and grandchildren.

Foreword

There are many approaches that assist us through the gift and challenge of life. Well Being: The Artfully Lived Life is a unique, transformational, creative, and innovative approach to celebrating and integrating "the masterpiece" of our inherent integrity, wholeness, and goodness. It is a systematically comprehensive approach to a) becoming intimately acquainted with the various dimensions of ourselves and b) unlocking and living the innate, often hidden core values and talents within us. The result is the opportunity to learn to live a more full and flourishing life!

This program can be used as an adjunct to psychotherapy or simply by readers interested in personal growth. ***Well-Being: The Artfully Lived Life*** intentionally incorporates evidence-based, empirically derived, practical and progressive concepts. The concepts are based on best practices from neuroscience, psychotherapy, and integrative medicine (mindfulness, guided imagery, etc.). It also includes evidence-based exercises, such as journaling and behavioral activities.

The intent is to help individuals identify and dismantle obstacles to well-being, then help them translate aspiration into action, and finally, to realize the full expression and manifestation of their unique selves.

Drs. Donna and Kim Rogers draw on decades of their professional experience as successful psychotherapists and scientists, along with their own personal life experiences, to inform the making of this exceptional program.

In short, Well-Being: The Artfully Lived Life offers a radically transformative program that is grounded in sound scientific and psychotherapeutic research and translated into loving, wise, and compassionate language. It is a program that applies healing interventions yielding real-world results, offering the reader confidence that the program can work for them!

Maya McNeilly, Ph.D.
Duke University, Integrative Medicine

Introduction

Think about where you are in your life – your feelings and beliefs, relationships with family, friends, coworkers, and your current physical health. Are you successfully directing your efforts toward what is important to you?

We often work with individuals and couples that are caught in thoughts and feelings that are uncomfortable or painful that come from past experiences. In fact, we often meet individuals who have not felt smart enough, successful enough, or attractive enough at some time in their lives. We find that often our clients don't know why they have come to feel inadequate in their lives, especially if they have tried to fix, ignore or escape these feelings. So, they are also often unaware of why they feel like they are stuck or perhaps have begun to engage in self-destructive behaviors such as alcohol, drugs, or non-stop screen time.

The Dalai Lama Haruki Murakami once said that "Pain is inevitable. Suffering is optional." As it turns out, the more we try to escape or ignore the uncomfortable thoughts and feelings, the more they come back to us. This cycle contributes to our suffering. There is, however, another way. In our experience with helping people, one of the first steps in assisting them is to discover what is most important to them and then help them develop the tools they need to align their thinking and behavior with their values. Next, we help them understand and chart a practical path they can follow to discover and choose thinking and behaviors that lead to well-being in their lives. We help them address the barriers that get in the way of self-discovery and well-being, such as difficulties with emotional dysregulation, childhood trauma, or a lack of tools or values that assist and guide them through life challenges.

We also explore the inherent qualities that are a part of each individual's unique personal make-up. We are all born with characteristics that define who we are. As our clients become aware of these qualities and begin to understand them, they also begin to better understand who they are, why they do some of the things they do, and why they love what they love. This information naturally leads them to begin to wonder about, question, and hopefully come to understand what they value, what they want to value, and whether or not their behavior reflects what they value.

Using concepts drawn from empirically evidenced therapies, the Artfully Lived Life program takes a unique experiential and process approach to discover who you are. You can use your strengths to create a values-guided life. One unique feature of the Artfully Lived Life Program involves understanding and coming to recognize how to best use the six domains of your personal life to create a balanced life experience.

Take a moment to imagine that your inner social being is an actual person. Who would that person be? Do you know this person? Can you give this person a name? Do you know what this person needs and wants? Or what this person most cares about?

Let's do the same with your inner emotional being. Who is this person? Do you know this person? Do you understand this person's needs and wants?

Suppose we were to do the same with your inner wisdom being, your inner physical being, and your inner thinking being. Could you answer these same questions? We are not suggesting the idea that we all have "multiple personalities". Rather, these aspects of yourself have always been with you. We will, however, encourage you to notice and explore these areas of functioning within you rather than from the automatic pilot we all usually feel most comfortable with.

Asking ourselves these questions helps us to understand a little better how little we know about ourselves. Without this understanding, it is difficult to meet our needs or identify the best choices for our well-being. We may also have excessively high expectations or expectations that are so low that we fail to reach our potential.

Mind-Body Literature

Based on the mind-body literature, we have expanded the "mind" component reference in the "mind-body" literature to include emotions, social interactions, thinking, and wisdom. Including the "physical" domain, we focus on five areas of functioning of the mind. We refer to each area as a "MindView". The Social MindView, for example, refers to the inherent or instinctive need for affiliation with others. In the Social MindView section, we explore more about what this means in our lives and how it can become de-railed.

The advantage of referring to separate areas of functioning of the mind is that there are tools, information, and coping strategies, that are available in the empirical research that are applicable and specific to each of the five areas. When they are addressed separately, we can also learn coping strategies for each area, which will, in turn, benefit the whole being.

We will also introduce you to the Observer-Manager which is the part of your brain function that steps back to keep track of the larger view of the five MindView areas. When we are aware and paying attention, the Observer-Manager offers suggestions, problem solves, provides guidance, and helps coordinate what is going on overall.

Together, these six MindView areas can begin to work cooperatively for your well-being in the same way a team works together toward a goal. We refer to this collective group as a Council. They are there to help and support you. With the creative use of the skills and strategies you will learn, your MindView Council can help you discover new ways to master life's challenges. With practice, it can become a valuable resource for decision-making as you strive to stay on track with your chosen values.

As you read this book, we are aware you may experience the need for "fixes" that we may or may not provide. However, life is quite a bit like learning to ride a bike in our vision. We can tell you what to do (how to pedal and how to stop the cycle), but we can't get into your mind to teach you how to balance your body on two narrow wheels. What we can do is encourage you to try. We will introduce what we refer to as The Artist's Tools, which will help you apply the changes to create a life of well-being. The Artist's Tools are acceptance, forgiveness, self-compassion, commitment, and gratitude. After learning about the six MindView members, your first task will be to learn about The Artist's Tools and how to apply them to the struggles you experience day to day. These tools will help begin the healing process by helping you discover the kinder and wiser person you already are within.

The Goals for this Workbook

The goals of Well-Being: The Artfully Lived Life program are to:

1) Introduce the skills and strategies you need to create a life of self-mastery, purpose, and vision.
2) Introduce you to the unique resources, capacities, and possibilities of your MindView members. Remember, we call this the MindView Council.
3) Help you integrate the information about the MindView Council into a better understanding of who you are and into a life that's purposeful, creative, effective, integrated, committed, forgiving, and accepting.

One of the strengths of this program is its focus on defining and creating wellness in your life rather than fixing something you may feel is wrong or broken. It's designed to propel you into a life of creative action and forward momentum. How? By using evidence-based strategies for developing skills and abilities for interacting with the world in such a way that you might benefit from whatever life has to offer you.

Wellness results from consistently and skillfully balancing environmental demands, our basic needs, and the management of our moment-to-moment experiences. It's not an end point. It's a process. We don't achieve it once and then forget about it. Instead, wellness can be defined as a skillful response to the problems we can solve. At the same time, we can accept our present life experiences as we move toward that which is most meaningful to us.

Discovering Your True Nature

Is it possible to discover your true nature? Absolutely! Granted, it does not seem likely right now. First, your experiences, knowledge, and the wisdom you have already gained in your life are a treasure trove of information you have available to you. The information and exercises in the chapters that follow can help you grow. As you complete the activities and practice the guided meditations, you will discover new ways to think about and integrate what you have learned in your life. As we go through each chapter, you will become more aware and familiar with who you really are. Your experiences will become valuable and meaningful resources to you as you need them.

Second, the meditations in this workbook will help you process your negative thoughts and feelings and choose behavior patterns that are more in line with your values and goals. Remember, the purpose of this program is to help you develop a healthier, more creative, and more effective way of being in the world. The best way to do this is to practice paying attention to what is going on within you. Awareness of your thoughts and feelings will help you begin wisely choosing more consistent responses.

Third, the information and tools are designed to help you discover and heal your inner nature. As you identify the values, goals, and actions that have guided your life thus far, your purpose in life will become more visible to you. Your goals in life will help to further consolidate who you are at the core and whether or not you are going in the direction that is the best fit for you. This workbook will also provide many of the tools you will need for your life journey.

Getting to know your true nature will arise as you complete the meditations, journal, and study the material in the Pause and Reflects. Remember, your true nature is likely hidden beneath some layers of protection right now, but it wants to be known by you. It wants to have a voice and to be a part of your life. The exercises in this program will allow your true nature to begin to emerge and to progressively gain a voice that will bring authenticity to your life.

A Little Bit About Why We Wrote this Book

With Kim's Ph.D. in research biochemistry and as an LMFT in marriage and family therapy and Donna's background in clinical psychology with training in developmental psychology and marriage and family therapy, we bring a relatively unique perspective to the problems that we see in practice. Combined, we bring over 35 years of experience to our practice with individuals, couples, and families who have changed their lives in positive ways using the principles and techniques of this program.

Acceptance and Commitment Therapy (ACT) and Mindfulness concepts have been two of the most prolific producers of research related to positive change and well-being in the last fifteen years. Together they offer a rich resource of information for defining, creating, and achieving a meaningful life that is inspired by committed action toward personal core values. The evidence-based concepts from Cognitive-Behavioral Therapy, ACT, Mindfulness, and Positive Psychology have been integrated into a framework that will allow you to come to a better understanding of who you are and who you are not.

So, for now, just be patient with yourself, and take your time. You have a lot to do. You do not need to rush into the healing process. We hope you integrate this information so that it becomes a part of who you are. The most important message we can convey to you is that you have time ~ so take it and enjoy the process.

Who Can Benefit from this Workbook?

It is a reality of being human that we will struggle sometimes. We don't mean struggle as in a bad day ~ we mean struggle as in hitting the wall and not knowing how to peel ourselves away from it. The Artfully Lived Life workbook is intended to be used by those who would like:

1) To develop a better understanding of who they are, and to examine and acknowledge their current strengths and limitations,
2) To define their values and goals, and to learn how to get out of their own way,
3) To learn new skills and strategies, as well as how and where to use them, and
4) To understand what it means to live a life of well-being and self-discovery rather than a life focused on eliminating discomfort.

The positive effects of moving toward our goals can counterbalance the discomfort. In the meantime, we are accomplishing what we want to achieve and doing what we want to be doing!

How to Study This Workbook

Well Being: The Artfully Lived Life program features five components:

1) The primary text is drawn from concepts common to empirically tested psychological therapies. Wisdom from modern and ancient masters and teachers, which has also begun to add insight and understanding to the clinical theory and practice of psychotherapy, is also included.
2) Pause & Reflect sections include exercises that help increase awareness. The more you write in these sections and journal your thoughts, the quicker you will integrate the information and progress through the program.
3) Guided Meditations contain experiential exercises specific to the chapter content. The written meditations are included at the end of the chapters. They are also recorded using binaural sound frequencies to create a deeper and more profound meditative experience. They can be found on Well Being: The Artfully Lived Life website. (www.theartfullylivedlife.com)
4) Journaling is encouraged throughout the workbook as it helps with processing and integrating the information. Space is provided in the Pause & Reflect sections. Additional pages for journaling are included in the Appendix section at the back of the workbook.
5) On Your Own Activities are suggestions for activities outside of reading and journaling. These activities can help you integrate new information and discover new ways to incorporate it into your life. They can be found at the end of each chapter.

The most significant benefit of Well-Being: The Artfully Lived Life comes from a commitment to reading the text, completing the exercises and reflections, and experiencing the guided meditations. The most important parts of the workbook are the parts you write (exercises and journaling) because they are personal to you and help you integrate what you learn into your own way of thinking and being. Some of the concepts you encounter in this workbook may be repetitive. There is a reason for this: thinking about these ideas in different contexts will help you integrate them as you create new and healthier habits in your life.

Although you may want change to happen quickly, it is essential to pace yourself. Give yourself time to think about how the material best applies to you and to find examples of these concepts and ideas as you go about your day. Personal transformation will occur as you find ways to make the information and ideas true for and about you. It is essential for you to read, complete the exercises, and practice the tools. As you set aside time each day to think about how you can use the concepts presented, you will experience positive and transformative changes in your life. You may need to re-do the workbook more than once. The more often you learn and practice something, the stronger the new behavior will become and the deeper the integration will be.

Why are the Guided Meditations so Important?

Thoughts spring from emotions, and emotions are often generated by thoughts. The critical thing to understand is that thoughts and feelings are not the same as facts. When thoughts are perceived as facts, we are likely to focus on what's wrong and how to change or fix it. We could find ourselves reacting emotionally to a situation when the real problem is our thoughts or perceptions about the situation.

The guided meditations offer the opportunity to bring clarity to our experiences, get to know the brain's inner workings, and understand some of the thoughts and feelings you experience there. The meditations will introduce you to new tools and strategies, new ways of thinking about yourself and your world, and new ways of interpreting and responding to the challenges you face.

You will begin to shift your thoughts 1) toward more acceptance and less negativity, 2) more focus on the process than the outcome, 3) toward more being than doing, 4) more choosing than reacting, 5) and toward more value-guided actions than emotion-guided reactions. These tiny shifts will help create a foundation for your life that will get you better results in nearly every aspect of your life.

Finally, the guided meditations will help create new neural pathways and new responses that will support the changes you want to make in your life. You will be learning to be kinder, more accepting, and compassionate with yourself and others. Most importantly, you will begin living your life with greater appreciation and gratitude for who you are as a unique and exceptional individual.

Listen to each meditation once per day for several days before moving on to the next chapter. This will allow you to better integrate the concepts into your life. Each time, after listening to the guided meditation, journal about your experience using the journal pages at the back of this book. This will help you to further integrate the material you are learning.

A Guided Meditation (GM) accompanies each of the chapters in this program, and sometimes there is more than one. The script for each meditation is included at the end of the chapter. It may also help if you read it once or twice before listening. Recordings of the guided meditations can be found at (theartfullylivedlife.com). The best time to listen to the GM is at the beginning of each chapter, and periodically throughout, so you're practicing the skills as you complete the workbook material. You can also improve your experience if you listen to the meditation while lying down in a comfortable position in a place where you feel safe. And during a time when you won't be disturbed. Earbuds or headphones will also help you get the most from these recordings, especially since binaural sound frequencies are included. The meditations are usually between 15 and 20 minutes.

The first GM is entitled "Introduction: Your Personal Space" and is designed to help you begin to discover, or re-discover, a sense of your inner self. Using a garden as a metaphor, you will be invited to ask yourself questions about who you are, what's important to you, and where you are going. What is your vision for your life? Have you thought about what is meaningful to you? And do you have a plan for getting yourself where you want to go? All that you are and need for your life is already within you.

We have included the first GM at the end of this section as a welcome to your experience with going to a meditative place.

Guided Meditation ~ Introduction: Your Personal Space

Lie down, get comfortable and close your eyes. Place your hand on the spot that rises and falls the most when you inhale. If this spot is on your chest, you are not using your full lung capacity. Put your hand on your stomach and take deep full breaths _ breaths that make your stomach rise more than your chest. Continue breathing slowly and deeply using your diaphragm.

See your breath as a pure white cloud. Coming in through the top of your head. As it swirls down through your body, it picks up all of the impurities, the tension, the fatigue, the pain, or the problems of the day. Imagine all of the impurities exiting out through your toes as you exhale. As your lungs are emptied, the cloud leaves your body and disappears out into space. Keep breathing slowly and deeply. Imagine the white cloud coming in at the top of your head, swirling through every part of your body. Down through your head and face, carrying away the tension. Down through your neck and shoulders. Down through your arms and into your hands and then your fingers, carrying away the pressures and the worries. Down through your chest and into your stomach and abdomen. Down through your buttocks and thighs. Down through your legs, into your ankles and feet, and carrying away the tension, worry, pain, or fear. Out through your toes. See these impurities exiting out through your toes and away.

If you find that your mind has wandered, don't let that bother you. Just remember to bring your attention back to your breathing. Breathing in pure, clear, cleansing oxygen, picking up the impurities, and exiting out and away through your toes. And now imagine that the oxygen that you breathe in turns a beautiful blue color. Calming, soothing… feel the color cleansing your body, your mind. Leaving your body feeling deeply relaxed. Your problems and worries washed away. Peaceful quiet, calm, lighter with each breath, almost as if you are floating. Just floating.

Imagine that you see yourself standing in the middle of a large field. The sun is warm on your skin. Imagine that you turn slowly in a circle with your arms stretched out to your sides. As you look past the tips of your fingers, you notice a sparkling shield begins to form. This is the boundary that protects your life space. In this space, you have the opportunity to consider what you are learning. You are perfectly safe here. This space is only for you, and anyone who comes here must be invited by you.

Now imagine that everything you are, is here with you within this safe, protected space. Your strengths and personal values, your achievements, your character – all that you are, is here with you.

Find a place to sit and be comfortable. You have within you a story about your life. Most of us don't spend enough time thinking about the good we have done. You have been kind to others. At times you have shown wisdom and compassion. You had strength when you needed it. You have made many good decisions and perhaps some bad ones, but you kept going. You have succeeded in taking good care of yourself. Take the time now to really see who you are. Yes, you have flaws, but they are just a part of the amazing being you are. Take the time to look for the positives within.

As we work together, you will begin to change your story. Because the truth is, you are good enough, smart enough, and enough of whatever you need to be already. You don't have to be perfect to be good enough. You are good enough just as you are. Our work together is not about helping you be a better person – it is designed to help you discover the person you already are.

Yet life also happens. None of us have a perfect understanding, the skills, or the strategies to deal with the obstacles we face. So, we do the best we can, and sometimes, that leads to what some people call failure. We forget that we did the best we could. We forget that we had few skills or guidance, and we just blame ourselves for failing. That is the first message we want to change. The idea of failure is a myth!

It is important to remember that everything that grows starts life as fragile. At over 300 feet, even the tallest Sequoia tree in the world was once a sapling. In fact, sequoia trees require fire to germinate! When they were exposed to the extremes of fire, weather, drought, natural disasters, and infestations, their roots grew deeper. Their bark became thicker, and their limbs and branches grew around the obstacles they confronted. In other words, they became more robust – more resilient by being challenged.

Our vulnerabilities nurture our potential and foster our growth. To blame ourselves for having flaws is to blame ourselves for the very things that help to improve our lives. Without them, there is no growth. You have a powerful brain that will help you turn struggles into experience and wisdom, and catastrophes into courage and strength.

Our job, then, is to learn from them and to keep learning from them. We can acknowledge our struggles rather than begrudge them and thank them for what they teach us rather than expend energy trying to rid ourselves of them. We can become kinder, more compassionate, and ultimately more loving as human beings toward ourselves and others because of them. Our vulnerabilities are the seeds that blossom into unique gifts, talents, and capacities.

Now, as you rest here in your personal space, just be present with your inner self. Notice your breathing, and as you breathe in and out, notice the air as it passes over your upper lip. Be present to whatever sights and sounds arise as you sit here in your space. It may be the sky's color or the color of the trees surrounding you. And what do you feel on your skin? Is it a cooling breeze or a breeze warmed by the sun? Let these sensations help center you, soothe you, and refresh you. They bring focus to your inner experience. Peaceful and quiet. Begin to see yourself in a new way.

Begin to see yourself from the inside out rather than from the outside in. See yourself from the inside–out. This is where you will find your center. Right here, right now, you are a courageous and powerful being about to embark on a new journey of accepting yourself from the inside out.

Chapter One: Getting Started

"The human brain is the most complex, yet fragile, organ in the universe. If <u>it</u> doesn't work right, <u>we</u> don't work right. It's that simple." ~Daniel Amen

Embarking on a New MindView

In a temple in Bangkok, Thailand, there is a golden Buddha statue. Its origin dates back to the 13th or 14th century. In 1767, to protect it from invaders, it was disguised under stucco and colored glass, and its' hidden identity lasted almost 200 years. In 1955, during relocation, it fell, and some of the plaster covering broke away, revealing its golden essence beneath. Surprised, the monks chipped away and removed the clay covering, revealing the statue's true nature – which represented spiritual enlightenment and energy. The golden Buddha had a purpose, value, and beauty when it was perceived to be made of clay because of its inherent nature, which is why it was treasured and valued for hundreds of years by millions of people. The discovery of its true hidden nature provided added richness and beauty to its people and their history. However, what the Buddha represented did not change.

We mention this story because it is so appropriate to the journey of the unveiling of your Masterpiece Within. Many of us have also been living with layers of hardened clay that cover our true nature. This clay covering is made up of stories about who you are, and experiences you've had that were not consistent with your true nature. They have been hiding your true nature for much of your life. Your true nature is the genuine person you are at the core, and that has existed since you were born. More importantly, though, it is your true nature that enriches the lives of the people around you. You just need the tools and skills to authentically express that part of who you are.

We, as humans, develop layers that protect us throughout our lives. For example, we might form a layer of anger that covers our sadness or hurt. We might develop addictions in response to painful memories or problems we do not know how to solve. Other layers might include defensiveness from feeling attacked by members of a chaotic family, or the deep insecurities that arise from growing up as a child with an abusive parent. All these layers separate us from our true selves. They also likely result in symptoms of depression, anxiety, trauma, and other mental health disorders that can severely affect our lives. The following exercise can help you think about your history through a lens of understanding the layers that cover your true nature.

This tale mirrors our journey to discover the "Masterpiece Within" Like the Golden Buddha, you may still be covered in metaphorical clay – the stories and beliefs that you have accumulated about yourself over time. These layers, concealing your authentic self, not only disconnect you from your true self but they can also lead to thinking and behavior disorders that can impact your life profoundly. Contemplating your personal history and the layers that cover your unique and brilliant inner being is a step towards uncovering your genuine self.

Exploring Psychological Wellness

Understanding psychological wellness involves delving into different psychological specialties. For instance, social psychologists examine human behavior in social settings, while cognitive psychologists focus on mental processes like reasoning and learning. In this chapter, we integrate insights from various fields, emphasizing Positive Psychology, Mindfulness, and Acceptance and Commitment Therapy (ACT). These approaches, vital to this workbook, will be explored through text, exercises, and guided meditations.

Positive psychology explores how individuals achieve optimal functioning, emphasizing happiness, meaning, and personal strengths to counteract distress and negativity. However, a challenge in this approach is our limited control over external stressors and negative influences.

Mindfulness, another key approach, helps change our stress response and enhances well-being. Defined by Jon Kabat-Zinn as "paying attention in a particular way: on purpose, in the present moment, and nonjudgmentally". Mindfulness involves attentive awareness of the present moment, acknowledging emotions without entanglement in our mental narratives.

Building on Mindfulness, ACT encourages embracing our full emotional spectrum. Avoiding difficult feelings can prolong and intensify them. By accepting both positive and uncomfortable emotions and focusing on purposeful action, we can find deeper meaning and purpose, avoiding the pitfalls of escaping problems.

In a clinical psychological practice, clients frequently present issues like flawed thinking, emotional instability, relationship troubles, and social challenges. Addressing these often involves developing skills related to these areas, guided by the principles of Positive Psychology, Mindfulness, or ACT.

Advances in Brain Science

Over the last two decades, groundbreaking research has dramatically changed our understanding of the human brain and behavior. Contrary to earlier beliefs that the adult brain's capacity is fixed, we now recognize that the brain not only grows but also thrives, especially under challenging, complex, or rewarding situations, provided these experiences are meaningfully interpreted.

Significant strides have been made in the last 25 years in understanding how the brain reacts to negative emotions and stress. This has sparked new approaches to brain health, including innovative ways to educate, nourish, and exercise the brain, thereby enhancing its capacity and vitality. The goal is clear; the more we improve our brain's functionality, the more rapidly we can progress and better our lives.

Recognizing, accepting, processing, and overcoming life's experiences are crucial for skill development. These skills enable us to focus on what brings us joy and fulfillment. Understanding our life's path provides us with clearer vision and a stronger sense of harmony. By navigating through challenges, we gain the tools needed to enrich our lives. Gaining insight into how our MindViews and brains operate can transform our journey, offering a fresh perspective on life itself.

^Pause & Reflect ~ Defining an Event^

1) Think about your life experiences and the challenges you're currently facing. Which of the following words describe you right now? Circle those. If you think of terms not listed below, write them in.

Chaotic	Ineffective	Unhealthy	Disorganized	Unhappy
Painful	Confusing	Disappointing	Directionless	Empty
Lonely	Frightening	Distrusting	Miserable	Threatening

2) Now, think of the obstacles you've already overcome in your life. What were they? Circle those. Add in those not listed.

Job loss	Child abuse	Cancer	Rejection	Illness
Addiction	Money worries	Heart break	Racism	Pain
Isolation	Work stress	Family stress	Mental Illness	Fear

3) Do you recognize the qualities listed below that may have helped you through those difficult times? Please circle those. Then add others.

Intentional	Persistent	Introspective	Patient	Determined
Hopeful	Resourceful	Courageous	Values	Tolerant
Stubborn	Focused	Faithful	Grateful	Empathetic
Committed	Accepting	Forgiving	Respectful	Compassionate

4) Now, go back to a time when you were happier, healthier, or stronger. Review the list again. What qualities did you see then? Please circle and add.

Intentional	Persistent	Introspective	Patient	Determined
Hopeful	Resourceful	Courageous	Values focused	Tolerant
Stubborn	Focused	Faithful	Grateful	Empathetic
Committed	Accepting	Forgiving	Compassionate	Respectful
Spontaneous	Wise	Discerning	Resilient	Open

5) What were your strengths? Did they help you? What kind of strengths were they? Did you notice them and feel proud of them?

Understanding the Brain's Neurophysiology

The brain is central to all aspects of our functioning and experiences. To understand its role better, it's useful to briefly explore its structure. Imagine the brain as a complex command center with different areas responsible for various functions.

At the front, above the forehead, are the prefrontal and frontal cortex, crucial for planning and problem-solving (cognition). The middle part of the brain, known as the limbic system, handles emotions and motivation. Motor control and balance are governed by the premotor and motor cortex.

The brain's functioning in social interaction, intuition, creativity, and spiritual or wisdom-related activities are generally located on the right side, while the left side predominantly handles analytical thinking, mathematics, science, language, and logic.

An imbalance between these two hemispheres can significantly impact our lives. Organizing, decision-making, and integrative cognitive behaviors, vital for a stable life, are rooted in the prefrontal and frontal cortex, drawing from other brain areas as well.

Using this knowledge, we can conceptualize the brain as a "MindView Council". In this metaphor, each "council member" represents different brain areas with unique needs and behavioral roles, working together in harmony for optimal functioning.

Integrating Recent Research in Neuroscience and Psychology

Recent breakthroughs in neuroscience, medicine, and clinical psychology have greatly enhanced our understanding of how to heal, optimize, and maintain the brain, our most complex organ. Let's explore these advances:

1. **Clinical Observations:** People often encounter challenges in specific life areas.
2. **Behavioral Domains**: These challenges align with behavioral domains identified by psychologists for study.
3. **Brain and Behavior Connection:** Generally, different brain areas correlate with areas of behavioral functioning.
4. **Brain Research Insights**: Research has pinpointed brain locations responsible for integrating information and behavior, essential for optimal response.
5. **The Council Metaphor:** Utilizing this knowledge, we can imagine a "Council", where each member represents a functional area of the brain, to understand the interplay of behavioral concepts.
6. **Cross-Disciplinary Findings:** By examining insights from various study areas, we gain a better grasp of our behaviors and how to enhance and improve them.
7. **Self-Awareness and Skills Development:** Increasing our awareness of our inner workings and using these research insights enables us to develop skills for better integration as individuals. These skills become internal resources we can rely on in our daily lives.

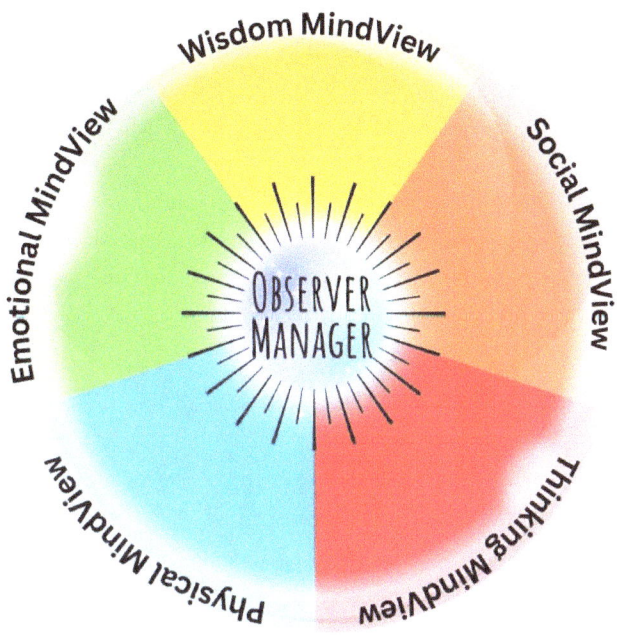

The MindView Compass which encompasses the five MindViews and an Observer-Manager. These six domains define and describe our behavior in everyday life. Write your daily activities on the MindView compass above.

Exploring the MindView Council

Like the Pixar movie "Inside Out", where emotions are personified in 11-year-old Riley's MindView, we can better understand mind-body behavior by visualizing different aspects of our psyche. Historically, the connection between emotions and health has been acknowledged for centuries, but it's only in the last thirty years that modern medicine has started treating the mind and body as interconnected yet distinct entities.

We've discussed the brain's physical characteristics and their impact on our behavior. But how do these relate to our thoughts, feelings, ethical beliefs, social connections, and spiritual needs? To simplify this, we introduce the "MindView Council" concept, inspired by the mind-body phenomenon. The Council comprises five members and an Observer-Manager: The Physical MindView, Emotional MindView, Thinking MindView, Social MindView, Wisdom/Spiritual MindView, and the Observer-Manager. Each member operates independently with unique skills and abilities, yet they also function collectively by cross-coordinating specific brain areas as needed.

The "MindView Council" helps us analyze life's challenges and our decision-making processes. Understanding these six MindView spaces enhances our ability to develop the skills we need for a better life.

The Observer-Manager plays a dual role. Firstly, it acts as an internal observation and guidance system, providing feedback on the thoughts, feelings, attitudes, and behaviors of the five Council members. Secondly, as the Manager, it oversees problem-solving, decision-making, and planning. It delegates routine tasks to the Council members and coordinates actions in line with their collective needs, functioning as the brain's executive center.

In harmony, the Observer-Manager and the five MindView domains guide us in making informed decisions, utilizing available skills and resources, and enacting values-guided actions. This synergy aids in maintaining stability, resilience, and well-being amidst life's challenges. As we progress through this material, you'll also learn about developing skills that may be outside of your repertoire.

Understanding the MindView Council Members

In this part of the chapter, we delve deeper into the five Council members, exploring how they collectively foster development, growth, and a balanced life. The Observer Manager plays a crucial role in monitoring and evaluating outcomes, and providing feedback for necessary adjustments to enhance well-being.

It's important to remember that the MindView Council is a general model, and each individual's experiences and characteristics may vary. Some traits and behaviors may be common among many, but your unique qualities might be subtle as we go through these descriptions. Pay close attention and journal your thoughts and experiences as you apply these concepts and skills; this will help your distinct personality and qualities to surface.

Reflecting on Your MindView Compass

The illustration above is referred to as your MindView Compass. It's a tool to help you reflect on your daily life, particularly how you allocate your time and energy. Consider the amount of time you spend on different aspects of your life. Is there an imbalance? For instance, do you find yourself focusing more on your Thinking MindView compared to your Social or Emotional MindViews, as is common for many people?

Even small changes, such as incorporating a few enjoyable activities in a neglected area, can significantly enhance your overall well-being. Alternatively, you might think about redistributing some of your time or energy to other areas that could improve your life in various ways. Sometimes, the mere act of being aware of how we spend our time can help us find a better balance.

The Physical MindView: This aspect relates to the health and functioning of the brain and body. Various brain centers, including the limbic system (often associated with emotions), are involved in physical actions. The limbic system initiates the desire to move, the pre-motor cortex generates movement impulses, and the motor cortex activates the necessary body parts. This intricate process, involving electrical and biochemical signals, links the brain and body, enabling us to perform complex activities like playing music, dancing, or engaging in sports.

In Well-Being: The Artfully Lived Life, exploring the Physical MindView involves focusing on fundamental aspects of brain and body health, such as exercise, diet, and sleep. We'll also look at ways to enhance life by paying attention to our physical well-being. Maintaining a healthy, strong, and active body through understanding and awareness is vital for the effective functioning of the MindView Council.

Linking Brain and Body Health to Cognitive and Emotional Wellness

Brain and body health are closely intertwined with our cognitive and emotional states. For instance, mental and emotional stress often manifests physically as muscle tension. Learning to identify, understand, and alleviate this tension is possible through practices like mindfulness meditation and progressive relaxation.

Innate qualities present from birth, which develop as we grow, play a significant role in this connection. These include temperament traits, language acquisition skills, the need for physical safety, and basic survival instincts like fight, flight, or freeze. Additionally, the instinct to procreate is a fundamental part of our makeup. Some individuals may have unique inherent physical traits, such as exceptional language skills or particularly easygoing temperaments. Understanding and nurturing these innate qualities is crucial for holistic well-being, as they influence both our mental health and physical responses.

The Emotional MindView is key to our emotional awareness and behavior. It involves feedback from various brain and body areas, highlighting the deep evolutionary roots of emotions in our survival. Emotions drive us to form connections, procreate, and protect ourselves.

Researchers have recognized six universal emotions evident across cultures: happiness, joy, surprise, anger, sadness, and fear. These emotions are thought to be evolutionary survival mechanisms, steering us towards activities that enhance survival and away from danger. Emotional bonds are crucial for finding a mate, reproduction, and nurturing offspring.

Emotions play a role in every life experience, acting like a compass or a magnet, guiding us toward what we desire or need. Whether joyful or challenging, emotions enrich our lives by highlighting what is meaningful and important.

Most of us are born with inherent emotional qualities, such as the capacity for love, spontaneity, joy, passion, independence, eagerness, compassion, and trust. Feeling emotionally safe and valued in our environment is also crucial. This sense of safety is not only vital for early childhood development and nurturing our inner potential but is also important in our adult lives. Feeling secure is foundational for developing the skills necessary for adulthood.

The Thinking MindView: This component of the Council is vital for learning, memory, decision-making, problem-solving, and intentional action. Located primarily in the frontal cortex, behind the forehead and eyes, this area is integral to processing and organizing information. The way we think is influenced by brain physiology, and conversely, our thought processes can impact our physical brain. For instance, chronic stress can lead to hormonal changes that adversely affect heart rate, blood pressure, immune function, and other bodily processes.

The Social MindView: This aspect of our MindView centers on our ability to connect with others. Our brains are inherently designed to live in communities, emphasizing our instinctual need for social structures that provide safety and resources. Healthy relationships are linked to better brain and body health, while harmful ones can trigger stress responses, impacting our health negatively. The Social MindView guides the Council by valuing connections and building relationships that benefit both individuals and the community. These connections are crucial for protection and survival. The inherent qualities of the Social Self include a desire for closeness and cooperative problem-solving. There's also an innate discernment ability, sensing whether surrounding behaviors are beneficial or harmful. Children, especially, show inherent trust towards adults, along with resilience, often viewing the world as a loving and forgiving place despite everyday struggles.

Challenges and Qualities of the Thinking MindView

In the Thinking MindView, difficulties often arise from distorted perceptions and interpretations. Many times, we don't critically assess the thinking patterns developed over the years, not realizing their potential irrationality. It's only when we become acutely aware of our thought processes that we recognize their flaws. Learning to modify these thought patterns can be transformative for our lives.

Like a camera lens bringing a scene into focus, the Thinking MindView sharpens our life perspective in ways we might not currently imagine. This part of our journey, centered on self-discovery, involves uncovering the amazing aspects of ourselves that we're yet unaware of.

The inherent characteristics of the Thinking MindView include curiosity, inquisitiveness, resourcefulness, teachability, and creativity. We are natural problem-solvers, and many of us possess an innate quality of persistence. We have a desire to understand our options and make our own choices. Achieving goals and gaining recognition for these achievements are also fundamental aspects of our Thinking MindView.

Exploring the Spiritual MindView, also known as the Wisdom MindView, embodies the deeper, wiser aspects of our nature. Its anatomical basis is less defined in scientific terms. Research, including MRI studies of meditating individuals, indicates activity in the right temporal lobes during moments of insight or spiritual awareness, but the exact nature of this MindView space remains somewhat elusive.

Your interpretation of the Spiritual MindView might vary - it could be an inner sense of knowing, wisdom, values, intuition, or a trusted internal guidance system. For many, it's a combination of these elements, often described as a "quiet inner voice".

Our values, beliefs, and social and moral codes are vital for survival and coexistence within a community, allowing us to live peacefully and safely among others with similar ideologies. Wisdom involves applying experience, knowledge, and cultural understanding to our decisions and actions.

The Spiritual MindView, being quieter than the other Council members, can be easily overlooked despite its significance. This underscores the importance of learning to "listen to your gut". The human MindView is a vast repository of information, knowledge, and experience, much of which lies beyond our conscious awareness.

Key qualities of the Spiritual MindView include discernment - the ability to differentiate good from bad. From childhood, we possess an inherent moral and ethical compass guiding our sense of right and wrong. Other qualities include kindness, authenticity, love, empathy, innocence, and hope in the goodness of others.

Understanding the Observer-Manager in the MindView Council

In the Well-Being: Artfully Lived Life program, we embrace Aristotle's idea that, "The whole is greater than the sum of its parts". While the concept of "MindView-body" health is familiar, it doesn't encompass all aspects of our well-being. The brain's evolution has been a continuous process of expansion and reorganization, raising the question: how does this impact our well-being today?

The Observer-Manager: This final member of the MindView Council plays a crucial role. The brain's primitive areas manage unconscious bodily functions like breathing, digestion, and heart function, along with survival instincts and species continuation.

The more advanced parts of the brain, the higher cortical areas, focus on attention, creativity, and planning, essential for protection and well-being. The Manager uses this information to direct attention, organize memory, make decisions, and take action.

The Observer acts as an internal system for reflection and guidance. It allows us to step back, observe our inner experiences, and integrate them into useful insights. The Observer provides feedback on what's effective or satisfying, and sometimes cautions us against potentially bad decisions.

However, there are times when we might not be immediately aware of the Observer, especially in emotionally charged situations. It's often later that we recognize the Observer's insights, offering perspective or wisdom. This part of our MindView is attuned to our identity, values, and goals, providing ideas and insights to achieve what matters to us. It subtly nudges us when our actions don't align with our values, guiding and redirecting our choices. When the Observer speaks, it's imperative to listen, as it offers crucial insights for our growth and well-being.

The Role of the Manager in the MindView Council

In the MindView Council, the Manager collaborates closely with the Observer. They process not only current information but also draw from past experiences. Their role is to manage the five Council members by aligning their input with real-world experiences. The feedback loop they create is essential for growth and evolution, enhancing self-worth, satisfaction, and the overall well-being of our core identity.

A practical approach to understanding the Observer-Manager is to reflect on past events. Often, our reactions in challenging situations are driven by intense emotions or negative beliefs, leading to emotionally reactive behaviors that may ignore the Observer-Manager's cautions. In hindsight, when emotions have subsided, we might recognize better ways to handle the situation, like thinking more rationally or improving communication.

The Manager acts as a guide, preparing us for potential issues and suggesting optimal actions. It consolidates knowledge and experiences from all Council members, offering informed advice on the best course of action. However, it's important to note that these are only suggestions, and it's up to us to decide whether to listen.

Attachment to Thoughts and Beliefs: A key question arises: why might we choose not to heed good advice? Often, this stems from a confusion between our true selves and our perceived selves. We may become attached to certain self-perceptions, hindering our ability to discern and listen to our wiser inner nature. Recognizing and trusting our innate ability to see beyond surface judgments is crucial. Empirical studies have shown that failing to align with our true selves leads to decreased satisfaction, fulfillment, focus, and personal integration. This is why the idea of "being true to yourself" holds such profound significance.

^Pause & Reflect ~ Describe an Event^

> Recall a recent event from the last few days. Perhaps you drove to work today or had a conversation with a family member. Can you identify each of the MindViews in that event? What was the event? _____
>
> Now think about what the Physical MindView experienced? _____
>
> What did the Emotional MindView feel? _____
>
> What did the Social MindView experience? _____
>
> What did the Thinking MindView think about? _____
>
> And through all of this, what did your Spiritual MindView notice? _____

Developing a Sense of Wholeness with the MindView Council

In the Well-Being: Artfully Lived Life program, our goal is to bolster the resources we possess and acquire new ones necessary for handling life's challenges. For instance, if the Observer maintains a presence in the current moment, despite persistent thoughts (Thinking MindView) or intense emotions (Emotional MindView) about the past, these thoughts and feelings won't define our identity (Observer) or control our actions (Manager). Instead, we have the freedom to choose our responses using the tools and strategies of the MindView Council. The key to progress in this program lies in conscious, active engagement and practice. While these skills may initially require effort to learn, they eventually become habitual coping mechanisms that enhance life quality.

The Observer-Manager plays a crucial role in shaping and integrating our "sense of self". Our identity, a blend of character traits and unique personality qualities, emerges from the integration of life experiences, inherent qualities, values, and ideals. Research shows that a lack of this integration can lead to various psychological, emotional, and life challenges, affecting both individual and community functioning.

Conversely, when there's congruence between our various selves and the Observer-Manager, we experience deeper integration and personal development. This alignment enriches relationships, makes life experiences more satisfying, and fosters a stronger connection with our successes, values, goals, and actions.

Exploring Happiness in Life

In our daily lives, we often don't consciously recognize the individual roles of the "MindViews" within our brain, as described in this chapter. The brain is dynamic, constantly adjusting to both internal and external stimuli, evolving throughout our lives.

A well-functioning brain offers vast resources. Yet, issues like distorted thinking, unregulated emotions, or harmful habits can disrupt its efficiency, leading to an imbalance among the five Council members.

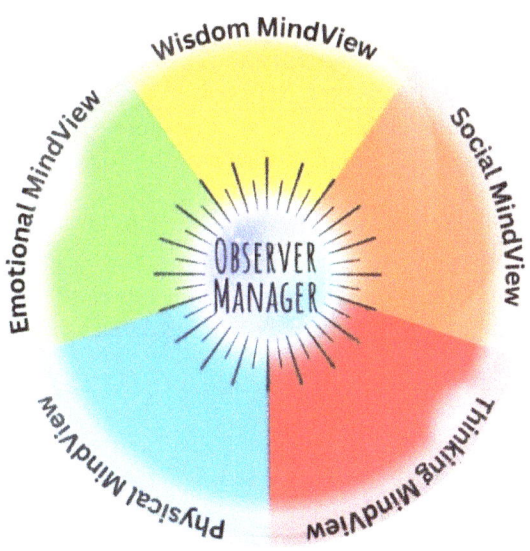

^Pause & Reflect ~ Your MindView Compass^

In the MindView Compass above, see if you can jot down a few words in each of the MindView Domain Sections that describe what you experienced in the event you mentioned above. Then describe the observations and responses that arose within your Observer Manager.

_____
_____
_____

^Pause & Reflect: The Five Council Members and Their Responses^

Physical MindView	The Physical MindView brings to the Council the ability to move, walk, talk, sing, dance, work, touch, hug, kiss, run, jump, drive, swing, draw, and write, among many other talents and skills. The physical systems ensure that the body functions in ways necessary for survival and comfort.
Emotional MindViewView	The Emotional MindView draws us with positive emotion toward experiences that enrich us and repels us with negative emotion from experiences that are harmful. Both are necessary for survival. Our Emotional MindView may also tend toward the avoidance of anything uncomfortable. The Emotional MindView experiences passion and compassion, interest and motivation, hope, joy and enthusiasm, etc.
Social MindViewView	The Social MindView brings to the Council the desire and ability to reach out to others, relate to them, understand them, and establish connections. The brain is "pre-wired" for belonging to a community, and it defines what is most meaningful through the connections it creates with others.
Thinking MindViewView	The Cognitive MindView brings skills to the Council, such as those required for learning, remembering, decision-making, problem-solving, and intentional action. The Thinking MindView is primarily located in the area right behind the forehead and eyes. It is responsible for the organization and integration of vast amounts of information.
Spiritual or Wisdom MindViewView	The Spiritual MindView is a much quieter member of the Council than the other four. It is often described as the "quiet inner voice". The Spiritual MindView (or Wisdom MindView) carries a deep sense of inner knowing, and insight regarding choices in the best interests of the individual.
Observer-Manager	Observer, overseer, advisor, planner, organizer, and problem-solver, it draws on the knowledge, skills, and experience of the other MindViews and then provides guidance and direction, as we navigate through our lives.

The concept of happiness has been widely discussed. What defines happiness? What are the characteristics and lifestyles of "happy people"? How do they perceive their world? What constitutes a life characterized by peace, introspection, and compassion, which many associate with happiness? The Well-Being: The Artfully Lived Life program draws from theoretical and empirical studies to explore these questions. Our journey through this workbook aims to delve into the most significant findings related to well-being. We will investigate these and other topics, progressing one day, one skill, one moment, and one loving action at a time.

Coming back to the garden metaphor, the needs and requirements of a garden can be pretty complex. If ignored, they can sabotage the health and vitality of whatever we plant there. In fact, very nearly every living organism will have needs that, if appropriately met, will contribute to their health and well-being.

In this Guided Meditation, you will have the opportunity to meet your MindView Council. It will be necessary to just be mindfully present with what you experience. Don't overthink this exercise. Let go of the need to fix or create anything. There is no right or wrong way to do this. Just be there non-judgmentally. After completing the Guided Meditation, complete the exercise below.

Journal Space

_____
_____
_____
_____
_____
_____
_____
_____
_____
_____
_____

- What did it feel like to create a sense of unity and cohesion within?
- Repeat this exercise at least three more times and journal everything you can about each experience.

GM Journaling ~ Chapter One: Getting Started

Now that you are getting to know the MindViews within you, try to express what you saw.

- What did you experience as you did this meditation? What changes did you notice in your mind and body?
- Can you describe your experience with each of your MindViews?
- Were they different? How? For example, did you notice some were stronger or more dominant than others?
- How have they been helpful?

Physical MindView _____
_____

Emotional MindView _____
_____

Thinking MindView _____
_____

Social MindView _____
_____

Spiritual MindView _____
_____

Guided Meditation ~ Chapter One: Introducing the MindView Council

Lie down, get comfortable, and close your eyes. Place your hand on the spot that rises and falls the most when you inhale. If this spot is on your chest, you are not using your full lung capacity. Put your hand on your stomach and take deep, full breaths – breaths that make your stomach rise more than your chest. Continue breathing slowly and deeply into your stomach.

See your breath as a pure white cloud. Coming in through the top of your head. As it swirls down through your body, it picks up all of the impurities, the tension, the fatigue, the pain, or the problems of the day. Imagine all of the impurities exiting out through your toes as you exhale. As your lungs are emptied, the cloud leaves your body and disappears out into space. Keep breathing slowly and deeply. Imagine the white cloud coming in at the top of your head, swirling through every part of your body. Down through your head and face, carrying away the tension. Down through your neck and shoulders. Down through your arms and into your hands and then your fingers, carrying away the pressures and the worries. Down through your chest and into your stomach and abdomen. Down through your buttocks and thighs. Down through your legs, into your ankles and feet, and carrying away the tension, worry, pain, or fear. Out through your toes. See these impurities exiting out through your toes and away.

If you find that your mind has wandered, don't let that bother you. Just remember to bring your attention back to your breathing. Breathing in pure, clear, cleansing oxygen, picking up the impurities, and exiting out and away through your toes. And now imagine that the oxygen that you breathe in turns a beautiful blue color. Calming, soothing, feel the color cleansing your body, your mind. Leaving your body feeling deeply relaxed. Your problems and worries washed away. Peaceful, quiet, calm, lighter with each breath, almost as if you are floating. Just floating.

From this deeply calm state, return to your personal space where you can see and experience the best of who you are. You are safe here. Now find a place to sit down and relax. This is your place of peace - your personal garden space. You might discover an area of green grass surrounding a big tree. Allow yourself to sit comfortably there in the grass, where you will soon meet your MindView Council and prepare to create a beautiful garden. There is a slight breeze that brushes softly across your face and hair.

Your inner world is made up of emotional and social needs, physical and thinking needs, and spiritual needs. There is also a part of you that can step back and observe what is happening within you without getting all tangled up in the details. We call that your inner Observer-Manager. All of these are parts of who you are.

Since they are part of who you are, will you welcome them into your space? Imagine a person walking towards you. It is your Emotional MindView. Invite your Emotional MindView to join you. What do you feel as you see your Emotional MindView? Can you embrace your

Emotional MindView and express gratitude for the richness and depth of experience it brings to your life. And if you notice faults or flaws, can you embrace them as well? The faults and imperfections have purpose and value. Even with them, your Emotional MindView allows you to experience passion, caring, interest, feeling, and drive, as well as despair, pain, and sorrow. All of these are the substance of experience, and, as such, they are worthy of your love.

Now, bring your attention to your Physical MindView. Invite your Physical MindView to join you. Your Physical MindView brings an awareness to your lifestyle – all of your healthy habits as well as perhaps some of the less healthy habits. What do you notice? Express gratitude for all that your physical MindView has done for you. And if you see faults or flaws, embrace them as well for the good they can bring into your life. There is so much potential here, waiting for the acceptance and compassion you can bring to it.

Now, see your Social MindView. Welcome your Social MindView to this circle of safety. Embrace your Social MindView. Your Council is beginning to take shape. Your Social MindView brings to your life the desire and ability to reach out to others, relate to them, and establish connections with them. Without the Social MindView, your world would be much smaller. Your Social MindView brings acceptance and compassion to your experiences, whatever they are. There is much you still have to learn about yourself and others around you. You gain much of this knowledge through interacting with others, thanks to your Social MindView.

Now, your Thinking MindView joins the circle of safety. Embrace and welcome your Thinking MindView. The Thinking MindView brings to your life the skills required for learning, remembering, decision-making, problem-solving, and intentional action and those used in teaching, guiding, and learning. Our thoughts provide a treasure trove of information about how we see ourselves and our world. They can focus and clarify our intentions. Be present to your Thinking MindView – it will bring kindness and compassion to your thoughts about yourself and the world.

Now, notice your Spiritual MindView. Embrace and welcome your Spiritual MindView. Your Spiritual MindView is a much quieter member of the Council than the other four. It's often described as the "quiet inner voice". Your Spiritual MindView carries a deep sense of inner knowing, understanding, and insight regarding choices that may or may not be in your best interests. It offers vast stores of information gleaned from your life's experiences. What do you notice about your spiritual voice? Sometimes you may have to listen very carefully to hear what it has to say.

And finally, your Observer-Manager joins your circle. This is the leader of your Council. This part guides you and gives you advice, but it can't do anything without you. Embrace your Observer Manager, who knows what you need, how you feel, and what's most important for your overall wellness. When we listen, our choices are likely to be more in line with our values. Your Observer-Manager is your best advocate. It will offer guidance if you will just be present and listen.

Now, your MindView Council is complete. Each of you, hold hands. You are a complete being now. You are a team. Be true to yourselves. As you go forward in your life and in the Artfully Lived Life Program, you will discover more about who you are and who you are not, what is essential, and what are unimportant attachments. Make the commitment to each other to keep moving forward as a team, depending on and trusting one another.

Everything you need is already within you. As you slow down and listen for guidance and wisdom from your MindView Council, allow yourself to see the brilliant being that you already are. It is time to rediscover what it means to be. Just be. Be what you are. You are enough.

Now, when you are ready, take a deep breath and come back to this room.

Chapter 2 – Tools for Uncovering Inner Wellness

Life isn't about waiting for the storm to pass.
It's about learning how to dance in the rain. ~Vivian Greene~

Many seeking wellness often find aspects of their lives imbalanced or painful. Typically, people seek help when the burden is too much to bear alone. However, not all discomfort is intense. Sometimes, we sense that our lives aren't progressing as we wish. Mental health is like a spectrum, ranging from flourishing at the high end to clinical depression at the low end. We might find ourselves closer to flourishing, moderately healthy, or leaning towards languishing at different times.

Corey Keyes (2010) introduced the terms "flourishing" and "languishing" in mental health. He described flourishing as feeling good and functioning well while languishing is the opposite. Studies indicate that the distribution of mental health statuses varies, with transitions through these stages being common in our lives. It means that many of us may experience periods of both flourishing and languishing.

Our current situation or past experiences don't doom us to stay at the lower end of the well-being spectrum. Various therapeutic approaches have shown that small behavioral adjustments through our MindView Council can enhance well-being.

We all experience negative thoughts and emotions as a natural part of our lives. How we respond to them is important. If we try to ignore them or hold on to them, they can create harmful cycles, leading to pain, low self-esteem, and self-loathing, overwhelming other aspects of our MindView like the Physical, Social, and Spiritual MindViews. It may lead to decreased activity, social engagement, and a reluctance to pursue values or goals, reducing life's rewards. These feelings can extend to others and the world around us, contributing to mental health issues. Individuals seeking treatment don't understand the root of their depression and may believe that being critical of themselves is beneficial.

Fortunately, new methods to evaluate psychological well-being can guide the healing process. Diener et al. (2009), developed a brief scale reflecting well-being, aligning with concepts like those in the MindView Council. The next Pause and Reflect section features this scale. It can be helpful to complete it at the beginning and end of the Well-Being: The Artfully Lived Life journey to measure progress.

^Pause & Reflect ~ Psychological Well-Being Scale^

Copyright by Ed Diener and Robert Biswas-Diener, 2009

1) I lead a purposeful and meaningful life.
   Disagree ○—○—○—○—○—○—○ Agree
2) My social relationships are supportive and rewarding.
   Disagree ○—○—○—○—○—○—○ Agree
3) I am engaged and interested in my daily activities.
   Disagree ○—○—○—○—○—○—○ Agree
4) I actively contribute to the happiness and well-being of others.
   Disagree ○—○—○—○—○—○—○ Agree
5) I am competent and capable in the activities that are important to me.
   Disagree ○—○—○—○—○—○—○ Agree
6) I am a good person and live a good life.
   Disagree ○—○—○—○—○—○—○ Agree
7) I am optimistic about my future.
   Disagree ○—○—○—○—○—○—○ Agree

Essential Tools for the Artful Journey

As we delve deeper into creating a Well-Being: The Artfully Lived Life, let's focus on the crucial tools needed for this personal journey. Just as an artist selects tools based on their medium, like clay and a pottery wheel for a potter or canvas and oil paints for a painter, we need specific tools for our journey of personal healing and self-discovery. Remember, art is a process, constantly evolving. The joy for an artist often lies not in the final product but in the journey of creation. Life mirrors this: finding joy in the journey itself is crucial, embracing successes, failures, lessons, and the anticipation of what lies ahead. This is a journey worth embracing that will lead to personal healing and self-discovery.

The first step in your healing journey is to learn and apply what we call The Tools for the Artist Within. While not physical, these tools represent principles and concepts passed down through wisdom traditions. They are tools and transformative agents that guide us in growing, developing skills, and living meaningfully, helping us pursue our goals without self-harm. They encourage a more enlightened perspective of ourselves, revealing deeper truths beyond the narratives we often construct about our lives.

Remember, art is a process constantly evolving. The joy for an artist often lies not in the final product but in the journey of creation. Life mirrors this: finding joy in the journey itself is crucial, embracing successes, failures, lessons, and the anticipation of what lies ahead. The first step in your healing journey is to learn and to apply what we call The Tools for the Artist Within. These tools will help you to discover the hidden inner core that you believe you are protecting by staying unaware. As you use and apply them, they will begin to create a profound sense of safety and acceptance within you, fostering an environment where you can truly be your authentic self.

Tools for The Artist Within

In this first step, we focus on five key tools for personal growth and well-being:
- **Acceptance** of life events as we experience them, including imperfections and mistakes as you engage in activities and pursue goals that give your life meaning and purpose,
- **Forgiveness** toward yourself and others for mistakes that are made as you are moving forward fully engaged in the present moment,
- **Self-compassion**, kindness, compassion, and care toward yourself as you refine your many abilities, as well as for others in your world,
- **A Commitment** to intention, focused action, and courage, even in the face of adversity,
- **And Gratitude** for all things, including the gifts of difficulties and experiences, as we strive to learn and grow.

Acceptance: Sometimes, we tell ourselves we want to create something. Still, when we try, our critical inner voice begins to analyze, judge, and question, possibly paralyzing our progress. The perfectionist in us wants to ensure that whatever we do will meet the approval of our inner sense of good enough. We may compare, measure, and minimize until, at last, we are afraid to do anything at all.

The idea of acceptance is to know that every aspect of life experience has meaning, purpose, and value – including and especially – mistakes! Acceptance must precede the lesson. We will not find beauty in a dandelion if weed is all we see.

In 1494, Michelangelo (Goldscheider, 1986) carved an angel from a large chunk of marble. When he saw the marble, he marveled at its beauty and said, "I saw the angel in the marble and carved until I set him free." He had a vision. He courageously embraced his image and did the best he could. You are a carver, too. You are the artisan of your own life. You can know yourself the way Michelangelo knew the chunk of marble. You can learn to see the beauty within yourself. With the right tools, acceptance, forgiveness, self-compassion, commitment, and gratitude, you can free the beauty within you.

We often harbor self-critical thoughts and grow up with misconceptions about ourselves. Yet, like the golden Buddha or Michelangelo's marble, we are inherently perfect and unique. The masterpiece within us exists already!

Change is about revealing this inner beauty, not altering our core selves. It's about removing the layers that obscure our true selves. Michelangelo took a risk with the marble; similarly, embracing change and mistakes is vital to our creative life process.

Remember, the answers are within you, waiting to be discovered. Embrace the journey, including the false starts, as each step brings you closer to wellness and reveals your inner masterpiece. And remember also, that acceptance means no self-judgment or labeling. It means allowing yourself to be whatever you are in this moment.

^Pause & Reflect ~ Acceptance^

At the beginning of their journey, we ask people to list their faults and flaws. They usually ask, "How long should it be?" But they can rarely think of more than a couple of their positive qualities. But let's start there anyway. List five things you do not like about yourself in the following lines.
_____
_____
_____

For a few minutes, sit with your eyes closed and imagine what it would be like to accept all of it! – even the most difficult things! What would it feel like to be in a place where you hardly think about that anymore? It does not mean you stop growing toward your full potential or think everything you do is perfect. How might it be to work toward your potential from where you look forward to being well rather than dwelling on your faults and flaws?
_____
_____
_____

Now, list your positive strengths, skills, and talents. This is not just work-related but also related to your life, your friends, your family, and your hobbies.
_____
_____
_____

Embracing Forgiveness

Forgiveness is a crucial part of our personal growth journey. It's inevitable that we make mistakes; they're a natural part of being human and crucial for learning. Mistakes represent hidden potential, and our response to these errors - ours or others' - is what truly matters. Without self-forgiveness, extending forgiveness to others becomes challenging. Holding onto negative feelings and seeking recompense can imprison us in the past, robbing us of peace and happiness.

Forgiveness is, in essence, a gift to ourselves. It's about reclaiming our right to joy and freedom, not about conceding defeat or necessitating reconciliation. Importantly, forgiveness doesn't have to involve another person. It is an internal act, a decision to release the need for restitution. Self-forgiveness is the key that empowers us to take control of our emotions and move forward.

Similarly, forgiving ourselves is vital. The past is immutable; we can't change who we were or what we did. We can learn from these experiences and make different choices now. Forgiving ourselves means accepting our limitations and acknowledging that we can't know or do everything. This realization isn't a sign of weakness but a step towards being the best we can be now. If we fall short of our expectations, we can adopt new values, set new goals, and devise new plans. Forgiveness opens the door to endless possibilities.

^Pause & Reflect ~ Forgiveness^

As you have been reading about compassion and forgiveness, painful thoughts or memories about events or relationships have likely come to the surface. Just briefly name them in the spaces below.
_____
_____

How have these events changed or damaged your life?
_____
_____
_____

Can you imagine shrinking them to the size of little pebbles? Notice how they feel as you hold them in your hand. Now imagine that you are surrounding them with light. They begin to glow. Visualize them beginning to transform into knowledge and courage. These are experiences that have helped to create you as you are today. And now they begin to melt away, leaving a puddle of water in the palm of your hand. Water nourishes your body and your life. How did these events help you to grow?
_____
_____
_____
_____
_____

The Power of Self-Compassion

Self-compassion is the gateway to forgiveness, a liberating journey that begins with understanding and accepting our human limitations. It's a realization that we can't always be everything to everyone, and that's okay. This understanding doesn't prevent us from learning from our mistakes but frees us from the heavy burden of guilt over our imperfections. Together, self-compassion and forgiveness guide us to the profound truth that life's purpose is to learn and grow, even though our errors.

Acknowledging our efforts with gratitude at the end of each day is vital. We should celebrate our successes and reflect on our shortcomings to foster growth. This practice of self-compassion and forgiveness nurtures creativity, potential, and personal development.

Self-compassion replenishes our energy and vitality, essential for our journey. Often, hurtful behaviors stem from the individual's own suffering. Recognizing this can ease the emotional load we carry, like removing stones from a backpack during a hike. Releasing the layer of blame and self-contempt frees up energy for healing and recovery.

Compassion can take many forms, such as kindness, empathy, validation, and care. It's often easier to offer compassion to others than to ourselves. For instance, we readily extend help to a friend in need or an injured animal, yet we may hesitate to show the same kindness to ourselves. Research shows that self-compassion is crucial for self-love, care, and overall well-being. It helps counter negative self-perceptions and unrealistic demands we place on ourselves.

Self-compassion replenishes our energy and vitality, essential for our journey. It's particularly important when we face stress or difficulties alone. By nurturing ourselves with kindness and supportive affirmations, we ensure that when we're with loved ones, we're emotionally present and able to share our best selves. When we are experiencing difficulties, self-compassion can bolster and strengthen our ability to cope and persevere. Flourishing can be the result rather than pain or despair.

Journal Lines

_____
_____
_____
_____
_____
_____
_____
_____
_____
_____
_____
_____
_____
_____
_____
_____
_____

^Pause & Reflect ~ Self-Compassion^

What are your thoughts about Self-Compassion?
_____
_____

Take a moment to think about the last time you listened to someone talk about their problems. How did it feel to listen to them talk? Were you able to listen patiently? Could you relate to what they said? Felt? Could you tell what they needed to hear from you? Did they need support, concern, validation? Were you able to give that to them?
_____
_____

Now, take a moment to think about the last time you had a similar conversation with yourself, about your own feelings? Can you answer the same questions as above? Could you tell what you needed in that moment? Did you need support, concern, validation? Were you able to offer these things to yourself?
_____
_____

We all need to know we are understood and cared about; these feelings often come up when no one is around. We are responsible for listening to ourselves and being there for ourselves. We can comfort ourselves when we (circle those that you can do, and when you do them, remind yourself that this is a self-compassion action because you deserve self-compassion as well):

Go for a walk	Take a nap	10-min meditation	Listen to music
Pray	Exercise	Read affirmations	Be on your side
Do a body scan	Accept yourself	Do something fun	Forgive yourself
Praise yourself	Show concern	Start a gratitude list	Eat a snack
Fix a cup of coffee	Listen to yourself	Take a warm bath	Enjoy nature
Review your values	Meditate	Work on a hobby	Study Your Strengths

Embracing Commitment and Courage

Commitment, the unwavering force that propels us toward our desires, is the cornerstone of our journey. Whether it's a personal aspiration, a sense of duty, or the pursuit of excellence in our various life roles, commitment defines our inner self and shapes our path to self-improvement and fulfillment.

Our commitments sharpen our understanding of ourselves, our goals, and the pathways to achieve them. Committing to something without believing in its possibility is like holding a paintbrush without paint. Belief and courage are vital here. The courage to pursue our commitments enriches and allows us to grow, enhancing our skills and leading us to new destinations.

It is not just a journey but a transformative experience waiting to unfold. It is recommended that you keep a journal of these experiences through these activities, you will notice subtle yet profound changes in your emotional, behavioral, social, spiritual, and cognitive patterns, bringing greater fulfillment to your life.

^Pause & Reflect ~ Commitment^

What are your thoughts about commitment? Are you willing to make a commitment to begin and complete this journey?
_____
_____
_____

Do you have a story about commitment from your life?
_____
_____
_____

Looking back on what you learned from your life experiences, what would you say to someone else who might be facing similar obstacles?
_____
_____
_____

How would you define courage?
_____
_____
_____

How would the need for courage be relevant to self-awareness and self-discovery?
_____
_____

Other words for commitment might be promise, pledge, obligation, guarantee, promise, and dedication. How do they apply to you? How can they help you?
_____
_____
_____

Courage is the strength to confront challenges, fear, pain, or uncertainty and is integral to commitment. Physical courage means facing physical challenges directly, while moral courage involves making choices that are right for you, even when faced with opposition.

Perseverance, a key aspect of commitment and courage, is about persisting in your path despite obstacles or setbacks. Transformation and personal growth are inherently rewarding, though these rewards are often not tangible. Without courage, the resolve for change might wane. Learning to set intentions and follow through with commitment and courage is a lifelong, invaluable skill.

Consider the many examples of commitment, courage, and resilience in the world around you. Can you think of any? Reflect and journal about them, drawing inspiration for your journey.

Cultivating Gratitude

Gratitude a cornerstone of the Well-Being: The Artfully Lived Life program, is not just a lofty concept. It's a practical tool that can transform our daily experiences. By shifting our focus from what we lack or the hardships we face to our blessings and positive aspects of life, gratitude helps us connect with something greater than ourselves. It could be a higher power or someone we admire, empowering us to reach our full potential.

Gratitude isn't just a feel-good sentiment. It has tangible benefits for mental health, backed by scientific research. It boosts brain chemicals that enhance mood and energy and alleviates depression. A grateful attitude enhances our relationships, making us more appreciative of others' strengths and less suspicious. People who practice gratitude often enjoy better sleep, health, less pain, and more vitality.

Our brains, a product of our evolutionary past, are wired to pay more attention to negative experiences. It was a survival mechanism that helped our ancestors avoid danger. But in our modern lives, this focus on the negative can overshadow positive events, making them harder to recall. This inclination towards negativity often extends to self-perception, where self-criticism feels more natural than self-acceptance. Expressing gratitude might feel unnatural or vain, even for actions we believe are expected of us. But it's a practice that can rewire our brains for positivity.

Yet, gratitude is essential for happiness. It triggers the release of oxytocin, known as the bonding hormone. Gratitude activates the prefrontal cortex, the brain area associated with positive emotions, moral cognition, and decision-making. Feelings of thankfulness foster closeness in human relationships, guiding our values-based actions and enhancing satisfaction with life. Gratitude also contributes to physical well-being, reducing fatigue, pain, and inflammation. Embracing gratitude, therefore, is not just an emotional exercise but a comprehensive approach to improving overall health and happiness.

The Tools for the Artist Within - forgiveness, self-compassion, commitment, courage, and gratitude - passionately and persistently applied will change your life for the better. Years of empirical research have shown these tools to heal and nurture growth within those who choose to embrace possibility.

Embracing Gratitude Amid Struggle

Dealing with struggles can often be challenging. Yet, gratitude teaches us that there is a balance in everything. With challenges, we might be aware of the growth and benefits they bring. Embracing uncomfortable situations can pave the way for greater beauty and understanding. As Kahlil Gibran eloquently put it, "pain is merely a wall separating two gardens".

When facing difficulties, it's beneficial to acknowledge the situation and then consciously shift our focus to something more positive or something aligned with our values. By concentrating on gratitude, we allocate less mental energy to negative thoughts. This shift diminishes the impact of negativity in our lives, allowing us to refocus on what truly matters with peace and creativity.

^Pause & Reflect ~ Gratitude^

What are the things you most appreciate about yourself?
_____
_____

What do you most appreciate about others?
_____
_____

Other words have similar meanings, such as thankfulness, giving credit, showing recognition, and acknowledgment. Describe how you experience and express these qualities toward anyone or anything in your life.
_____
_____

No one you love is without flaw. Can you look past the imperfections to see them with grateful eyes?
_____
_____

If not, what is stopping you? Journal.
_____
_____

Integrating the Metaphor for Healing

In Chapter One, we introduced the MindView Council, comprising five members and the Observer Manager. To visualize their interplay, think of your hand: four fingers, an opposing thumb, and a palm coordinating movement. The fingers symbolize the Council members, representing different internal capacities or MindView. The palm, acting as the Observer-Manager, directs these capacities as the hand wields its tools. This metaphor helps us understand our inner workings.

The metaphor of two hands working together, symbolizing protection, safety, and strength, ties together the concepts we've explored: the MindView Council and The Tools for the Artist Within. These concepts guide you in identifying the starting point for your healing and the tools necessary for recovery. By understanding your inner workings in terms of the five MindViews: Social, Emotional, Thinking, Physical, and Spiritual (or wisdom), you can understand more about what healing need to take place within you and which MindView might needs your attention to healing. Then, you can begin to heal by applying the five Tools for the Artist Within to the areas with your inner workings. These tools can help heal the deepest of hurts and wounds by focusing your attention, on where you most need it.

Imagine the hands as a metaphor. The Observer-Manager, like the palm, receives, coordinates, and integrates the actions of the five Council members, akin to how a palm works with the fingers and thumb. This analogy helps us grasp the complex interactions within the MindView Council.

Each Council member brings resources that are beneficial not only individually but also to the other members. For instance, physical exercise can alleviate stress and depression, benefiting the Emotional MindView. Cognitive tools from positive psychology enhance emotional well-being. Empirical evidence shows the emotional uplift from physical touch, the multifaceted benefits of socializing, and the healing effects of spiritual practices.

Using the Tools for the Artist Within can significantly aid in healing. The upcoming Guided Meditation offers a chance to create a safe, nurturing space within yourself, shielded from negative thoughts and fears. These tools - self-compassion, forgiveness, self-acceptance - can help repair damage to your core being by reconnecting you with your true self.

We introduce these tools early in the workbook to allow ample practice while exploring other concepts. More skills and guidance will be provided as we learn to navigate life's experiences. Through the exercises and skill development, you'll gain a deeper understanding of yourself, better equipping you to craft an Artfully Lived Life and achieve the well-being you seek.

Journal Lines

_____
_____
_____
_____
_____

^Pause & Reflect ~ Goal Statements^

It is my intention to accept both my successes and failures, and to forgive my mistakes with a compassionate heart, as I commit to focused action, even in the face of adversity. I openly express gratitude for opportunities to create peace, & healing, as I move forward in my life.

- **I Accept** myself as I am. Acceptance will free me to be more open to risks and change. My imperfections are potential in disguise. I can greet my learning process with courage. It gives my life direction and purpose. As I learn acceptance for myself, I will also come to accept others as they are. _____

- **Forgiveness** will create the safety I need in my life to become the person I choose to be. I can be more forgiving toward myself and others by _____

- **I choose compassion** and kindness toward myself today. I can be kinder and gentler toward myself and others by _____

- I am making a **Commitment** to courage and focused action, even in the face of adversity by _____

- I have used the creative resources of my MindView Council throughout my life, and I express **gratitude** to my inner being for _____

Journal Lines

_____
_____
_____
_____
_____
_____
_____
_____
_____
_____
_____
_____
_____
_____
_____
_____
_____
_____
_____
_____

Guided Meditation ~ Chapter Two: Tools for the Artist Within

Before we move on to the following Guided Meditation, take some time to think about the stories you tell yourself that have not been helpful. You will refer back to these unhelpful stories as you go through the Guided Meditation that follows. In this guided meditation, we hope to set the stage for positive growth by introducing The Artist's Tools: acceptance, forgiveness, self-compassion, commitment, and gratitude for who you are. It is our belief that these tools will help to free up your creativity and increase your energy for discovering what is most important in your life.

Journal Space

_____

☘ What would it be like to think of your MindView council as your inner family?

Some of them may need more attention than others, and still others can make big contributions. Journal about what this would be like.

GM Journaling ~ Chapter Two: The Tools for the Artist Within

☘ Describe your experiences with your MindView Council since you journaled last.

☘ What were the unhelpful stories you and your MindView team weeded out of your garden space?

☘ What was it like to have a team support you?

☘ How might The Artist's Tools assist you in your efforts to be more accepting and compassionate toward yourself?

☘ Did you begin to experience a sense of compassion and healing within the part of you that has been suffering?

Guided Meditation ~ Chapter Two: Tools for the Artist Within

Lie down, get comfortable and close your eyes. Place your hand on the spot that rises and falls the most when you inhale. If this spot is on your chest, you are not using your full lung capacity. Put your hand on your stomach and take deep full breaths. Breaths that make your stomach rise more than your chest. Continue breathing slowly and deeply into your stomach. See your breath as a pure white cloud. Coming in through the top of your head. As it swirls down through your body, it picks up all of the impurities, the tension, the fatigue, the pain, or the problems of the day. Imagine all of the impurities exiting out through your toes as you exhale. As your lungs are emptied, the cloud leaves your body and disappears out into space. Again, the white cloud comes in through your head. Imagine it swirling down through your body, carrying away the tensions and the worries – the impurities exiting with your breath. Down through your chest, your buttocks, and thighs. Down through your legs, ankles, and feet, and carrying away the tension, worry, pain, or fear out through your toes. See these impurities exiting out through your toes and away.

And now the cloud of oxygen turns a beautiful blue color. Calming, soothing, feel the color cleansing your body, your mind. Leaving your body feeling deeply relaxed. Your problems and worries washed away. Peaceful, quiet, calm, lighter with each breath, almost as if you are floating. Just floating. Deeply relaxed.

From this relaxed place, go to your garden space. Again, no one can come here unless you invite them. Everything within this protective shield is your personal space. Everything that you are is here with you.

Find a place to sit down and relax in this beautiful place. It can be a place you have already created or something new. You are comfortable here. There is nothing here that will bother you. And from this deeply relaxed place within you – think of a time in your life when you learned how to do something challenging. It might have been learning to ride your bike, or when you learned a new sport. It might have been something in school that was really difficult. Remember how badly you wanted to know that new skill. You would think about it, and you would make time for it in your day.

Take a moment to think about what it was. It might have been learning to ski or learning to horseback ride. It probably started with your imagination or seeing someone else doing that amazing thing and wanting so badly to do the same thing.

You accepted that you didn't know how to do it, and you dared to try, anyway. It didn't even occur to you to worry about your mistakes because the priority was to learn. It started with a Commitment to accomplish that fantastic feat before you. Perhaps it was doing something you loved, so you didn't notice how much time it took. But, you would practice, and practice. You made so many mistakes but kept trying because you accepted mistakes as part of the process.

Perhaps you had someone in your life who encouraged you to keep trying, or perhaps you learned because you wanted to. Either way, you dared to keep trying. When you made mistakes with self-compassion, you forgave yourself, learned from them, and then kept trying. And as you practiced, you got better. Your confidence grew, and so did your self-esteem. And then, when you got it right, it felt so amazing to be doing that thing that you thought was impossible. You were so grateful that you didn't quit and for the opportunity to learn and grow.

It is time now to apply your experience to your inner work. The Artist's Tools are Acceptance, Forgiveness, Self-compassion, Commitment, and Gratitude. You may also use the new tools and skills from this chapter. Learning to accept internal difficulties and become aware of what they are is a challenging but essential commitment.

It may not seem possible or easy to think of your inner nature with compassion, forgiveness, or acceptance, especially considering your current beliefs about who you are. In fact, you may feel you deserve punishment. That is okay. But we want to correct this message. Whatever your story is, whatever it is that has caused you so much difficulty, it is time now to start clearing it away.

Let's go now to your garden space. There are weeds here that are blocking new growth. Can you tell what they are? Are you ready to begin to clear them away? One by one, see the ideas or stories that have hurt you and watch them as they shrink away. Smaller and smaller. Shrinking. Until they are nothing but molecules. Now send those molecules outside of your MindView. Out. Now blow them away. Out and away. We want to make this inner garden space a place where you are safe to grow.

It may take a while to get used to what it's like not to have all of those ideas and stories in your MindView, and for a while, they may want to keep coming back. But that is okay. That is normal. Your brain will feel like you need them to help you be a better person. But you don't. Each time the negative thoughts, feelings, or beliefs come back, imagine yourself shrinking them. And shrinking them. Until they are nothing but molecules. Send them out of your head and blow them away. Just blowing them away.

Now notice the presence of your MindView Council. They are here to support you and to remind you that you are more than the labels. You are more than words. In fact, no amount of words could ever describe all that you are, your value, or your worth.

Now imagine that self-compassion is like a warm, healing rain that washes away sadness, low self-esteem, and hurt. As it washes these away, you begin to feel stronger and renewed. Peaceful and complete. New insight and understanding begin to open to you. Just receive whatever your MindView Council chooses to share. And when you have completed this guided meditation, journal all that you experienced. Remember that each time you return to this garden space, you will experience new healing. Each day is a new beginning.

Now, when you are ready, take a deep breath and come back to this room.

Well-Being: The Artfully Lived Life

Chapter 3 – Understanding Well-Being and Shaping a New MindView

"The great thing in this world is not so much where we stand as in what direction we are moving." ~ Oliver Wendell Holmes

Our journey to understanding ourselves starts early in life. As children, everything was new, and we were learning what we liked and disliked, seeing the world with fresh eyes. Over time, our interactions with others helped form our belief systems, acting like filters through which we view and interpret the world. These beliefs, influenced by our cultures, religions, family backgrounds, and education, shaped-and continue to shape our understanding of ourselves and our place in the world.

Self-understanding involves developing ideas about how our MindViews work, shaping our social interactions, relationships, and overall life functioning. Skills like empathy, the ability to understand and share someone else's feelings, emerged from our own experiences. Empathy, along with hope, kindness, forgiveness, and gratitude, are crucial for maintaining relationships and are innate qualities present from early life.

Our life experiences also taught us "rules of thumb" – basic behavioral templates. Over time, these evolve into stories that continue to form our sense of identity, or "me-ness". A healthy sense of self develops from successfully applying these behavioral templates. Children learn these rules within their family and society, and as they apply them, they build self-esteem. This growth is nurtured by positive interactions, where attempts at new skills are met with support and validation, which are key to emotional health and well-being for both children and adults. A supportive environment fosters creativity, independence, confidence, and self-esteem.

Conversely, if a child encounters unpredictable rules or harsh reactions to their learning attempts, they may struggle to develop a sense of freedom, safety, and self-assurance. Exposure to negative behaviors like name-calling, judgment, or violence can lead to trauma in both children and adults. Many who experience such environments struggle with confusion and despair, internalizing the negative labels and judgments imposed on them. These "negative scripts" can be detrimental, especially without a strong sense of self-identity to counteract these harmful judgments.

Overcoming Negative Scripts and Embracing Well-Being

Negative scripts can be challenging to overcome. We tend to wholeheartedly believe them, trusting our feelings as absolute truths. In therapy, clients are encouraged to step back from these perceived truths and distinguish themselves from the people or situations that fostered these negative scripts. This process involves activating the Thinking MindView, helping individuals understand that external labels cannot fully define their complex selves. Recognizing our depth and complexity is the first step in recovery, using The Tools for the Artist Within.

Well-being doesn't mean rewriting the past or changing who we were. It's about altering our perspective, how we interpret and process emotions, and how we view our past coping strategies. Reflecting on the Golden Buddha's story, the clay covering served a protective purpose for centuries. When it was eventually removed, the true beauty beneath was revealed, inspiring millions.

Similarly, the symbolic layers of mud and clay that have covered your life might have served a purpose once. Now, it might be time to assess whether these layers still hold value. The choice is yours. If you've experienced pain and hardship, you also possess the power to learn from these experiences and let them go. As you acquire new skills and move forward, you can find a renewed sense of balance and well-being.

Exploring the Essence of Well-Being

Earlier, we introduced three influential approaches to well-being: Mindfulness, Acceptance and Commitment Therapy (ACT), and Positive Psychology. While each has unique perspectives on human flourishing, they also share commonalities, collectively providing a comprehensive understanding of how to live a meaningful life through committed actions toward well-being.

Achieving wellness will require dedication to learning and practicing the right tools and skills. Mindfulness, ACT, and Positive Psychology have established principles that guide our understanding of human flourishing. This chapter offers insights into well-being based on extensive research, which is essential as you apply The Tools for the Artist Within and learn the strategies in subsequent chapters.

Mindfulness: Mindfulness teaches that life is filled with joyous and challenging experiences. An open, curious attitude allows us to accept and approach all experiences with kindness and compassion, instead of judgment or avoidance. Mindfulness skills involve

a) nurturing curiosity and acceptance of present thoughts and feelings, recognizing their potential for learning and meaning,

b) accommodating complex emotions like fear or anxiety without struggle, and

c) focusing on present experiences.

Mindfulness has gained significant attention in psychology and medicine, with numerous clinical trials supporting its effectiveness. Regular mindfulness practice has been shown to help manage stress and alleviate anxiety, depression, trauma, and pain symptoms. Long-term mindfulness practice benefits emotional regulation and overall well-being.

Research also indicates that mindfulness improves memory, brain function, and brain structure, reduces stress hormones and enhances immune system function. Incorporating daily mindfulness practice, whether alone or alongside other therapies, can significantly benefit mental and physical health.

Embracing Mindfulness for Stress Reduction

The Mindfulness-Based Stress Reduction Program (MBSR), created by Jon Kabat-Zinn in 1990, promotes seven key principles for a new approach to daily life:

1. **Affirmation of Self:** Recognizing that as long as you're breathing, there is more right with you than wrong.
2. **Present Moment Awareness:** Often, we dwell in the past or future, over which we have little control. MBSR emphasizes awareness of the present moment, including sensory experiences like sight, sound, taste, and touch.
3. **Acceptance:** Accepting the present moment, even if it's challenging, helps us move beyond judgmental expectations and reactions.
4. **Alternative Approaches to Challenges:** Often, we either avoid unpleasant experiences or obsess over them with negative thinking. MBSR suggests these strategies are counterproductive. Instead, it promotes facing these experiences directly.
5. **Turning Towards Discomfort:** Rather than avoiding or holding onto negative aspects of challenging experiences, MBSR encourages us to open up to them, and then let them pass like a train crossing our path. By accepting and learning from these experiences, we increase our resilience, insight, and wisdom.
6. **Positive Redirecting of Energy:** We can focus our energy more positively by approaching our experiences with kindness and compassion, we can focus our energy more positively.
7. **Non-Doing Mindfulness:** Mindfulness involves simply being present with ourselves in each moment with compassion and without judgment.

Incorporating these seven principles into daily life can transform how we perceive ourselves and the world. As we practice kindness and compassion, letting go of judgments and struggles, we focus more on the present and the inherent qualities within us. Cultivating attitudes like non-judging, patience, trust, acceptance, and letting go becomes instrumental in life transformation and developing well-being. These qualities serve as guideposts, influencing our life choices and steering us toward greater well-being.

Understanding Acceptance and Commitment Therapy (ACT)

Acceptance and Commitment Therapy, like Mindfulness, aims to cultivate psychological flexibility. This flexibility aids in confronting life's challenges with acceptance, openness, and present-moment awareness, enabling us to see them differently. Through committed action and employing effective skills, we can move beyond difficulties to focus on what truly matters to us.

ACT employs a values-based behavioral approach where mindfulness skills (such as acceptance, openness, and present-moment awareness) are applied to identify core values and goals. This approach enhances our ability to concentrate on significant aspects of our lives, rather than getting caught up in self-narratives. Integrating ACT with mindfulness offers dual benefits: first, by overcoming emotional barriers like avoidance, negativity, or self-judgment, and second, helping us remain present and committed to our values despite challenging feelings.

ACT suggests that well-being is achieved by

1) accepting unwanted thoughts and emotions, allowing them space within us rather than trying to exclude them,

2) detaching (or defusing) from these thoughts and feelings instead of attempting to change or fix them, and

3) maintaining present-moment awareness by focusing non-judgmentally on our current interactions with the world. This approach highlights that our attention is a choice.

A personal example to illustrate this concept is the experience of stubbing a toe. It's a painful yet common incident. Both children and adults instinctively understand that such accidents happen, and there's little to do other than express discomfort and move on. For instance, after stubbing his toe, Jacob might momentarily feel the pain but then quickly refocuses on preparing for the prom, shifting his attention from the discomfort to the excitement of the upcoming event. This scenario exemplifies the principle of present-moment awareness, as discussed in Jon Kabat-Zinn's MBSR program.

Navigating Life Stories and Embracing Change

Over time, layers of life history and stories accumulate, and just like that Tibetan Buddha, they begin to obscure our true selves. We begin to form attachments to false ideas about who we are and what we are like. When we observe our thoughts and emotions from a distance, we gain some perspective and awareness regarding the transient nature of these false beliefs and the impermanence of the thoughts and perceptions that have shifted our interpretations of who we are over time.

This perspective shift enables us to "defuse" or neutralize judgments and labels. These emotional experiences, similar to a stubbed toe, may cause pain but don't define our essence. They occupy space within us, but coexist with everything else that matters to us. Like the excitement of an upcoming event such as a prom, the next moment, goal, or joyous occasion awaits our attention. Focusing on these positive aspects and learning to neutralize negative judgments can become a powerful tool for well-being.

Adopting a "beginner's mind" attitude is an effective way to release negativity and judgment. This mind set involves approaching each moment without preconceived notions, habitual thinking, or labels. Starting fresh with a new perspective opens us to alternative possibilities, solutions, discoveries, and conclusions, leading to quicker and more flexible problem-solving and resolution.

ACT also promotes committed action for self-care to enhance psychological well-being. Adopting and maintaining lifestyle changes like healthy eating, regular sleep, exercise, and reducing harmful habits like alcohol and nicotine use can be challenging. The psychological flexibility developed through ACT assists in managing the discomfort associated with thoughts, feelings, and physical sensations during these lifestyle adjustments.

Personalizing Your Journey to Well-Being

Embarking on this journey to well-being has a variety of approaches. Your unique inner masterpiece will start to reveal itself as you develop and refine these skills. Creating your well-being is a personal endeavor, shaped by your actions and insights, rather than being dictated by past events or external circumstances beyond your control.

We understand that this is a substantial amount of information to take in. In the upcoming pages and chapters, we'll guide you in applying these principles to your understanding of well-being. However, before diving deeper, gaining a clearer perspective on what specific areas of this program would be most important to focus on. The upcoming activities are designed to help you understand your MindView Council and how it currently functions in your life. They also assist in identifying where to direct your energy moving forward. If you commit to this program, it will become increasingly relevant and meaningful to you. The strategies you learn will enhance your interaction with the world. The next section includes a questionnaire to help you gain deeper self-awareness and understanding of your MindView Domains.

Synthesizing Insights for Personal Growth

Having explored the new MindView perspective, take a moment to reflect on your insights. Identify your strengths and areas for improvement. Remember, the goal isn't perfection; it's about self-awareness and using it to make adjustments, set goals, and watch your progress toward the best version of yourself.

Imagine observing an artist in their studio. You'd notice the preparatory steps and techniques needed for even the simplest artistic creation. Similarly, understanding the steps and strategies required to bring your vision to life makes the seemingly unattainable achievable.

Navigating Life's Challenges for Well-Being

We often find ourselves focusing more on certain areas of our lives while neglecting others, sometimes as an automatic response to coping with pain, fear, or anxiety from past experiences. However, trying to evade or eliminate these negative feelings in specific areas of our lives (MindViews) is only sometimes the approach. Instead, embracing a balanced and enriched life can infuse optimism and hope into our journey of growth and change.

Well-being isn't about sidestepping life's challenges; it's about finding meaning and purpose in our problems and focusing on positive aspects to transform our experiences into something fulfilling. A life of well-being doesn't mean a life without issues. It entails facing life's inevitable problems with effective problem-solving and resolution skills and understanding that difficulties are a natural part of life. While these challenges sometimes seem overwhelming, they don't have to overpower us. We have many tools and skills at our disposal to address these problems.

If you encounter a problem that seems too daunting or find yourself overwhelmed, remember that you are on a path of learning and self-discovery. Achieving well-being involves a readiness to grow and change, engaging in what we value most, and reconnecting with activities that foster hope and optimism. This journey also demands commitment and consistent practice.

MindView Questionnaire

1) I know there is a part of me that always seems to be looking out for me.
Disagree ○──○──○──○──○──○──○──○ Agree

2) When I am with others, I find I do not trust them, and I find it hard to open up.
Disagree ○──○──○──○──○──○──○──○ Agree

3) I generally take things at face value. I don't always wait for the facts.
Disagree ○──○──○──○──○──○──○──○ Agree

4) When I need to make big decisions, I am able to consider all aspects, as well as the others who will also be affected.
Disagree ○──○──○──○──○──○──○──○ Agree

5) I have a sense of wisdom that I've gained from my life experiences.
Disagree ○──○──○──○──○──○──○──○ Agree

6) I am able to tell when my behavior is not in my best interest and make adjustments.
Disagree ○──○──○──○──○──○──○──○ Agree

7) My life feels purposeful and meaningful to me.
Disagree ○──○──○──○──○──○──○──○ Agree

8) I consider myself to be resourceful when it comes to accomplishing my goals.
Disagree ○──○──○──○──○──○──○──○ Agree

9) I have a strong support system that I can turn to when needed.
Disagree ○──○──○──○──○──○──○──○ Agree

10) I feel good about the world I live in and hope to make it a better place.
Disagree ○──○──○──○──○──○──○──○ Agree

11) I have very strong emotional reactions, sometimes so strong I can't control them.
Disagree ○──○──○──○──○──○──○──○ Agree

12) I value healthy lifestyle choices and am willing to commit to them, even when hey are uncomfortable.
Disagree ○──○──○──○──○──○──○──○ Agree

13) When I feel physically unwell, I also feel unwell in other ways.
Disagree ○──○──○──○──○──○──○──○ Agree

14) Gratitude and appreciation are what keep me going during difficult times.
Disagree ○──○──○──○──○──○──○──○ Agree

Reflecting on Wellness Principles

As we transition to the next Guided Meditation in Chapter Three, it's important to pause and reflect on the insights you've gained about wellness. Consider the various wellness principles we've explored. Identify which of these principles you found most enlightening and consider how to apply them to your life. Reflect on the ways these principles could be beneficial to you. Also, recognize any current obstacles or challenges that might be hindering you from utilizing these principles effectively. This reflection will help you engage more meaningfully with the upcoming Guided Meditation, allowing you to focus on the most relevant and useful principles for your personal growth and well-being.

Journal Space

‌ What would it be like to consider your MindView Council as an inner support system? Again, some of them may need more attention than others, but as imperfect as they may be, they can still have your back. Journal your thoughts.

GM Journaling ~ Chapter Three: Guiding Principles

‌ As you imagined yourself in the midst of your personal space what did you notice? _____

‌ Describe your experiences with your MindView Council. _____

‌ Were you able to become more aware of how the wellness needs are so different for each MindView Space? _____

Journal Lines

_____
_____
_____
_____
_____

Guided Meditation ~ Chapter Three: Embracing Guiding Principles

Find a comfortable position, either sitting or lying down, and gently close your eyes. Rest your hand on your stomach and take deep, full breaths. With each breath, imagine a stream of pure white light entering through the top of your head. Visualize this light as it flows through your body, gathering any impurities, tension, fatigue, or the day's burdens. As you exhale, picture these impurities leaving your body through your toes and vanishing into the void.

With each inhalation, the white light continues to cascade through you – from your head and face, easing tension, down through your neck, shoulders, arms, and fingers, washing away worries. It flows further down, through your chest, hips, thighs, legs, ankles, and feet, cleansing as it goes, and exits through your toes, taking all negativity with it.

Now, envision this light transforming into a serene shade of blue. Feel its calming and purifying energy, relaxing your body and mind, carrying away concerns and leaving behind a state of peace and tranquility. Imagine yourself floating in this quietude.

Transport yourself to your personal Garden space, a place where you and your MindView Council have dispelled negative thoughts. It's a blank canvas, ready for your creative touch. In this space, embrace your inner Artist's Tools: acceptance of your whole self, forgiveness, empathy, and compassion. Let these qualities fill every part of you, permeating every cell, infusing your mind and body with love, care, self-acceptance, and self-compassion. Release any lingering fears or worries with each breath, sinking deeper into a state of calm and peace.

Contemplate how you want this Garden space to reflect your essence. It could be a vibrant rose garden, a serene cactus garden, or even a contemplative Zen rock garden. Envision a space that brings you comfort and healing. Find a spot in this Garden where you feel most at ease. Maybe it's sitting on the grass, leaning against a tree, or on a bench surrounded by your favorite flowers. Take a moment to just be present in this space.

In this next phase of the meditation, let's explore the guiding principles for each member of your MindView Council. Focus on your Spiritual MindView, the part of you that connects with your core values and what truly matters in your life. Take a moment to listen inwardly. What messages is your Spiritual MindView conveying to you? Reflect on the values that significantly enhance your well-being.

Now, shift your attention to your Emotional MindView, where the guiding principle is acceptance. Can you be present in this moment without judgment? Visualize allowing any uncomfortable thoughts and feelings to arise, acknowledging them, and then letting them drift away like clouds in the sky.

Turn your focus to the Thinking MindView, which in the Artfully Lived Life is about learning to react with less emotion and more mindfulness. Strive to remain calm and centered. Make choices that align with your values, drawing on the collective strength of all your MindView resources.

Lastly, contemplate the guiding principle of the Social MindView. This principle is about understanding how your thoughts, feelings, and beliefs shape your interactions with others. It influences the depth, quality, and intimacy of your relationships. Spend a few moments considering how this principle manifests in your social connections

Let's now focus on the Physical MindView, where the guiding principle involves making healthy lifestyle choices. This includes following a committed action plan for diet, exercise, sleep hygiene, and abstaining from harmful substances. Remember, your physical health is a crucial component of your overall well-being.

Next, consider the Observer-Manager MindView, which plays a pivotal role in self-regulation. This involves the willingness and determination to commit to your action plans. The Observer-Manager is always mindful of your complete self, including your values, goals, intentions, and choices, ready to support you in your journey.

These Guiding Principles can steer you through life's challenges, helping you to accept difficulties as part of your journey. Learn to let challenges pass without struggle, practicing non-judgment and self-compassion.

Visualize feeling the warmth of the sun on your skin as you sit in your Garden space. Take a mental snapshot of this serene place, noting the vibrant colors and soothing scents of the flowers, trees, and plants. Here, in this safe haven, The Artist's Tools of acceptance, forgiveness, compassion, commitment, and gratitude shield you from internal and external judgments. When pain arises, these tools will bring peace and well-being.

Let this Garden be a space of healing and acceptance, initiating your personal restoration process. In real life, we often turn to our inner resources when we need or desire something. Right now, focus on what you need, allowing yourself to embrace these changes. Spend a few moments with the transformations you are inviting, feeling their healing and strengthening effects.

Check in with your MindView Council, each part benefiting from The Artist's Tools. Feel the Physical MindView growing stronger, the Emotional MindView becoming more peaceful and stable. Acknowledge your Social MindView evolving through relationships, and your Thinking MindView integrating these changes. Focus on your Spiritual MindView, feeling renewed and restored.

Take this time to connect deeply with your core self, experiencing healing and rejuvenation. Repeat this meditation whenever you feel down or when old habits resurface. Remember, these are just habits with deep roots, but as you continue these meditations, they will gradually lose their hold, becoming distant memories.

When you're ready, take a few deep breaths, gently open your eyes, and return to your surroundings, carrying with you a sense of renewal and clarity.

Chapter 4 – Where We Get Stuck and How We Move On

"When I let go of what I am, I become what I might be." ~Lau Tzu~

Understanding Our Challenges and How to Overcome Them

So far, we've covered a lot of ground on what it means to be well. We examined three approaches to achieving well-being: Mindfulness, Acceptance and Commitment Therapy (ACT), and positive psychology. Through these, we've gained insights into wellness, including what constitutes healthy activities. However, discussing well-being also means acknowledging the need for change in our thinking and choices.

Reflecting on history, we find an example in Plato's accounts of Socrates, a Greek philosopher living around 400 A.D. Socrates was put on trial to encourage his students to think critically and question established beliefs. Given the choice between prison, exile, or death, Socrates famously said, "The unexamined life is not worth living". He believed that life without the freedom to think and question – to seek answers to life's challenges – wasn't a life worth living, and he chose death over losing this freedom. Socrates felt that without striving for understanding, life lacked purpose and meaning.

In our time, we have the gift of agency or free will, allowing us to pursue our dreams and purposes. But do we fully utilize this freedom? Sometimes, our ego resists change, preferring to maintain the status quo. However, to grow, we need to let go of old, destructive ways of thinking about ourselves and our world. Growth and change can be thrilling, motivating, and uplifting. It can also be challenging, requiring new resources and skills. Embracing exploration and discovery can deeply enrich our life experiences.

This chapter will delve into the four common barriers that hinder progress: low self-esteem and self-blame stemming from past experiences, the harsh inner critic born from negative thinking and toxic environments, the challenge of releasing old patterns, and the fear associated with letting go of familiar thoughts, feelings, and beliefs. We'll explore these obstacles and discuss strategies to move past them.

Defense Mechanisms – A Barrier to Well-Being

Defense mechanisms are a barrier to well-being. They operate similarly to an Inner Critic, but they function oppositely by keeping us unaware and unable to receive important information that may be important and meaningful. While the Inner Critic can make us feel inadequate, defense mechanisms subconsciously shield us from stressful or emotionally taxing situations. By distorting the exchange of information between ourselves and our environment defense mechanisms allow us to deny information, repress memories, and blame others for our errors. They are barriers that often stem from misjudgments or exaggerated perceptions of emotional threat, and they subtly shape our reactions and decisions, especially under pressure. Understanding and managing our defense mechanisms is integral to building the kind of confidence that supports lasting well-being and personal transformation. Certain defense mechanisms can also trap us in a cycle of stagnation. For example, avoidance can foster a fear of change, creating a loop without progression. In conflicts, we might resort to blaming others or projecting our faults onto them. We will talk about this more in Chapter 13.

Consider a workplace scenario: you're unfairly blamed for a mistake. If you are unable to correct your boss publicly, you will internalize the blame. Later, this frustration might manifest in your personal life, leading to unnecessary conflicts with your partner by releasing the emotions meant for your boss onto your partner (projection). You might also avoid the conflict altogether by internalizing it as a personal attack and refusing to discuss it (avoidance).

A healthier approach would be to embrace vulnerability, and discuss the real issue with your partner or friend. Choosing open communication can build intimacy rather than conflict, helping you to step out of the shadow of defense mechanisms and into a space of authenticity and growth.

When we fail to recognize or confront our most harmful defense mechanisms, they often solidify into formidable obstacles blocking the path to well-being. These mechanisms, while sometimes appealing and cleverly executed, are primarily tools for coping with negative emotions like sadness and pain. However, they frequently breed suspicion and distrust, stemming from maladaptive behaviors developed in response to emotionally taxing or threatening experiences in our past.

While there's ongoing debate about the exact nature and number of these mechanisms, the central issue remains; they provide only a temporary shield from discomfort but at the cost of dampening our overall life experience, including joy, authenticity, and personal growth.

Research has pinpointed over 20 common defense mechanisms that serve to protect our self-esteem and assist in managing anxiety and depression. These mechanisms range in their effects and visibility. Some are quite primitive, with clear drawbacks, such as denial or aggression. Others like avoidance or forgetfulness, might seem less harmful often manifesting in social or personal situations.

The frequency and intensity of these defenses determine their placement on a spectrum from mildly to moderately dysfunctional. Although they may offer temporary relief from challenging emotions, ultimately, they hinder our ability to align with our core values and long-term objectives. They prevent us from receiving information that may be helpful or meaningful in our lives.

The journey from relying on defense mechanisms to embracing authenticity may seem daunting, but it's often more achievable than many believe. Your work in this program has likely initiated significant changes. It is also worth noting that our defense mechanisms are often more apparent to others, such as friends, family, and partners than to ourselves. When loved ones point out our potentially self-destructive behaviors, it's beneficial to consider their observations with an open mind.

Clinical evidence underscores the importance of being present to our emotions, allowing them to pass, and then choose actions driven by our values. This approach fosters personal growth and well-being. In contrast, defense mechanisms, anchored in self-protective emotions and behaviors, are generally considered maladaptive. They mask the root of our issues, and dampen our capacity to experience positive emotions, thoughts, and connections fully.

Cultivating Inner Stability in Our MindView Systems

Embracing wiser choices and behaviors leads to equanimity and inner peace. Individuals who grasp this concept tend to transcend reactive patterns, flowing harmoniously with life's rhythms. They tap into their intuitive understanding and grow more attuned to their surroundings. This heightened awareness allows them to foresee potential challenges and unearth solutions that might not be immediately apparent to others.

Life inevitably brings its share of pain and frustrations. Sometimes these either arise from unforeseen obstacles, or simply because we haven't yet mastered the necessary strategies to tackle them. This is precisely why we need to prepare internally. We can turn pain or adversity into wisdom by honing our problem solving skills. This wisdom, born from our struggles, can significantly alleviate - or even eradicate - future suffering. Thus, challenges and contentment are interlinked aspects of our journey towards well-being, as long as we are learning from our experiences.

Acknowledging that emotions such as peace, joy, happiness, sadness, and suffering are fleeting, is a powerful act of self-compassion, and it embodies the concept of equanimity. Although equanimity is a principle deeply rooted in Buddhist traditions, it holds universal, secular value. It's the capacity to fully engage with all aspects of life while maintaining composure amidst intense emotions or pain. This equilibrium prevents us from losing our inner and outer balance during life's trials or helps us swiftly restore it. Imagine navigating through life's ups and downs with this level of steadiness and poise!

Personal Significance and Well-Being

Well-being is commonly perceived through two lenses: happiness and a sense of meaningfulness. Happiness is often associated with feelings of comfort, joy, and a sense of security. In contrast, a meaningful life is usually marked by its significance, purpose, and a sense of equilibrium. The dynamics between these aspects can differ across cultures, and according to age and life stages

A life of happiness typically unfolds in stable social, financial, and political settings. This implies that such a state of being is more readily achievable for those in higher socioeconomic strata, who often enjoy robust, consistent interpersonal relationships. Yet, these conditions are not universally accessible. Adopting flexible MindViews rooted in optimism, gratitude, and an appreciation for life's moments can extend the reach of happiness to broader segments of society.

In his seminal work, "Man's Search for Meaning", Viktor Frankl (1946, Reprinted 2006) asserted that finding meaning in life is the most significant pursuit for any individual. Frankl, argued that our personal beliefs shape and define how we interpret life's challenges. A loss of meaning can greatly impair our ability to comprehend and navigate through life's adversities.

Throughout this book, we have emphasized the concept of a psychologically rich life, one that encompasses diversity, interest, adaptability, and an inquisitive spirit. Embracing the idea that our perspective is not the sole valid viewpoint fosters our ability to evolve and adjust as life changes. Through alternative perspectives and the insights gained from our experiences, we recognize that our perception of life events can contribute more to our distress or instability than the events themselves.

While confronting uncomfortable emotions can be challenging, the obstacles created by rigid thinking patterns can sometimes feel overwhelming and hopeless. Therefore, understanding and cultivating cognitive flexibility is highly beneficial. By critically evaluating our thought processes, we can adapt our interpretations and reactions to reduce feelings of helplessness or vulnerability. This is what taking responsibility for our thoughts entails. Life rarely presents issues in black and white or in absolute terms of good and bad. Dialectical thinking, or the ability to view issues from multiple perspectives, enables us to see that every situation in life has both positive and negative elements. We have the power to choose not to be victims of circumstances that seem beyond our control. At the very least, we always have the autonomy to determine our perception, interpretation, and response. Our attitudes, beliefs, and opinions, in the end, are ours to shape.

Navigating Self-Esteem and Overcoming Its' Challenges

Self-esteem is essentially our sense of self-worth or worthiness. It's how we perceive value, often compared to others like peers or family members. We frequently seek validation and ask ourselves, "Am I good enough?" However, this approach can be flawed, as it bases our worth on others' opinions or our performance in specific tasks at specific times. It's crucial to remember everyone has varied abilities in areas they value. Focusing too much on others who may be more skilled than us can be disheartening. Conversely, self-esteem compared with less skilled individuals can lead to complacency and hinder our progress. Our true worth cannot be accurately measured by others' perceptions, as they can't fully understand our entire potential.

Building self-esteem comes from confronting challenges with the intent to overcome them. We gain self-esteem by observing our efforts toward a goal, regardless of the outcome. Success is not always guaranteed, but recognizing the learning opportunity in every attempt brings us closer to our goals. We can then identify areas for improvement and persist through a problem-solving approach.

The Observer Manager within us witnesses this cycle of success, failure, and perseverance. There is a profound satisfaction, pride, and gratitude in the effort and courage it takes to continue despite setbacks. Applying these lessons across different aspects of our lives fosters growth, self-esteem, and a sense of empowerment. This approach nurtures a positive desire for achievement and becomes an integral part of our value system. The Observer-Manager is then able to confront other challenges and face them with confidence and welcome the opportunities to grow.

However, if self-esteem solely depends on others' approval, we become susceptible to their criticisms and judgments, leading to feelings of inadequacy. This reliance can be damaging over time, causing individuals to adopt a "false self" to shield themselves from hurt. These "conditions of worth" become deeply rooted and can perpetuate into adulthood. For instance, if we fail at a task and undervalue our effort or problem-solving, we might be discouraged from trying again. Narrow criteria for success can lead us to abandon our goals, and further diminish opportunities for building self-esteem.

Using The Artist's Tools to Overcome Self-Esteem Challenges

Consider the example of dieting, especially for those significantly overweight. It is a challenging and often disheartening experience because weight loss is not a linear journey. If one's self-esteem hinges solely on consistent weight loss, fluctuations can lead to immense frustration and a sense of failure, often resulting in giving up and self-criticism.

Realizing that the process of trying, problem-solving, failing, and trying again is integral to success and changes our perspective. Every effort, irrespective of the immediate outcome, is an opportunity to learn, refine, and improve. This is where The Artist's Tools - self-acceptance, forgiveness, self-compassion, commitment, and gratitude - become crucial, motivating and inspiring even in small victories.

Take the example of a technical coder at a major tech company, responsible for a team but plagued by feelings of unworthiness and self-doubt. He believes he is less skilled and liked compared to others. This self-image has roots in his childhood, where he was unfavorably compared to siblings and friends, leading him to internalize a belief of inferiority. As an adult, he perpetuates this narrative, impacting his professional and personal life.

Our self-perceptions are often shaped by the words and beliefs we've internalized over time, almost like a script we unknowingly follow. Like the coder, we might not realize we're replaying these scripts from our past. It's important to recognize that not all of our negative thoughts reflect the truth. Studies suggest that a significant portion of our thoughts can be negatively skewed. That's why learning to accept ourselves, flaws and all, is a vital step towards well-being.

The Artist's Tools are especially beneficial in this context. Regularly practicing acceptance, self-compassion, commitment, forgiveness, and gratitude can revolutionize our existence within ourselves. Instead of fixating on past shortcomings, focus on being present and engaged in your current life. Embracing this MindView can lead to a profound transformation in how we view and live our lives.

Understanding and Managing the Inner Critic

One of the brain's greatest abilities is learning from experience. But, if we misinterpret our experiences as evidence of our unworthiness or incapability, we may start to believe that we're powerless to improve our situation or influence the world around us. This perspective can paint a bleak picture of an unfriendly world that resists our efforts to make sense of it. However, it's crucial to remember that these perceptions and feelings don't doom us to an unhealthy or flawed existence. With the right tools and goals, the unhealthy and inaccurate perceptions can be mended, forgiven, and let go.

Consider our primitive brain, which evolved to ensure our survival. There was a time when being constantly alert to danger was necessary for survival. In our modern, relatively safer world, our perceived threats are often internal, leading to a heightened sense of self-criticism. The Inner Critic frequently emerges first in response to our life's challenges, sometimes manifesting as harsh self-blame and sometimes serving as a helpful cautionary voice.

In clinical practice, however, the Inner Critic is often a significant barrier to healing because of its persuasive nature. As with the technical coder's story, our experiences can become deeply embedded, almost like a repetitive script or song. When the Inner Critic is active, we might become overwhelmed by its negativity and overlook any positive aspects it might offer. This can lead to hopelessness, fear of making mistakes, and tendencies to give up or self-sabotage before even attempting new behaviors.

Another challenge with the Inner Critic is its potential to color our perceptions of others. This critical voice can breed distrust or suspicion towards people, including friends, family, colleagues, or partners. Therefore, establishing a healthy relationship with our Inner Critic is vital for our overall well-being. In the upcoming Skills and Strategies Chapters, we will delve into how to cultivate a positive relationship with this aspect of ourselves. For the time being, our focus is on shedding as much of the negative influence of the Inner Critic as possible, which will be the subject of our next discussion.

Releasing the Past to Embrace the Present

It's essential to reemphasize a critical point we discussed earlier: the layers of life history and narratives that have shaped our identity over time are often old attachments to stories that have distanced us from our true selves. While some of this fear and apprehension may have been justifiable, much of it also stems from the uncertainty of change - releasing an old way of being and embracing a new one without a guarantee of success.

When we step back to objectively observe our fears and emotions (adopting the observer perspective), we begin to recognize the transient nature of these moments. This altered perception helps us to understand that our current pain or negative feelings do not define our entire being. We learn to say to ourselves, "This pain is not me", "I may feel bad, but I am not fundamentally bad", and "These thoughts are just thoughts; they do not encapsulate my entire identity". This realization empowers us to release the past and choose what is in the present. It's akin to learning to swim; we must first let go of the pool's edge to move forward.

Utilizing the Total Truth Healing Letter for Emotional Release

A crucial tool in your journey to emotional healing is the Total Truth Healing Letter (Canfield, 2015). This exercise is designed to help you release the negative thoughts and pain that may burden you, regardless of whether they stem from your inner critic or painful life experiences. The key here is to separate the pain arising from your experiences from your intrinsic worth and value. Imagine this pain as an infection in a wound, hindering your healing; the Total Truth Healing Letter acts like an antibiotic specifically targeted for your use.

Embarking on this exercise can be demanding and uncomfortable due to its introspective nature. It requires time and emotional investment. You'll be asked to write letters to each person or situation that has caused you harm, including addressing your inner critic. Remember, these letters are for your eyes only, not meant to be delivered or shared. Allow yourself to fully engage with your emotions during this process, taking the necessary time.

Writing these letters offers a chance to articulate your hurt and pain before symbolically letting them go. While memories and feelings, at times, may resurface, continue to apply The Artist's Tools and engage in writing or journaling. Over time, the impact of these memories will gradually diminish in intensity, frequency, duration, and their power to disrupt your life, and they will be replaced by The Artists Tools.

If, during this exercise, you find yourself overwhelmed by intense memories or emotions, or if it becomes disruptive, please pause the process. Such reactions could indicate underlying significant trauma that may require the guidance of a counselor for effective resolution and reprocessing.

Crafting the Total Truth Healing Letter

The aim of this exercise is to compose a Total Truth Healing Letter. Again, it's important to remember that this letter is solely for your own benefit and is not intended to be sent to the person or situation it addresses. As you embark on this task, follow the detailed outline provided. Allow yourself the freedom to write as extensively as needed, using as much paper as required for your expression.

While writing your Total Truth Healing Letter, visualize the person or event you are addressing as though they are right before you, enabling you to speak directly to them. This approach lends a sense of immediacy and authenticity to your words. After completing your first letter, take the time to read it aloud to yourself at least twice. Vocalizing your thoughts and feelings can be a powerful part of the healing process.

Next, engage in one of the guided meditations that seems most appropriate for your current state of mind. This meditation should help you process the emotions and thoughts that have arisen from writing the letter. When you feel prepared, move on to the next individual or situation on your list, continuing this process until you have addressed each one.

This exercise is your opportunity to express all the thoughts and feelings that you might never have had the chance to communicate before. It's a chance to be completely honest and unburden yourself of unspoken words and unresolved emotions. Jot down some names of those you would like to write to.

Journal Lines

_____
_____
_____
_____
_____
_____
_____
_____
_____
_____
_____
_____

^Pause & Reflect ~ Total Truth Healing Letter^

The purpose of this exercise is to write a **Total Truth Healing Letter. It is not to be given to who it is addressed. It is only for you!** Follow the outline provided below. Please make it as long as you need and use as much paper as will help. While you are writing this **Total Truth Healing Letter,** imagine the person or event in your mind as if they are in front of you and you are speaking to them directly. When you are done with the first letter, read the letter out loud to yourself – two or more times. Then go to one of the meditations that will be most helpful. When you feel ready, go on to the next person on the list, until you have written to them all. This is your chance to say all of the things you never got to say.

Make a list of the people or situations that have hurt you. Then rate them from the Most (5) to the Least (1) amount of hurt they caused.
1) Choose something in the middle to start with (not the worst).
2) Start your letter with Dear _____, The hurt you caused was when _____
3) At the time I was (age, size, situation, vulnerability) _____
4) I felt so (betrayed, tricked, shocked, angry, frightened, ashamed – write down every feeling you experienced at that time _____
5) I thought (write down what you believed to be true before, during, and after the fact about yourself, about the event, life, and way you saw yourself _____
6) I've never been able to shake the (idea, belief, feeling, regret) _____
7) But now that it is down on paper, I can begin to see _____
8) I know now I can forgive myself because I was _____, and you were _____
9) Those feelings (in #6) were never mine, and I do not want them any longer!
10) And I no longer must believe _____ about myself!
11) As I return this pain back to you, I can forgive you for _____
12) I can now turn this wounding over to my Artist's Tools compassion, gratitude, commitment, forgiveness, acceptance, and the healing that it deserves._____

Embracing Acceptance and Moving Forward

While preparing this section, I revisited Dr. Russ Harris's thoughts on willingness in "The Happiness Trap" (2008). Despite having read it numerous times, it struck a new chord with me. Suffering from severe lower back pain for years and undergoing multiple procedures with no relief, I believed I was managing well with my focus on well-being, values, and resilience. But then, Harris's words resonated differently:

"I don't know anyone who wants to feel discomfort. The idea here is to be willing to feel it... Willingness simply means that you're allowing it... By making room for your feelings and willingly feeling them, you'll change your relationship with them."

I realized that my understanding of willingness had not extended to accepting my pain. This revelation shifted my approach, allowing me to apply The Artist's Tools - Commitment, Acceptance, Self-Compassion, Forgiveness, and Gratitude - to my situation. I recognized that while my pain was unpleasant, giving it control over my well-being was even more detrimental. By accepting and allowing it to be what it is, I also create freedom from engaging with the pain and to release it as meaningless in my life. In other words, just as Russ Harris has said - because I've made room for its co-existence, I no longer struggle with it. Instead, I can move on and focus on what is more important.

Confronting the Fear of Change

Our struggles with problems often involve our entire being - physically, emotionally, spiritually, and socially, impacting all aspects of our lives. Wisdom suggests that it's not the problem itself that harms us but our response to it. Through the MindView Council, we've learned to blend our inner qualities like an artist mixes colors, and we've discovered how The Artist's Tools can be used to support and elevate us as we engage in our daily lives.

However, one of the most significant challenges in this journey is the fear of change. It's not necessarily the difficulty of the actions themselves, but the challenge lies in making the choice to change. The most common fear is: "What if this is all wrong? What if I really am as flawed as they said? What if I am the failure I see in the mirror?" How do we persuade someone that the negative self-image shaped by emotions or the Inner Critic is not the truth? The answer lies within. It is a choice each person must make - to see themselves in a new, more positive light.

Overcoming Fear to Unlock Your Potential

In her influential book "Feel the Fear and Do It Anyway", Susan Jeffers (1987) discusses three levels of fear. The first level includes tangible fears from real events like natural disasters, personal loss, or significant life changes such as career transitions. The second level involves internal fears—fear of rejection, vulnerability, failure, and the like - impacting self-image and various life aspects. However, it's the third level that is most daunting: the fear encapsulated in the thought, "I can't handle…"

This level of fear arises from past experiences we found overwhelming or from a diminished belief in our ability to cope. Even in nurturing environments, cautionary messages like "Be careful!" can inadvertently instill a sense of self-distrust. Combined with life's challenges - mistakes, accidents, relationship issues, illness, and stress - this can evolve into a profound fear of engaging with the world. Recognizing that we can't change the past or our ingrained beliefs and feelings, which have become habitual, the question becomes: What can we do differently to effect change? Let's summarize:

1. **Utilizing the MindView Council:** Each MindView, Emotional, Social, Physical, Thinking, and Spiritual, can significantly contribute to well-being. Imagine each MindView as a color on an artist's palette; if certain "colors" are lacking, we can balance our "masterpiece" by drawing on the strengths of other MindViews. This approach allows us to leverage existing strengths, qualities, and inner dialogue for immediate benefit and a new perspective of ourselves.

2. **Applying the Artist's Tools:** Like using brushes to apply paint, The Artist's Tools help shape our masterpiece. These tools - self-compassion, forgiveness, acceptance, commitment, and gratitude - support us in making desired changes, allowing for self-kindness and appreciation of the growth process.

3. **Envisioning Well-being:** You've explored what well-being looks like for you and how to achieve it. Learning to recognize and accept fears and challenges as they are, rather than letting them define you, focuses your energy on what truly matters.

The central message is the impact of being tethered to the past and burdened by old emotions. Such attachments hinder access to the full capacity of your creative mind, where limitless possibilities reside, freeing yourself from these binds, and doors to new opportunities and potential open wide.

Transitioning from Old to New Perspectives

Our lives consist of numerous challenging moments that ebb and flow, often without conscious awareness. Memories and emotions from our past can be unexpectedly triggered, seeping into our daily lives with varying emotional intensity. The impact of these memories can range from mildly disruptive to profoundly life-altering

To navigate this, we must learn to step back and detach from the labels and judgments we place on our thoughts and accompanying emotions. This involves utilizing our Observer MindView to objectively assess our thoughts, feelings, and behaviors. Such detachment facilitates better decision-making through our Manager MindView. It's like coming to a crossroads where we can choose to recognize our strengths and achievements, listen to and learn from our inner critic, and increase our self-awareness. This process helps us understand how we are wired to learn, make decisions, cope with challenges, manage emotions, and adapt to new information. It allows us to reframe our perception of ourselves during times of adversity, recognizing the strengths and skills we have exhibited.

Resilience and the Artist Within: Negative thoughts and resistance to uncomfortable situations are part of the brain's survival mechanism, and facing these difficulties can be daunting. When memories and emotions are triggered, the inner critic often magnifies them in the present, leading to feelings of helplessness, worthlessness, or loss of control. It's estimated that up to 90% of people experience at least one traumatic event in their lifetime (Norris & Stevens, 2007).

Resilience is the ability to recover from significant stress or adversity. It encompasses attitudes, behaviors, values, and lifestyles and involves various brain regions like the amygdala, hippocampus, and nucleus accumbens, as well as hormones and neurotransmitters. Genetic factors and neuroplasticity play roles, too. Many resilience skills are innate and present from birth.

Resilience is multifaceted, involving all aspects of functioning in life. It is bolstered by the collective resources and skills of the MindView Council, encompassing Social, Emotional, Thinking, Physical, Spiritual, and Observer-Manager MindViews. These include values, morals, and skills crucial for well-being. The Artist's Tools - acceptance, commitment, compassion, forgiveness, and gratitude - further enhance resilience. External resources such as relationships, role models, religion, and ethics, contribute to resilience. Prolific writers, like Schiraldi (2017), highlight the importance of forgiveness, social intelligence, meaning, moral character, self-esteem, and gratitude. Others, like Southwick & Charney (2012), emphasize the necessity of hope and facing fears for resilient living. Each of these perspectives, and others, have been incorporated into the text and exercises in this workbook.

Cultivating Willingness, Hope, and Resilience for Positive Growth

Willingness, hope, and resilience are key drivers propelling us through life's myriad experiences. Trusting in our ability to succeed and adaptively modify our thoughts, expectations, and behaviors enhances our chances of success. This approach cultivates a more affirmative perception of ourselves.

As adults, developing psychological flexibility and resilience is crucial. It's not the existence of negative or challenging circumstances that define our happiness, but our ability to accept life's experiences without judgment and remain focused on the present. Embracing life's moments as they occur opens the door to creative progress. Many of these skills and abilities are inherent within us, waiting to be consciously nurtured. By making deliberate, patient choices and practicing self-compassion, acceptance, and forgiveness - as taught through The Artist's Tools - we can steadily progress.

Chapter 2 highlighted the importance of support from others, a valuable resource for resilience. Social support, emotional regulation, spiritual practices (religious and secular), physical and cognitive health, and overall brain well-being significantly contribute to resilience. Beyond thoughts and intentions, these elements offer substantial support for building resilience. By considering the contributions from MindViews, you will find many strategies for staying grounded in the present rather than dwelling on past pains or failures.

An inevitable question arises: How do we truly "bounce back" when the same concerns linger at the end of a stressful period as they did at the beginning? How do we release the "old stuff"? The upcoming Pause & Reflect exercises address this by guiding you to detach from past beliefs that spawn sadness and pain, furthering your journey of letting go and moving forward positively.

Discovering Your Artist Within

Now, it's time to connect with the most knowledgeable guide for your inner world: your Artist Within. For our journey in this program, the Artist Within symbolizes a blend of your observer-manager, your inner guide, and the positive aspects you've always known deep within yourself. Think of it as a combination of wisdom, guidance, and self-recognition all in one.

The Artist Within serves as your internal compass, a voice of wisdom guiding you towards your best interests and well-being. Take a moment to contemplate this idea. Who could this Artist Within be for you? If it helps, imagine this entity as a close friend or a loving family member. The key here is to tap into the essence of this inner presence. Who might this be in the core of your being? Jot down any thoughts, images, or feelings when you consider this question. This exercise is not just about identifying this internal guide but also about fostering a deeper connection with that part of yourself that intuitively seeks your well-being and growth.

^Pause & Reflect ~ Feedback from the Artist Within^

It is time for feedback from the one entity who knows you better than anyone else: your inner self. For the purposes of this program, we are going to refer to your inner self as your Artist Within. The Artist Within of a combination of your observer-manager, your inner guide, and the good things you have known about yourself deep down, all wrapped up in one. It is there to act as an inner wiser voice. You might think of it as an inner compass. Whatever it is to you, it has your well-being and best interests in mind. Stop for a moment a try to imagine who this might be. If you need to imagine this person as a best friend or family member who loves you, that is just fine for now. Just try to reach for the feeling of who that person might be within. Then write down whatever comes to mind. Describe what you see.

_____
_____

What would it be like to have someone like this in your life all the time, wherever you go? Someone who encourages you to do your best but reminds you that perfection is not required. You are good enough just the way you are. How might your life be different?

_____
_____

Can you imagine your Artist Within being there for you during the difficult times in your life, perhaps giving you strength?

_____
_____

Again, close your eyes and imagine your Artist Within. Remember it is your inner compass. Now, ask yourself if your Artist Within has a message for you. What would it be?

_____
_____

Does your Artist Within have advice for you regarding the next steps toward well-being?

_____
_____

Reflecting and Progressing on Your Journey

As you move forward in your journey, regularly revisit the reflections and decisions you've made in the above sections. Reviewing your progress and intentions will serve as a valuable reminder and guide you toward your aspirations. Remember, the path to success and achievement is rarely a straight line. It's completely normal for your efforts to seem scattered initially. Embrace this phase as an essential part of learning and personal growth.

In the upcoming chapter, we'll delve deeper into identifying your values and goals. We'll provide guidance to help you clarify your objectives and the values that underpin them, along with actionable steps to achieve these goals. Additionally, we will assist you in creating a "Journey Map". This map will serve as a strategic plan, outlining your destination, the route to get there, potential obstacles, and key points to be mindful of along the way. This proactive approach will equip you with the tools and foresight needed to navigate your journey effectively. The steps for moving forward with the skills you've learned are outlined below.

Step One: Initiate Action. Start by identifying your goals. Consider what you want to achieve and remember that progress takes time. Begin with small steps, allowing yourself the patience to see your efforts unfold.

Step Two: Embrace Emotional Responses. Understand that fear, sadness, discomfort, and pain are natural reactions. When these feelings arise, remind yourself, "This is my mind signaling care and caution. It shows that my life and well-being matter to me."

Step Three: Utilize Your Artist's Tools. If you feel overly anxious or alarmed, turn to the Artist's Tools for support. These include affirmations that reinforce your strength and ability to handle challenges. Recall your positive affirmations to soothe and reassure yourself.

Step Four: Concentrate on Personal Change. Acknowledge that you can only control your own emotions, decisions, and actions. Direct your energy towards areas of your life where you can make an impact and avoid wasting effort on things beyond your control.

Step Five: Define and Embrace Your Values. Reflect on and establish your personal values. Embrace these values, as they are unique and form the foundation of your decisions and actions.

Step Six: Transform Mistakes into Learning Opportunities. View mistakes not as failures but as chances for growth and improvement. Learn from each misstep and use these insights to evolve, rather than to indulge in self-blame.

Step Seven: Adopt a Beginner's Mind. Approach each moment with a fresh perspective, full of curiosity and openness. Look for new possibilities in your current situation and respond with compassion, gratitude, and acceptance. This mindset can transform how you perceive and interact with the world around you.

^Pause & Reflect ~ Success Review^

1) Make a list of five affirmatives in your life. They can be anything about you that you feel good about and has meaning for who you are. <u>Ex: I am a good cook, or I learned to read,</u> <u>I graduated from high school or college, etc.</u>

   A _____
   B _____
   C _____
   D _____
   E _____

2) From the list below circle at least ten skills that were <u>necessary</u> for you to accomplish what you did in number 1. Circle them as skills, even if you didn't feel you had mastered them 100%. Add any skills that are not listed below.

Patience	Tolerance	Forgiveness	Kindness	Maturity
Discipline	Persistence	Determination	Courage	Selflessness
Strength	Intelligence	Communication	Resourcefulness	Faith
Strong	Independence	Self-sufficiency	Hard-work	Loyalty
Work Ethic	Willingness	Teachable	Friendly	Loving
Flexible	Compassionate	Open-Minded	Analytical	Conscientious

3) Now, putting the words above into sentences, create a paragraph that describes you, your efforts, and the accomplishments you have made in your life up to this point. Start your paragraph with the phrase, "I am a person who . . ."
   _____
   _____
   _____
   _____

4) What did this teach you about who you are? What are your strengths?
   _____
   _____

Journal Lines

_____
_____
_____
_____
_____

Guided Meditation ~ Chapter Four: Moving Forward

We are hard-wired within our neural networks of the brain to survive and to thrive… to make our lives meaningful and worthwhile. Research has shown that using our imagination (like we will in this guided meditation) to write new ideas into our thoughts creates neural networks that are very similar to those that are formed as a result of an actual experience. This means that our imagination is a powerful resource. If you learn to distance yourself from disturbing thoughts, beliefs, and feelings and slightly rewrite small fragments in your imagination, you can create a very different outcome in your life. At some point, you may have thought to yourself, "I wish that this or that person was different – look at what they have done to my life. My life is such a mess, and I am a victim of their behaviors". This is not the process we are suggesting here. By using The Artist's Tools, we can positively rescript an imagined outcome that can help us take responsibility for our thoughts and feelings in the present moment.

GM Journaling ~ Chapter Four: Moving Forward

- As you imagined yourself in the midst of your personal space what did you notice? Have you begun to notice any changes since you first started coming to this place?

- Are you becoming more familiar with your mindviews? Do you think it is helpful to get to know each of your mindviews? Can they be helpful to you in your life?

- Can you see yourself moving ahead more easily with the help of The Artist's tools?

- Think about the Steps Forward chart. Is the idea of flexibility and resilience, and how to apply them in your life, beginning to make sense to you?

In this Guided Meditation, you will have the opportunity to rewrite your story in much the same way. Before doing the exercise, ponder one or two changes that might make a difference. If you had, or still do have, an alcoholic, addict, or abuser in your world, how might you use your imagination to re-write that part of your story? How might your outlook on life be different if you were to write your Artist Within into your life story to allow you to feel safe? Using your imagination to help you emotionally heal in this way can be thought of as suturing your skin until a wound heals.

As you reflect on your life, you will be asked to focus on one or two things that you would like to rewrite, and then imagine how you or your life might have been different. We will then focus on the masterpiece within you that is waiting to be discovered. You may need to repeat this guided meditation many times to reach the full potential of the exercise. Be persistent with it; it will be worth the time and energy.

Guided Meditation ~ Chapter Four: Moving Forward

Lie down, get comfortable and close your eyes. Place your hand on your stomach, and take deep full breaths. Continue breathing slowly and deeply. See your breath as a pure white cloud. Coming in through the top of your head. As it swirls down through your body, it picks up all of the impurities, the tension, the fatigue, the pain, or the problems of the day. As you exhale, imagine all of the impurities exiting out through your toes. They disappear out into space. Again, the white cloud flowing down through your head and face, carrying away the tension, down through your neck and shoulders, down through your arms and into your hands, and then your fingers, carrying away the tensions and the worries. Down through your chest, your buttocks and thighs, your legs, ankles and feet, and out through your toes. See these impurities disappearing out into space.

And now the oxygen turns a beautiful blue. Calming, soothing, feel the color cleansing your body, your MindView. Leaving your body feeling relaxed. Your problems and worries washed away. Peaceful, quiet. Just floating.

Now go to your Garden space.

Your Artist's Tools are here within you. Acceptance of all that you are. Forgiveness, empathy, and compassion surround and heal you as you breathe it in. Allow forgiveness, empathy, acceptance, and compassion to flood into every cell of your body. Infusing your MindView and body with love, caring, self-acceptance, and self-compassion. Let go of concerns or fear. Relax with each breath. And, with each breath, go even deeper into calmness and peace.

Now find a place here where you can sit and be comfortable. Perhaps you are sitting in the grass, with your back against a tree, or on a bench overlooking a patch of your favorite flowers. Just notice.

Let's recall the guiding principles for each member of your MindView Council. The guiding principle for your Spiritual MindView is to identify your values. The guiding principle for your Emotional MindView is acceptance without judgment. The guiding principle for your Thinking MindView is to defuse negative content while responding in a way that is consistent with your values. The guiding principle for your Social MindView is awareness of the filters through which we interpret and judge the world around us. The guiding principle for the Physical MindView is to follow a healthy diet, exercise, sleep, and abstinence choices. The guiding principle for the Observer Manager is to be aware and available to the MindView council, and to help to self-regulate and to self-stabilize, with the goal of maintaining personal resilience.

Notice the slight breeze that is so relaxing, and feel the sun on your skin as it warms you.

Now, look around your Garden space. It is beginning to take shape around the change you have requested. Your Garden as you envisioned it is beginning to emerge. You might notice the different scents from the flowers, trees, and plants. The colors of the vegetation are so bright and beautiful that they fill you with wonder. Now notice that it is the breeze, the warmth of the sun, the scents, and the colors of the vegetation around you that are bringing these changes to you. Notice those changes taking place within you. They are enveloping you. They permeate through every muscle, tendon, and cell of your body. Repairing you, healing you, restoring you. Allow these changes to just flow through you.

Growth and change can be exciting, motivating, and inspiring. It can also be difficult. However, just as weeds grow in our beautiful garden space and must be pulled and discarded, sometimes thoughts and feelings can arise that seem to interrupt our progress or block our way.

These weeds in your inner garden may take the form of low self-esteem, self-blame, or a brutal inner critic. What might be blocking the growth in your garden? When we observe thoughts or feelings that tell us, "you can't do this, or you are not good enough for that", you can just acknowledge them, give them some space and distance, and then give them to your observer manager. The Observer-Manager knows who we are and the facts of the situation. The Observer-Manager can help us decide what to do with a comment that does not match what we know about ourselves. We make the decision about who we are. Hurtful thoughts or remaining painful memories are just stories. Remember to shrink them away. Make them smaller and smaller until they are nothing but molecules. Then send them outside of your head and blow them away. And in their place are The Tools for the Artist Within – Acceptance, Forgiveness, Commitment, Self-compassion, and Gratitude.

One step at a time, we learn to prepare our MindViews to move forward. We learn to accept our emotions, and we learn to calm them when we become reactive.

By applying our Tools for the Artist Within, we develop self-compassion, self-acceptance, and gratitude. Then we can take charge of our lives by focusing on what we can change and by using our resources.

We are only responsible for our own behavior, responses, and choices. When our behavior is in line with our values, we create the moral strength, meaning, and purpose that brings value to our lives. It also provides protection against the unintended consequences of choices that are not in line with our values.

Finally, practice the beginner's MindView, knowing that every choice and action will bring about a new beginning. The Beginners MindView reminds us to let go of what we think we know and be teachable in ways that will create well-being.

And now, coming back to your garden, notice how beautiful it is. Listen to the sound of the wind through the trees. Feel the sun on your skin and how it warms you. Notice the scents from the flowers, trees, plants, and the beautiful colors of the vegetation. All of it brings peace and calm to your life. Notice the sense of peace and calm that is taking place within you. Enveloping you and permeating through every muscle, tendon, and cell of your body.

Acceptance, forgiveness, compassion, commitment, and gratitude, repairing you, healing you, restoring you. Allow these changes to just flow through you. Remember that in real life, we do this all the time. Right now, you are asking the universe for what you most value. Just allow yourself to be present to those changes. Now, when you are ready, send them out into the universe.

Your willingness, hope, and your ability to bounce back by using your skills and tools are already within you. Your observing self says to you, "You have everything you need already within you that will help you to master and adapt to your life experiences. All you need to do is look within and trust what is there". Flexibility, resilience, durability, and the desire to thrive are already hard-wired into your brain. Your life experiences, along with the power of your MindView Council, and The Tools for the Artist Within, can help you to manifest your potential.

Flexibly accepting life's experiences without self-judgment while learning from them and staying focused on what is happening right here and now will give us the space we need to move forward in a creative way. Take some time now to focus inward. Be present to the core of who you are.

Repeat this guided meditation whenever you feel sad or discouraged or whenever the old stories begin to return out of habit. That is all they are . . . habits, old stories that have deep roots. Keep yanking them up or shrinking them. Most importantly, keep visualizing the masterpiece you are creating.

Now, take a deep breath or two, and when you are ready, open your eyes, and come back.

Chapter 5 – Mapping My Journey

"Only one who devotes himself to a cause with his whole strength and soul can be a true master." ~ *Albert Einstein*

Our idealistic visions of a flawless existence often paint a picture where life is devoid of challenges and discomfort. In this romantic scenario, families are always nurturing, careers are fulfilling and stable, and health and happiness are guaranteed. We imagine a world free of conflict, where kindness and generosity are universal, and every aspect of life aligns perfectly with our desires. However, reality often diverges from this idyllic vision, presenting us with a complex tapestry of experiences that include setbacks and triumphs.

Understanding that life is a blend of various experiences and acknowledging that perfect harmony is an unattainable ideal are crucial first steps. Accepting that challenges and setbacks are inherent parts of growth can empower us to face life more resiliently. By setting realistic goals and aligning them with concrete action plans, we can journey through life's ups and downs more effectively. Every effort, no matter its scale, contributes to progress. Remember, personal growth is a non-linear journey marked by learning and adaptation. Embracing commitment, compassion, acceptance, forgiveness, and gratitude can guide us through difficult moments and mistakes, fostering resilience and self-awareness.

Creating a Life Guided by Values

Values are the compass that directs our journey, shapes our perceptions and guides our actions. They influence our beliefs about appropriate behavior and determine what deserves our focus, time, and energy. By understanding and prioritizing your values, you will set the stage for living a life of purpose and intention.

Reflecting on questions like, what principles do I uphold? What impulses do I resist? What aspects of myself am I most proud of? What drives my decision-making? It will allow you to delve into the core of your being. These inquiries are not just about making choices that feel good but about aligning with deeply held beliefs that give your life meaning and direction.

Our personal values are the foundational elements that help us to concentrate on what truly matters. They enable us to move beyond transient pleasures to embrace the essentials of life. Moreover, these values provide a framework for enduring life's challenges and recovering from setbacks. They help us see beyond immediate obstacles, offering a broader perspective to evaluate our actions and experiences.

In essence, how we interpret and overcome life's trials and our ability to find meaning and purpose despite adversities are testaments to the strength and clarity of our values. By embracing and living according to these values, we forge a life that is not only meaningful and purposeful but also resilient in the face of life's inevitable ups and downs.

^Pause & Reflect ~ Values Search^

Thinking:

Alertness	Ambitious	Open-Minded	Flexible	Curious
Analytical	Practical	Responsibility	Teachable	Creative
Stability	Intelligence	Self-sufficient	Organized	Perceptive
Attentive	Accomplishing	Accountability	Accuracy	Genius
Educated	Professional	Recognition	Reasoning	Teamwork
Decisiveness	Determination	Skillfulness	Smart	Inquisitive
Learning	Logic	Organization	Success	Innovation
Challenge	Clever	Leadership	Justice	Mastery

Emotional:

Insightful	Safe	Thoughtful	Accepting	Respect
Thankful	Accountable	Trusting	Intuitive	Loving
Generous	Compassionate	Empathic	Kind	Caring
Amusement	Fearless	Expressive	Contentment	Courage
Intensity	Purpose	Hope	Sincerity	Sharing
Sensitivity	Happiness	Creativity	Courage	Serenity
Peace	Reverence	Tranquility	Optimism	Passion
Grace	Gratitude	Satisfaction	Thankful	Inspired

Physical:

Courageous	Healthy	Hard-working	Clean	Active
Persistent	Coordinated	Capable	Busy	Adventure
Fitness	Strength	Productivity	Discipline	Effort
Discipline	Dedication	Hard Work	Health	Skill
Careful	Cleanliness	Competition	Growth	Diet
Rigor	Balance	Capable	Strength	Beauty
Fortitude	Teamwork	Toughness	Valor	Victory

Social:

Appreciative	Balance	Communication	Belonging	Polite
Independent	Humorous	Justice	Leadership	Loyal
Considerate	Respectful	Cooperative	Helpful	Peace
Family	Fun	Polite	Humor	Spontaneous
Teamwork	Confidence	Sharing	Social	Sharing
Sensitivity	Harmony	Dignity	Charity	Honor

Spiritual:

Maturity	Mindfulness	Honesty	Wise	Integrity
Prayerful	Aware	Purpose	Believing	Present
Hope	Compassion	Forgiveness	Faith	Meaning
Altruism	Clarity	Giving	Humility	Dedication
Consciousness	Devotion	Peace	Discovery	Equality
Support	Unity	Selflessness	Meaning	Stewardship

Exploring Personal Values. Reflect on the challenges you've faced and triumphed over in your life. Consider the strengths and qualities you exhibited during those times. For the upcoming exercise, think about the values and attributes that you just selected in the previous exercise. These are values you've shown in the past, those you possess now, and particularly those you aspire to develop.

As you work through the next exercise, you're encouraged to identify and embrace the values that align with your aspirations and life goals. This process is not just about recognizing your past strengths but also about shaping the person you want to become. Consider sharing the insights from this exercise with your loved ones. Engaging in this dialogue can be a valuable exercise, offering insights and fostering understanding in various aspects of your life and relationships.

Of the values you circled in each category above, you will write a mission statement that best describes your chosen values. An example for each category is provided for you in the next Pause and Reflect.

Envisioning a Values-Driven Future

Take a moment to delve deeper into your self-perception, principles, and motivations. Reflect on what truly matters to you and the type of internal environment you aspire to cultivate. Most importantly, consider whether your actions are in harmony with your stated values.

Close your eyes and project yourself one year into the future. Visualize how you see yourself living out these values in your daily life. What changes or achievements do you envision? Document these reflections in the upcoming Pause and Reflect section. If you find this challenging, think about a person you deeply respect or admire. Imagine how they might approach this exercise. Use their example to clarify your vision and align it more closely with your core values and aspirations.

Crafting Your Personal Mission Statement

Having reflected on your core personal values, the next step is to articulate your mission statement. This exercise is on the following page. This statement is a concise declaration of your fundamental identity and values. It encapsulates your principles, your aspirations, and the essence of what drives you. Consider what matters most to you – what principles guide your actions, what ideals you strive to uphold, and the inner atmosphere you aim to cultivate. In other words, where would you like to be 1 year, 3 years, and 5 years from now?

Your mission statement serves as a guiding beacon, offering direction and clarity in both prosperous and challenging times. It ensures that your decisions and actions consistently align with your deepest values and objectives. Think of it as your personal ethical compass that helps you navigate life's journey in a way that is true to who you are.

Craft a statement that is brief yet powerful, ideally encompassing two or three sentences. It should be clear, compelling, and it should contain a sense of motivation. This statement should stir passion and ignite creativity, constantly reminding of what you stand for and why you do what you do. Let it reflect of your innermost self, capturing the essence of your unique perspective and approach to life.

^Pause & Reflect ~Mission Statements^

The words I chose for my Thinking MindView are: _____
_____

My mission statement for my Thinking MindView is (ex: it is important to me that I get an education so I can pursue a career that will create safety, allow me to be self-sufficient, and provide a sense of direction and purpose for my life.)
_____
_____

The words I chose for my Emotional MindView are: _____
_____

ೞ My mission statement for my Emotional MindView is (ex: I want to learn about, and demonstrate acceptance, compassion, respect, and kindness toward myself and others, and to learn to be accountable for my own behavior.) _____
_____

ೞ The words I chose for my Physical MindView are: _____
_____

ೞ My mission statement for my Physical MindView is (ex: It is important to me that I show respect for my body by taking care of my physical health, and remaining active and involved):
_____
_____

The words I chose for my Social MindView are: _____
_____

ೞ My mission statement for my Social MindView is (ex: It is important to me that I nurture assertive, authentic, respectful, honest, friendly, and cooperative relationships.)
_____
_____

The words I chose for my Spiritual MindView are: _____
_____

ೞ My mission statement for my Spiritual MindView is (ex: It is important to me that I allow creativity, mindfulness, wisdom, integrity, purpose, hope and faith guide my life.)
_____
_____

Embarking on Your Journey Map

With a clear understanding of your core identity and personal mission, you're now equipped to create your Journey Map. This tool is designed to strategically plan and navigate your path of personal development. Reflect on the key attributes you've identified in yourself and consider the changes you wish to implement in the coming weeks. This process will help concentrate your efforts towards these objectives. The Journey Map serves five primary functions:

> **1. Identifies your aspirations**: It helps you to identify your life's principles, aspirations, and direction for your life.
> **2. Goal setting:** Define the objectives you aim to achieve by the program's conclusion. These goals resonate with your core values and represent meaningful milestones in your journey.
> **3. Navigating Pitfalls of Impulse:** Recognize and document impulsive behaviors that typically derail your progress. These are the distractions or temptations that sidetrack you from your path and hinder your growth.
> **4. Overcoming Swamps of Habit**: Identify entrenched, habitual behaviors that are counterproductive or self-destructive. These are the chronic patterns that obstruct your success and fulfillment. The focus here is on cultivating character traits that counteract these habits, paving the way for more constructive actions.
> **5. Use Your Journey Map:** Regularly refer to it to stay aligned with your goals, monitor your progress, and adjust your course as needed. It's a dynamic tool that evolves with you. It reflects both your challenges and triumphs as you advance toward personal fulfillment.

Your Journey Map will be a constant guide and reminder throughout this program. If you have difficulty identifying your goals, or values, ask someone close to you to help you. Sometimes, our best friends and family know us better than we know ourselves.

Living with Purpose: The Impact of Values and Goals

Identifying our core values and setting goals is a pathway to actualizing our deepest aspirations. Embracing our values and living by them, even amidst challenges, offers profound satisfaction and a sense of accomplishment. This process reflects the essence of living a purposeful life. Viktor Frankl, a Jewish psychiatrist and Auschwitz survivor, illustrates this concept poignantly. His experiences during the Holocaust, as detailed in his seminal work, reveal a powerful truth: those who clung to a sense of purpose and meaning amidst the horrors of the concentration camp were often the ones who persevered the longest. This observation underscores the vital role of a belief system or values in providing a foundation of purpose and meaning, even in the direst circumstances. Frankl's insights show us that values-guided thinking and behavior can be life-sustaining in extreme situations and bring direction and significance to our everyday existence.

Life's journey is undoubtedly challenging and requires unwavering commitment and effort. However, those who have weathered these trials often attest that the rewards and fulfillment derived from such dedication surpass the hardships encountered. This testament to resilience and purpose highlights the transformative power of living in alignment with our values and pursuing our goals.

From Values to Vision

Now, using the mission statements that you wrote in the exercise above, take a few minutes to clarify your thoughts about who you are, your ideals, what you stand for, and why you do what you do. What is most important to you? What kind of an inner environment do you wish to create? Most importantly, do your behaviors currently match your values? If not, how might you change them? Close your eyes and think about how you envision yourself one year from now, then describe what you see in the Pause and Reflect below. If you have difficulty with this exercise for some reason, then think about someone you greatly admire. How might they complete this exercise?

^Pause & Reflect ~ From Values to Vision^

> Thinking about my Philosophy of Life, the most important things to me are:
> _____
> _____
>
> The way I envision my future is: _____
> _____
> _____
>
> The changes that I would most like to see are: _____
> _____
> _____
>
> If I had a life compass, to complete my journey it would guide me toward a place where: _____
> _____
> _____
>
> My very best self is someone who: _____
> _____
> _____
>
> What gets in my way is: _____
> _____
> _____

From Vision to Focused-Action

You are now ready to move on to the Journey Map. Just as there is no such thing as a perfect person in this imperfect world, you are also imperfect. Most people have a lot of trouble with this.

The concept of Acceptance in The Artist's Tools allows us to be "good enough" no matter our starting point here and now. However, the truth needs to include an awareness of both strengths and weaknesses, or we set ourselves up for failure before we even get started. The Journey Map allows us to include those difficulties and habitual behaviors that get in our way and interrupt our progress.

In this exercise, you'll organize the work you'd like to do and what you'd like to achieve into a map that will guide your progress. Using the values you chose at the beginning of this chapter as a reference point, think about the changes you'd like to make in the next few weeks.

The Journey Map Exercise can help you accomplish four things:
1. Identify the values that guide your life choices.
2. Identify goals that you would most like to achieve.
3. Identify the Pitfalls of Impulse, which are the impulsive behaviors that often pull you off track and make it difficult to progress toward your goals.
4. Identify behaviors that tend to be habitual and difficult to interrupt – the Swamps of Habit. These chronic, self-destructive behaviors can rob you of the opportunity to succeed in anything at all. Interestingly, they often include habits we have developed to help us avoid difficult or uncomfortable feelings.

Be careful to choose only a few values and goals, perhaps one or two from each council member that you feel are most important to work on first. Your completed Journey Map will anchor and guide your progress through this process. Use it often as a reference.

Before we begin, let's review The Tools for the Artist Within in terms of how they might apply to this process. These tools change the internal experience of defining meaning and purpose for our lives from goal-oriented to process-oriented. It is the "how" of the Journey Map that we are interested in, not just the "what". Your thoughts and feelings are part of you, but they do not define you. It is the hope that these tools will help you to change your relationship with your thoughts, feelings, and beliefs without necessarily trying to change or avoid your feelings.

The essential Tools for the Artist Within are:

- **Acceptance** of imperfections and mistakes as you engage in activities and pursue goals that give your life meaning and purpose,
- **Forgiveness** toward yourself and others for imperfections and mistakes you make as you are moving forward fully engaged in the present moment,
- **Self-compassion**, kindness, compassion, and care toward yourself and for others as you refine your many abilities, and others in your world.
- A **Commitment** to intention, focused action, and courage in pursuing our path toward growth and change, even in the face of adversity,
- And, **Gratitude** for all things, including our strength and courage, and the gifts of joy, difficulties and experiences, as we strive to learn and grow.

As we identify values, develop goals, then take steps toward accomplishing them, we are actualizing the deepest and most meaningful intentions within us. As we learn to live by our values, we will begin to experience the benefits and rewards of the efforts and sacrifices we make, even when it becomes difficult.

Journey Map Exercise

Step One: What are your Values? Values are purposeful expressions of what is most important to us. They are qualities of being in our skin and our lives, and every action we take is related to what is most meaningful to us in that moment. Values that are chosen become purposeful pathways that guide our lives in directions that are enriching and fulfilling. Ideally, our values guide the goals we set. The difference between a goal and a value is that a goal can be accomplished or completed, whereas a value is never completed. For example, we don't complete and check off our list of the value of being a good partner or friend. It is an ongoing process.

Everything we do is guided or influenced by what's important to us. When we define these values so that they become comprehensible and usable to us, we avoid drifting without direction. Behaviors not consciously guided by goals often result in misdirected or wasted energy.

Journal Lines

_____
_____
_____
_____
_____
_____
_____
_____
_____
_____
_____
_____
_____
_____
_____
_____
_____
_____
_____

JOURNEY MAP

Swamps of Habit
Chronic Self Destructive Behaviors

Focusing on my failures, avoiding painful emotions by drinking or watching television, pornography. Making excuses and rationalizing my choices. Refusal to take responsibility for my temper and bad choices. Failure to be teachable.

Example

Personal Values

1) (Thinking) Continue my education so I can have a career I enjoy
2) (Emotional) Create Loving Relationships in my Family
3) (Physical) Develop the Personal Qualities of Health and Well-Being
4) (Social) Contribute to the Community in which I Live
5) (Spiritual) Live a Life of Honesty and Integrity

Goals

1) (Thinking) Explore areas of interest to me.
   Sign up for classes and/or training programs
   Develop and practice good study habits
   Learn to listen to the Observer Self
2) (Emotional) Learn to better control my temper
   Spend time with my family
   Learn to be a good listener
   Learn to be more patient
3) (Physical) Better manage my stress
   Develop a more healthy life style and stick to it
   Start a savings account for rainy days
   Quit Smoking
4) (Social) Choose a charity that I can work with
   Explore the needs within my community
   Set aside time to be involved in my child's school
   Learn communication & problem solving skills
5) (Spiritual) Learn to be more appreciative
   Explore ideas that help me grow as a person
   Be more aware of my mistakes and take responsibility for them.

Action Steps

Thinking Action Steps
Go to the University and talk with an advisor
Set up a daily schedule and follow it
Find a job that will work with my class schedule
Set aside time for daily meditation & do it

Emotional Action Steps
Dinner together every night and talk about stuff
Schedule a weekly family time to talk & play
Have a weekly date night with my partner

Physical Action Steps
Join and go to a gym at least 3 times per week
Follow a healthy eating plan
Talk to my doctor about smoking cessation

Social Action Steps
Join a club or other venue in our area
Start scheduling activities with friends.

Spiritual Action Steps
Set aside time for reading, prayer, or meditation
Write down a personal code of ethics and post it
Attend spiritually uplifting activities with family & friends

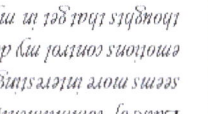

Pitfalls of Impulse
Impulsive Reactions We Use When Stressed

Lack of commitment, laziness, being distracted by what comes along or seems more interesting. Limited self-discipline, letting my temper or other emotions control my decisions. Obsessing over problems and/or negative thoughts that get in my way. Procrastination.

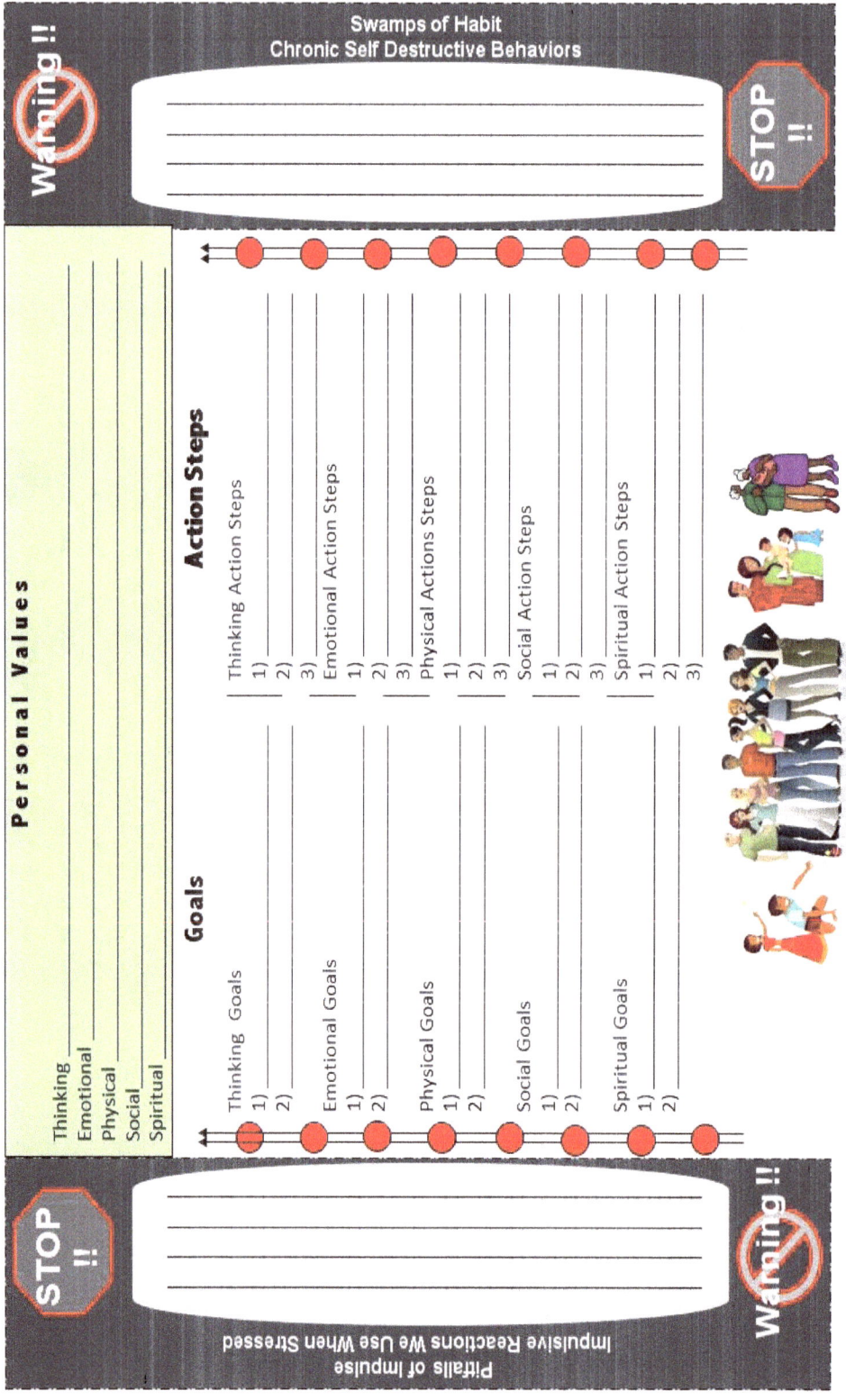

The Journey Map's exercise purpose is to give you an opportunity to make conscious choices about your values. Values describe the Why–"why is it important to do what I'm doing?" For example, "Why do I work hard? Because I want to have a successful career." Goals describe the what – "what skills do I need for a successful career in my field?" Action steps describe the How "How am I going to attain these skills?" The Journey Map exercise will allow you to identify all three.

Staying true to your values might be difficult at times, but no more difficult or painful than the trouble or disappointment will likely to encounter without them. The following exercise is just a template you can follow as you refine your journey map.

After selecting your values, goals, and action steps, the next two parts of this exercise will give you the opportunity to look at some of your impulsive behaviors, or habits that may be getting in the way of achieving your goals.

^Pause & Reflect: Step One ~ Journey Map Values^

Some possible examples might include the following:

Thinking
- Experience a lifetime of learning and growth
- Use my talents and abilities to provide a comfortable living
- Nurture curiosity, creativity, and flexibility

Emotional
- Enjoy a loving and enduring relationship with a partner
- Exercise empathy in my relationships with others
- Appreciate beauty in all things
- Exercise faith in my ability to experience joy

Physical
- Maintain a safe environment for myself and my family
- Develop the personal qualities of health and well-being
- Choose self-sufficiency whenever possible
- Respect the earth and all of its creatures

Social
- Contribute to the community in which I live
- Enjoy relationships with friends that are guided by healthy boundaries
- Live with honesty and integrity in my relationships with myself and others

Spiritual
- Manage whatever challenges may arise in my life with peace and equanimity
- Exercise compassion and forgiveness with myself and others

Spend some time with the examples provided below on the journey map. The Pause and Reflect exercises on the next several pages will help guide you as you complete your journey map that follows. Consider what might give your life the greatest sense of direction and purpose, then use the tables to guide you as you create your own Journey Map. If your values, goals, or action steps are not listed, take the time to create your own. Your efforts with this exercise will be well worth it in the long run.

^Pause and Reflect ~ Journey Map Goals^

> **Some possible examples might include the following:**
>
> **Thinking**
>   Develop creative and effective problem-solving skills
>   Practice understanding perspectives different from my own
>   Sign up for classes and read material that enhances my knowledge base
>   Learn mindfulness skills and how to tap into guidance from the Observer Self
>   Learn something new everyday
>
> **Emotional**
>   Learn more healthy ways of managing emotional or psychological symptoms
>   Develop the ability to be less avoidant of discomfort and difficulty
>   Appreciate beauty in all things
>   Exercise faith in my ability to experience joy
>
> **Physical**
>   Develop a healthier life style and stick with it
>   Set up a savings account, retirement fund, and college fund
>   Choose self-sufficiency whenever possible
>   Respect the earth and all of its creatures
>   Be mindful and sensitive to wastefulness and disrespect for natural resources
>
> **Social**
>   Learn and use good communication skills
>   Reach out to others who have similar interests and values
>   Educate myself about boundaries through reading, discussion, or therapy
>   Develop the skills for managing conflict and creating collaboration with others
>
> **Spiritual**
>   Spend time noticing and enjoying the beauties of people, animals, and nature
>   Explore beliefs and philosophies that edify my life
>   Demonstrate understanding as I learn from my mistakes
>   Express appreciation and gratitude for my life and all that I experience

Step Two: What are your Goals? Goals are general statements that define the pathways we can take to realize values. For example, a value of "Creating Loving Relationships" would not include a goal of "Retiring at age 50" or an action step of "Set up a 401k." Values create motivation and inspiration. Goals are the expression of the inspiration that we act on. They have a beginning, a middle, and an end. They are measurable; they are realistic and achievable. Goals can also be further broken down into mini-goals or action steps based on a weekly, monthly, or yearly timetable.

However we go about selecting goals, it is important to understand that striving toward and achieving goals enhances our self-esteem, fosters confidence, and brings clarity and meaning to our actions. If, for some reason, we are unable to achieve the goals we set, we have the opportunity to benefit from the lessons we learn as we go through the process and use that information to re-formulate our action steps. Either way, they keep us moving toward meaningfully expressing our values.

Step Three: Action Steps. Every goal requires planned, directed efforts for accomplishment. Considering the goals you've identified, what steps must you take to achieve them? One way of identifying an appropriate action step is by considering the time, date, and place you will complete the action. If it can be scheduled, purchased, or investigated, then talk about when, where, and how to do that. Be specific!

Step Four: The Pitfalls of Impulse. We use the Journey Map like a road map. The goals, values, and action steps guide our direction, and, as in every journey, obstacles, detours, and unexpected road conditions interfere with our progress. Similarly, in our lives, we make repetitive choices that can sabotage our efforts to achieve our goals. These are labeled *Pitfalls of Impulse* because they're choices we make in response to stressors in the immediate environment. When based on avoidance, the choices are usually reactive and nonproductive. They may feel like the right choices at first, which is why these choices are so deceptive but those that arise from intrusively negative emotions – such as fear, negative thoughts, attitudes, beliefs, expectations, etc. They are usually unintentional and appear with little or no forethought.

Examples of these pitfalls are listed in the Pitfalls of Impulse Pause & Reflect. Choose those that apply to you and enter them in the section of the Journey Map labeled Pitfalls of Impulse. Add any others not listed that may interfere with your journey.

Among personal challenges you may face are self-defeating tendencies such as criticism of yourself, others, and the world around you. Failing to accept aspects of yourself or others can undermine or even block your ability to change your life. For example, a lack of self-acceptance might lead you to question or minimize the importance of your insights or intuition. If you're experiencing conflict or intensely negative feelings toward yourself or others, you might also have difficulty clarifying the problem or solution.

Unmet or unrealized expectations create feelings of frustration and disappointment. Judgments and assumptions interrupt your ability to get information and find solutions that bring about resolution. All of these are obstacles that can get in the way of identifying and achieving your purpose and manifesting your values. Other impulsive behaviors that can get in the way include the tendency to "let it slide" or to convince oneself that change is not necessary. The phrase, "That's just who I am", is a trap that many people fall into. The reality is that we are never the same person from day to day. We are always changing and growing because our brain is always active, alert, and helping to manage our lives. Every new word we learn and every new thing we experience will ultimately change us. So, we might as well be the masters at the helm of our ship, or better yet, the masters of our own work of art. By growing in directions that will be of benefit to our lives in the long run, we are making effective choices about where we end up. Otherwise, like a ship without a rudder, we leave our futures up to chance, or worse, we become comfortable with familiar, destructive thinking and behaviors that are not compatible with our values.

^Pause & Reflect ~Journey Map Action Steps^

> **Some possible examples might include the following:**
>
> **Thinking**
> > Schedule time for daily reading/study and mindfulness meditation
> > Respond promptly to work assignments
> > Develop a consistent daily schedule of meditation time
>
> **Emotional**
> > Schedule weekly therapy with experts for learning to better manage my symptoms
> > Journal my successes, failures, and lessons learned each day
> > Schedule a weekly family day including fun activities and time to talk to each other
> > Schedule a weekly date night and talk time with my partner
>
> **Physical**
> > Remember to check doors and locks and to set the alarm system at night
> > Choose and practice a daily meal plan with 5-pound weight loss rewards
> > Exercise or go to the gym three to four times per week
>
> **Social**
> > Join clubs or other activities for networking and enjoying friendships
> > Schedule play dates with friends at least twice per week
> > Choose social activities that reflect healthy boundaries
>
> **Spiritual**
> > Write a personal code of ethics and post it where I can see it every day.

A final thought about learning to be the master of our world: if we are clinging to the idea that change is not possible or necessary, this choice may affect not only ourselves but also close relationships. Impulsive thinking and emotion are notoriously problematic concerning trust, communication, and healthy boundaries that are necessary for fulfilling relationships. Personal transformation, by contrast, can be a life-changing experience. If people in meaningful relationships are learning these tools and discovering personal values, purpose, and meaning together, the process can enrich and deepen the intimacy in a relationship and in a family unit exponentially.

^Pause & Reflect ~Journey Map Pitfalls of Impulse^

> **Some possible examples might include the following:**
>
> **Thinking**
> - Making premature judgments or assumptions without information
> - Running negative thoughts through your MindView over and over with no positive result
> - Negative or judgmental thoughts that lead to self-or other-condemnation
>
> **Emotional**
> - Avoidance reactions that prevent us from addressing and benefitting from experiences
> - Reliving negative emotional experiences from the past
> - Blaming self or others to avoid feeling painful emotions
>
> **Physical**
> - Setting unrealistic expectations then giving up when they don't work out
> - Rationalizing the use of substances or other distractions to avoid emotional content
> - Crossing others' physical boundaries through physical means
>
> **Social**
> - Defensiveness, denial, and/or refusal to accept responsibility in relationships
> - The kind of defensiveness that interrupts the ability to truly listen to, and hear another person's point of view because you are so invested in your own ideas
> - Crossing thinking, emotional, physical, social, spiritual boundaries to meet our own needs
> - Lack of honesty and integrity in my relationships with myself and others
>
> **Spiritual**
> - Procrastination, thoughtlessness, or pessimism
> - Perfectionistic expectations that do not allow for growth through making mistakes
> - Rejecting the wisdom of change out of a sense of pride or entitlement

Step Five: Swamps of Habit refers to chronic self-destructive behavior patterns that are difficult to pull ourselves out of – once we fall into them. They drain us of vast amounts of time and energy. They become chronic and emerge as a result of unsuccessfully struggling with the Pitfalls of Impulse. They are more destructive behaviors that are either aimed toward oneself or others who are closest to us.

^Pause and Reflect ~ Journey Map Habits^

> **Some possible examples might include the following:**
>
> **Thinking**
> >   Destructive uncontrolled/untreated behaviors, beliefs, and expectations
> >   Thoughts and beliefs that are detrimental to the self or others
>
> **Emotional**
> >   Lack of empathy, narcissism, and/or self-centeredness
> >   Personality patterns or disorders that violate healthy/appropriate boundaries
>
> **Physical**
> >   Violence toward self, others, pets, or property
> >   Addictive behaviors, including substances, pornography, rage, and/or dominance
>
> **Social**
> >   The verbal expression of hatred or contempt toward people or situations
> >   Excusing, minimizing, or passive-aggressive behaviors
> >   Behaviors that violate the law and/or the rights of others

Look at the examples of the Swamps of Habit in the following Pause and Reflect. If your difficulties aren't listed, think about what patterns hold you back and add them to the list. What choices or actions have you taken that weren't good uses of your time or energy? Are they distracting you from what is most important to you and creating barriers that make your life more difficult? Are they behaviors that set fires that you later must put out? Have you tried to stop them but found it was much more difficult than you expected? Don't worry. Most people have been confronted with some form of these behaviors at some point in their lives. For now, just acknowledge that they are a part of your life, and they exist for a reason. It doesn't matter how or why. There is no need for blame, justification, guilt, or shame. All that matters is that these habits are not working for you in your life now. For some people, they might have begun as protective mechanisms for other types of problems, and for others, they might have been sincere efforts toward problem-solving. In any case, identify any that you are aware of and enter them on the outer left side of the Journey Map labeled Swamps of Habit.

Step Six: Your Community. Finally, to complete your Journey Map, write down the people you would like to include on your journey. The people you list at the bottom of your Journey Map represent your community, those who are close to you. It is these people that you wish to have with you when you reach your goals. People in your community help to keep you grounded because they likely share similar goals, values, and personal qualities. Members of a healthy community provide support, inspiration, compassion, and encouragement for one another as they journey together. Maintaining and protecting the community you belong to is one of the most important keys to your personal success and happiness. And, between those individuals, at the bottom of your journey map and the goal box at the top, imagine a road. The road represents the journey of time and effort as well as the trials, errors, restarts, and successes you will experience along your way. As with any journey, there will be obstacles, roadblocks, and interruptions of life that will have the potential to disrupt progress and success. Be prepared for them. They will happen. This is also where The Artist's Tools will be so helpful. With acceptance, forgiveness, self-compassion, commitment, and gratitude, you have the ability to achieve well-being in your life. As you continue to grow with this goal-oriented process, you will experience a lifetime of refining your values, renewing your goals, and exploring new ways to achieve them.

As you share this process with your loved ones, they will benefit as well. They will see a more centered, self-assured you, and they will likely want to follow your example.

From Where You are Today to the Masterpiece You Can Be

The work you have just completed with the Journey Map represents the goals and dreams of your core self.

You have mapped out:
- a vision of your potential,
- why it is important to work toward your potential,
- how you will get there, and
- how you will avoid the types of choices and behaviors that will de-rail your success.

The journey that will take you from where you are today to the masterpiece you will be one day will not go in a straight line. Rather, it will be a spiraled journey of steps forward and steps backward. You will constantly be re-evaluating, redesigning, and renewing your commitment and efforts toward your values and goals. It sounds arduous, but there is also great joy to be found in this process.

Journal Lines

_____
_____
_____
_____
_____
_____
_____
_____

^Pause and Reflect ~ Journey Map: My Summary^

> Thinking about what you have learned from the Journey Map process, can you find a way to summarize your experience?
> _____
> _____
>
> Go back to the Vision Pause & Reflect exercise at the beginning of this chapter. How similar is your initial vision to the Journey Map you created?
> _____
> _____
>
> Did you experience any surprises or new discoveries about yourself? What were they?
> _____
> _____
>
> Write a short paragraph that summarizes your values, and goals, and how you hope to achieve them. _____
> _____
>
> Do you have a better idea of how or what might sabotage your success? Jot down a few words to summarize your thoughts. _____
> _____
>
> How might this process be useful in other areas of your life? Could others around you, or close to you, benefit from this exercise? Can you find someone, perhaps a friend, family member, or significant other, who might enjoy creating a Journey Map of their own? A Journey Map partner can greatly enhance the experience as well as the enjoyment as we share our struggles and successes with someone who is on the same journey.
> _____
> _____

^Pause & Reflect: Your Council Compass Values^

The final step in your Journey Map exercise is to transfer your goals and action steps to your Council Compass. Take a few minutes to write them in the sections of each MindView space. Then look for balance. What do you see? Are you finding better balance than the first time you completed this activity in Chapter One? What adjustments could you make to improve it?

Now that you have your Artist's Tools, you've learned about your council and all that it has to offer, you've learned about what it means to be well, to flourish, and what can get in your way, and finally, you have identified your goals and action steps. Let's move on to the last and most important discovery: Who you are as a person!

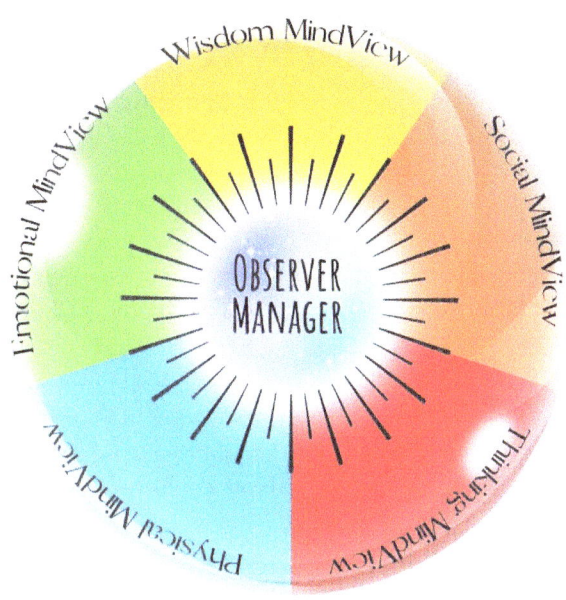

What are your goals and action steps? Write them in.

    This chapter introduces a guided meditation designed to help you visualize the transformative journey you are about to undertake. Envision the successes, challenges, and the profound joy you will encounter along this path. The purpose of this meditation, coupled with journaling prompts, is to facilitate a deeper understanding and integration of the concepts you are exploring. The effectiveness of this meditation is directly proportional to the effort and intention you invest in it. As you engage in this meditation regularly, allow yourself to fully immerse in the process, visualizing each step of your journey with clarity. The journaling aspect is not just a form of reflection but a tool for internalizing and personalizing the insights gained. This process is designed to be a cornerstone in your journey of self-discovery and personal growth. Dedicate yourself to these practices and observe the transformative impact they have on your journey towards realizing your fullest potential.

Journal Lines

_____
_____
_____
_____
_____
_____
_____
_____

Journal Space

GM Journaling: Ch. 5 - Journey Map
- What did you experience as you did this meditation?
- When you think about where you are going in your life, what do you see?
- When you envisioned yourself one year and five years from now, what did you see?
- What values and goals will help you?
- What habitual or impulsive behaviors are most likely to get in your way?
- Would it be wise to get help to deal with them? How could you do that? When will you do that?
- When you see yourself as having achieved your vision, how did you feel?
- How can you help yourself stay true to your values and goals?
- Do your values help you to better understand what brings a sense of meaning and purpose to your life?
- Can you begin to see how these goals might improve and enhance your life? How could you make those changes happen?
- Knowing what is at stake, do you think it might be worth it to begin working on accomplishing your goals?

Journal Lines

Meditation- Journey to Self-Discovery ~ Chapter 5: Guided Meditation in the Garden of Creativity

As you begin this meditation, find a comfortable position, lying down with your eyes gently closed. Place your hand on your stomach, and take slow, deep breaths. With each inhalation, visualize a pure white cloud entering through the top of your head, swirling through your body. This cloud collects all the day's tensions, fatigue, and worries. As you exhale, imagine these impurities leaving your body through your toes, vanishing into the ether.

Feel the transformation of the breath into a calming blue hue, bringing serenity to your entire being. Your body relaxes, and your mind becomes peaceful and still, floating in tranquility.

Now, in your mind's eye, step into your personal Garden space. This is a realm where your Artist's Tools - acceptance, forgiveness, empathy, and compassion - reside within you. Breathe in these qualities, allowing them to permeate every cell, infusing your mind and body with love, care, self-acceptance, and self-compassion. With each breath, sink deeper into a state of calm and peace.

As you explore this garden, find a comfortable spot. Perhaps it's a bench under a tree or beside a gently flowing stream. Along the path, absorb the beauty around you - the vibrant colors, the fragrant scents, the gentle sounds of nature. Notice how the path leads you to a clearing, revealing a workshop.

Approach this workshop, your secret haven for creativity and self-exploration. Before entering, take a moment to walk around its exterior, familiarizing yourself with this space that belongs solely to you. As you step through the front door, you're greeted by a mirror. Pause here. Look at your reflection. What do you see? Who is the person gazing back at you? Just observe.

Moving further into the workshop, you find a welcoming workbench equipped with an array of art supplies - vibrant papers, colorful markers, pens, and paints. Each piece is untouched, waiting for your creative touch. Picture frames lean against the wall, ready to frame the masterpieces you will create here. This workshop is a sanctuary for crafting your life's vision and discovering your true self.

Settle into a comfortable position, eyes closed, and take deep, soothing breaths. Feel the tranquility enveloping you as you reflect on your childhood. Recall how you observed and absorbed the words and actions of those around you, shaping your understanding of yourself and the world. Recognize that some of these early impressions may still impact you in a negative way, while others filled you with a sense of security and belonging.

In your mind, walk over to the workbench in your special workshop. Here, you find an array of artistic tools – markers, pens, pencils, paper, and blank canvases. Some canvases already bear the strokes of your past experiences; others await your creative touch. Settle in, feeling the comfort and possibilities that surround you. Choose your tools and canvases.

Begin by thinking about one of your most painful stories. How did it make you feel? How would you represent this on paper? What colors? What textures? Now begin to create it. Recall the affirmations you've learned: "You were good enough when you were born, and nothing has changed that." Understand that labeling yourself negatively based on past choices, reactions, or others' opinions is as unjust as blaming a tree for bending in a storm. Life's events happen to everyone; these harsh words and beliefs are not your truth. Now tear up this painful memory and discard it in the trash bin. Remember, these old stories linger only because of their familiarity, not their accuracy. Whenever negative thoughts or hurtful stories arise, take a deep, cleansing breath, exhale, and mentally shrink these thoughts to mere molecules, blowing them away from your Mind.

Now, with a fresh stack of paper or a canvas, begin to artistically represent your values. Select colors, designs, and scripts that resonate with you, creating a visual representation of each value. Once completed, envision framing and arranging them in a beautiful row on the wall before you.

Step back and admire this visual array of your chosen values. Each one is a testament to your journey and the person you are becoming. Feel the emotions that arise as you gaze upon them, recognizing the beauty and strength in the values you've embraced for your journey.

As you delve deeper into relaxation, bring your focus to a collection of smaller papers spread across the workbench. These symbolize the goals that are consistent with your values. With each deep breath, visualize your goals, inscribing them onto these papers, aligning each beneath its corresponding value on the wall. This arrangement reflects the dynamic nature of your journey; goals and action steps might evolve and change as you progress, and that's perfectly okay. It's part of the growth process to reassess and adapt your goals as needed. Remember, progress is a series of steps, some forward, some sideways, and even some back. It's all part of moving towards your values. If you find the journey overwhelming, focus on one value, one goal, and one action step at a time, simplifying the process to make it more manageable.

After detailing your goals and steps, take a moment to step back and observe the tapestry you've created above your workbench. Admire the cohesion of your values, goals, and actions steps. Feel the pride and excitement stirring within you as you contemplate the adventure that lies ahead.

Now, in your mind's eye, envision your future self. In this future, outdated and negative narratives no longer hold sway. They've been replaced by a continuous mindful awareness of your chosen values, goals, and actions. These elements collectively infuse your life with purpose and meaning. As you focus on these goals and steps, your life's trajectory shifts. You are actively crafting your future with every mindful decision, shaping it to mirror your potential. Feel a newfound sense of health and well-being radiating from your core.

Whenever old, negative thoughts resurface, pause, and breathe deeply. Visualize shrinking these thoughts until they're mere specks, then release them, letting them drift away. This practice helps you maintain focus on your values and goals.

Take one more look at the gallery of your values, goals, and actions steps. Let them serve as a constant source of inspiration and encouragement. Following your journey map, your life is becoming more intentional, meaningful, and enriching, not just for you, but for those around you as well.

As you continue to relax and breathe deeply, imagine the evolution of your values and actions into seamless, instinctive behaviors. Envision scenarios where life's challenges might distract you from your path. In these moments, you'll sense an internal alarm, signaling when choices might misalign with your higher purpose. This awareness is your guide, ensuring you stay true to your values and goals.

With a spirit of commitment, acceptance, compassion, forgiveness, and gratitude, any deviations from your path can be corrected. Your journey map is not fixed; it's a living document, adaptable as you grow and learn. This flexibility is the key to transforming your life, one decision, one step at a time.

Now, it's time to leave the workshop. Feel the profound inner transformation. Imagine yourself in a year, in five years, having fully embraced your values-guided life. With ongoing practice and dedication, the masterpiece within you will gradually unfold.

As you step out of the workshop, notice your reflection in the mirror once more. Observe the changes in how you see yourself. With a final glance, step out into your garden, knowing your workshop is a safe sanctuary within you, always accessible on your journey to a healthier, more fulfilled, and loving life.

When you're ready, slowly bring your awareness back to the present, carrying with you the insights and tranquility from this meditation.

Chapter 6 – Exploring Your Inner Artist: What is an Identity?

"Setting boundaries is a way of caring for myself. It doesn't make me mean, selfish, or uncaring (just) because I don't (want to) do things your way. I care about me, too."
~Christine Morgan

Reflect on the concept of possession and its role in self-identity. Common phrases like "I have a car" or "I have a career" are often used to describe ourselves. But what do these statements truly represent? Is it about ownership, the investment of time and effort, or something deeper? These expressions serve more as social identifiers than genuine reflections of our core values, purpose, or internal meaning. They provide a surface-level definition of who we are to others, yet many of us struggle with the profound question: "Who am I?" and "What is the purpose of my life?" There's often a hesitation to define ourselves definitively, perhaps due to the fear of being incorrect.

Imagine, however, fully embracing and owning a definition of yourself that you find correct, acceptable, and desirable. How would such self-assurance transform your life?

Our interactions often lead us to recognize our unique traits and differences. Unfortunately, it's more common to focus on perceived flaws rather than strengths. Challenges in life lead to the development of coping mechanisms and personality traits, which may hinder or help us in achieving our goals. Viewing these traits objectively, through the lens of the MindView Compass, and employing The Artist's Tools - acceptance, forgiveness, compassion, commitment, and gratitude-can prevent the usual self-condemnation that accompanies low self-esteem.

By consistently practicing mindful observation of ourselves with The Artist's Tools, we gain deeper insights into our identity. This chapter aims to guide you in understanding your inner self more clearly. This clarity will illuminate how you perceive yourself, your decisions, and the skills needed to create the desired well-being.

Consider this analogy: learning about your inner workings is akin to understanding the basics of driving. We might know which pedal accelerates and which one brakes from a young age, but navigating out of challenging situations requires skill and understanding. My early experience with a car at three years old, inadvertently rolling down a hill, was thrilling yet lacked the skill to resolve the situation safely. Similarly, understanding the intricacies of our identity and personality requires more than surface knowledge; it demands skillful exploration and application.

Understanding Identity and Its Formation

Research on identity suggests that it is shaped by five core processes during our interactions with the world and others (Adams, 1996):

1. Self-Definition: This is how we articulate who we are to ourselves and others.
2. Meaning, Direction, and Values: These aspects pertain to what matters to us and guide our actions.
3. Personal Control: This involves our sense of agency.
4. Consistency: This refers to the continuity of our self-perception over time.
5. Personal Skills and Abilities: We recognize these capacities in ourselves.

These processes are crucial in forming our identity, which will be discussed in depth in the following sections.

Defining Identity

Identity encapsulates our self-perception and the descriptions we share with others about who we are. It's centered on what brings meaning and purpose to our lives, our values, and how these elements guide our choices. It also includes the principles that drive our decisions, focus our attention, and motivate our actions.

Consider how we introduce ourselves to someone new. The characteristics we share, such as academic pursuits, aspirations, and values, paint a picture of our identity. For instance, a student discussing their agricultural studies and aspirations to teach sustainable practices globally reveals their intellectual pursuits, a desire to help others, and a commitment to environmental stewardship. These chosen highlights are indicative of the person's core identity attributes.

As life progresses, we construct narratives about our experiences and roles, whether as heroes, victims, or other archetypes. These stories shape our beliefs about ourselves. However, the danger lies in the potential for inaccuracies and distortions in these narratives, which can negatively impact our self-esteem and hinder healthy identity development.

Research suggests that struggles with identity can lead to:
- **Ineffective coping strategies.**
- **Reduced stress tolerance.**
- **A propensity to avoid challenging experiences.**
- **Tendencies to harshly judge one's emotions or actions.**
- **Issues with self-esteem, depression, or anxiety.**
- **Challenges in developing empathy for others.**
- **Difficulties in identifying life-guiding values.**

The next Pause & Reflect outlines the characteristics that contribute to the growth and development of a healthy sense of identity. These tools and strategies will all be introduced and discussed in the following chapters.

^Pause & Reflect ~ Complete the "I am a person who . . ." statements below.^

	How the Mind Creates a Sense of Identity and Wholeness:
Thinking MindView	Curious, resourceful, teachable, creative, OLIVE Problem-Solving, Values-Guided Thinking, Thinking and identity, mindful awareness. I am a person who is: _____
Spiritual MindView	Discerning, authentic, Intelligent, wise mind. Spiritual principles as a personal stewardship, the spiritual journey is a life that is defined by principles. I am a person who is: _____
Emotional MindView	Emotional IQ for setting boundaries, strategies for creating inner safety, recognizing triggers, emotional boundaries. I am a person who is: _____
Social MindView	Social IQ skills, Assertiveness & Social Boundaries, attending, speaking, & Listening skills, social skills and Problem Solving. I am a person who is: _____
Physical MindView	Lifestyle choices that fit, committed action, commitment to wellness, sleep & activity hygiene, it's the brain and body that keep score. I am a person who is: _____
Observer Manager	Overseer, advisor, planner, organizer, with an attitude of curiosity, receptivity, creativity, and meaningful perseverance, mindfulness of the whole person I am a person who is: _____

Therefore, it's vital to develop a genuine understanding and acceptance of ourselves, as this forms the bedrock of healthy identity growth. Misconceptions and distortions about oneself can profoundly impact personality development and perception, highlighting the importance of nurturing a well-rounded and accurate sense of identity.

Exploring Identity Through the Lens of the MindView Council

While research offers broad insights into human behavior and emotional adjustment, a more nuanced understanding can be achieved by examining these aspects through the MindView Council. This approach can help pinpoint and address specific issues affecting each Council member, fostering recovery of self-esteem and identity. If you identify with having identity-related challenges, the tools and strategies discussed in this book, along with the guidance of a therapist, can support your healing journey.

It's possible to have a sense of identity even with low self-esteem. Our life experiences often teach us about our values, such as love and care for animals, which can be extended to relationships with friends and family. These experiences shape our identity, even as we grapple with questions about our worth within these groups.

The shaping of identity often follows one of three paths:

1. Positive Reinforcement of Self-Worth: Individuals who are encouraged to see self-worth and accept failures as part of life are likely to face experiences with resilience. They often have a strong sense of self-esteem that supports continuous growth and a clear connection to their ingrained values and behaviors that bring joy.

2. Positive Experiences with Lack of Support: Some may have positive experiences but lack support in developing self-worth, and they may face criticism or undervaluation from others. Such individuals might internalize a view of themselves as problematic, despite positive family or social experiences. There are numerous variations within this category, with each uniquely influencing the individual's perception of their identity.

3. Survival in Harsh Environments: For those in particularly hostile environments, survival becomes the primary focus, overshadowing the development of a distinct sense of self. These individuals may adopt a defensive approach to life, where their identity either retreats for survival reasons or remains underdeveloped.

In all of these scenarios, identity is present but may be influenced differently based on the environment and experiences. Recognizing and nurturing an identity, regardless of its path of development is crucial for personal growth and well-being. By understanding these varied paths to identity formation, we can begin to explore and reclaim our sense of self, even amidst challenges.

^Pause & Reflect ~ Identity, as I am Today^

Consider the three scenarios regarding self-esteem and identity above.

Which group do you most identify with?
_____

Why did you choose the scenario you did?
_____

How have your experiences affected your self-esteem?
_____

Do you have a sense of your identity? Can you describe who you are?
_____
_____

Exploring Self-Definition

Self-definition is our unique way of identifying ourselves, based on our standpoints, on vital issues and experiences in life. It's about recognizing our individuality rather than seeing ourselves merely as reflections of others' perceptions. Particularly after enduring challenging experiences, either in childhood or adulthood, it's common to self-scrutinize harshly, often viewing oneself negatively.

Recall your journey in Chapter 4, where you began differentiating yourself from your past pains or adverse experiences. These experiences, regardless of their nature, do not define your essence. They are external events that happened to you, separate from your individual identity. Those with an underdeveloped sense of self often misinterpret others' emotions, behaviors, and intentions, and react defensively to non-threatening situations, missing out on valuable learning and growth opportunities. Complete Pause & Reflect ~ Self Definition.

Individuals with a fragile sense of self typically have lower self-esteem, less confidence, and are hesitant to embrace life's challenges. This often translates to relationship instability, increased emotional reactivity, and unnecessary anger. It's crucial to recognize that self-definition is not static; it evolves. The work you have embarked on is instrumental in enhancing both your self-definition and self-esteem.

In the upcoming Pause and Reflect activity (Values, Meaning, & Direction), we invite you to compose a paragraph about yourself, focusing on five of your achievements and the skills you utilized to attain them. As you review your description, observe the patterns in how you perceive yourself. Draw upon this chapter to gain a clearer understanding of your identity.

^Pause & Reflect ~ Self Definition^

Things I most admire most in others are _____
_____
Qualities I would most like to exemplify are _____
_____
When I was young I use to say, when I grow up I want to be _____
_____
Things I am most afraid of becoming are _____
_____
These thoughts tell me I am a person who values _____
_____
When I meet someone new, I describe myself to them by telling them _____
_____

^Pause & Reflect–Values, Meaning & Direction^

> Consider the questions in the section above and write a paragraph about who you are in terms of what is most meaningful to you, what you value, and what directions you have chosen in your life. _____
> _____
> _____
>
> Have these choices brought you the peace or joy you have been seeking? and if not, what might be modified to achieve the outcome you desire?
> _____
> _____
> _____

Aligning Values with Life's Direction

Our natural inclination is to gravitate towards environments that mirror our past experiences, where we can utilize our talents, pursue interests, and express our core values. We are instinctively drawn to challenges and roles that invigorate us and avoid what we find unfamiliar. How we define ourselves and adhere to our values acts as a navigational tool, influencing our decisions and life paths. Those lacking a strong sense of direction often experience higher levels of depression and lower self-esteem, feeling less competent in various life domains, such as career, relationships, and parenting.

The sense of meaning and direction is vital for cultivating a purposeful life. This sense of purpose can often shape our goals. Achieving these goals reinforces our belief in our capabilities, fostering hope, pride, self-worth, and an awareness of our potential.

Journal Lines

_____
_____
_____
_____
_____
_____
_____
_____
_____
_____
_____
_____
_____
_____

^Pause & Reflect ~ Physical Boundaries^

Consider the following boundaries. Where do you see yourself? What might be some good goals to work on?

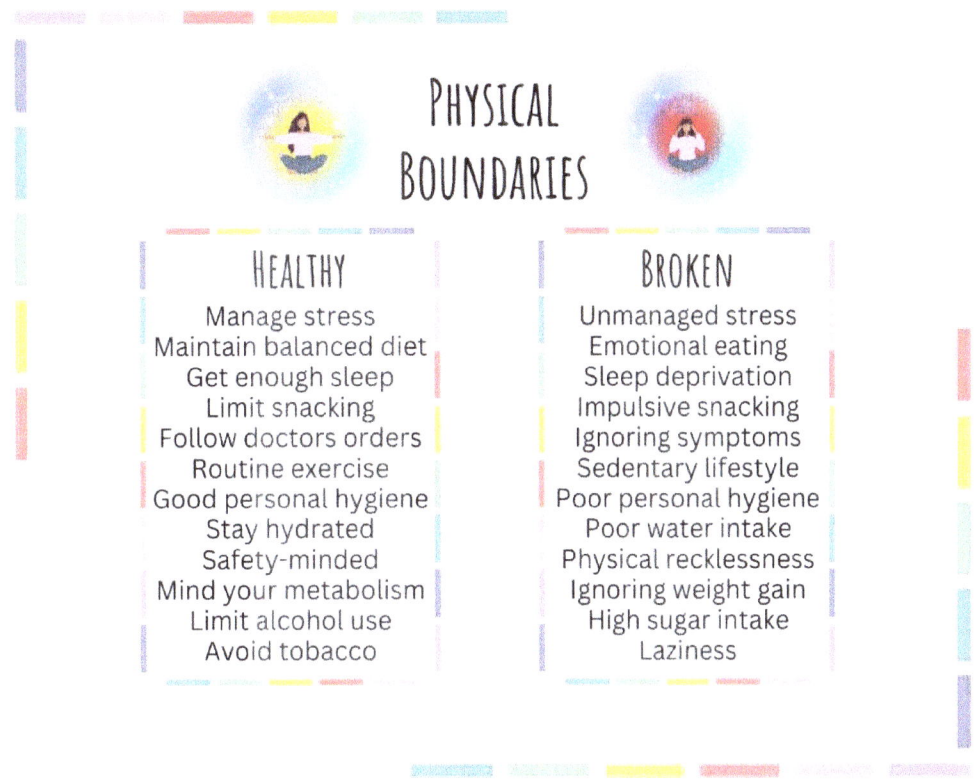

To discern our personal meaning, values, and direction, examining our choices and actions is insightful. Every action we take either brings us closer to our true selves or distances us from our potential. Recall the work that you accomplished in Chapter 5, where you defined your values and goals. To strengthen your identity, consider whether your actions are congruent with your values.

Another approach to uncovering our unique sense of meaning and direction is to explore our inherent gifts and interests. We all differ in our attractions and aversions. For instance, some may be intrigued by the natural world of insects and reptiles, while others may be captivated by human behavior or the mechanics of how things operate. Discovering these personal affinities helps us set meaningful goals and monitor progress towards them.

This goal-setting process is crucial for personal growth, self-esteem, and evolving identity. There's a dynamic interplay between our actions, personal development, and what we find meaningful, continuously shaping our identity.

^Pause & Reflect ~ Personal Boundaries^

On the lines in the figure below, jot down the boundaries you maintain currently on the left side of each line for each MindView domain, and on the right – enter the boundary you would like to begin maintaining.

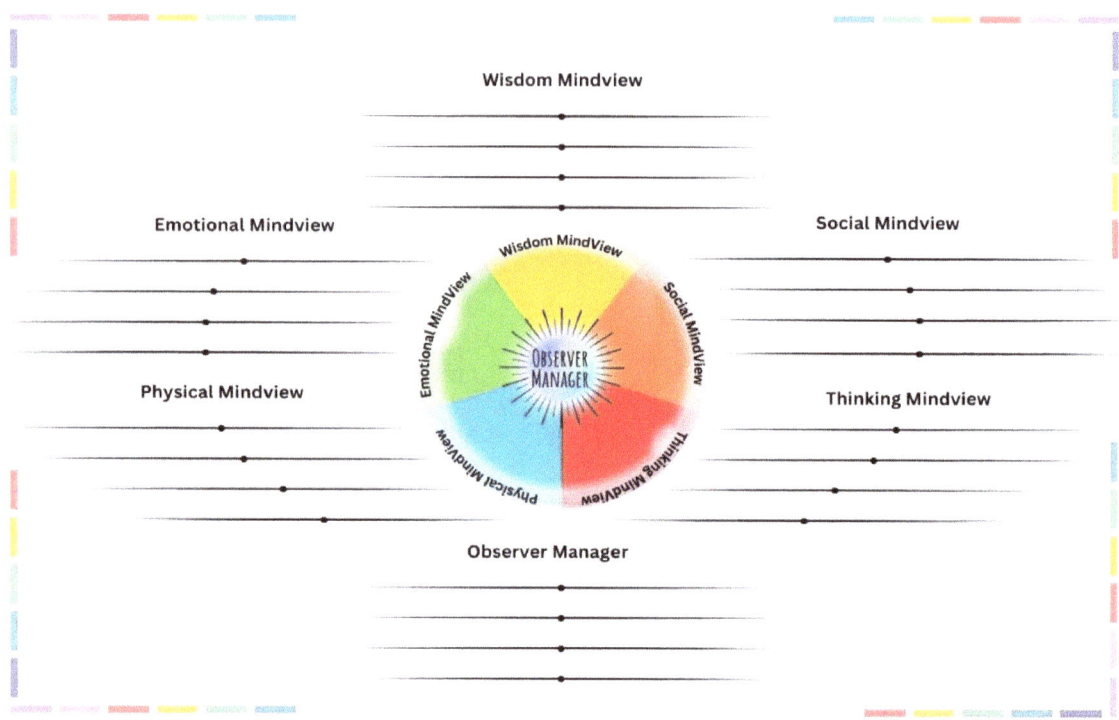

Finally, consider your core values. Reflect on the three most significant aspects of your life. Are you more spiritually inclined or secular? Do you view yourself as altruistic or pragmatic? Understanding what predominately guides your decisions is essential in aligning your actions with your values.

Mastering Self-Regulation

Self-regulation is our capacity to modulate our emotions and behaviors, enabling us to respond appropriately to our feelings and the emotions of others. It may involve focusing on tasks even when they don't pique our interest and managing impulsive reactions. Those proficient in self-regulation often exhibit enhanced social skills, better managing their interactions with the world.

On the flip side, behavioral dysregulation manifests as a struggle to control the impact of emotions on thoughts and actions, often leading to responses that are incongruent with one's values and objectives.

Poor self-regulation is linked to heightened risks of depression, anxiety, and substance abuse. Additionally, those with dysregulated behaviors tend to have conflict-ridden relationships, display immaturity and anger, and struggle to adjust socially. Dysregulation can lead to reckless behaviors, escalating stress and conflict in relationships, and overshadowing the skills needed to cope with stress and trauma effectively.

A world perceived as predictable and manageable fosters the ability to tackle life's hurdles, cultivate healthy relationships, and enjoy overall satisfaction and well-being. A sense of control and adept self-regulation also bolsters self-esteem, and confidence in our competence and effectiveness in life.

We typically learn self-regulation through socialization from family, school, and peers. However, in environments marked by dysfunction, these crucial skills may not be adequately taught or modeled. Key components of effective self-regulation, some of which have been outlined in previous chapters, include:

- Developing self-mastery skills through goal setting.
- Upholding healthy lifestyle habits, such as regular exercise, sufficient sleep, and nutritious eating.
- Avoiding substances that alter the mind.
- Implementing relaxation or meditation practices.
- Managing thoughts through cognitive reappraisal and other techniques.

These skills form a critical foundation for self-regulation, enabling us to navigate life's challenges with resilience and adaptability.

^Pause & Reflect: Self-Regulation^

Consider the following behavioral ratings. Score yourself on each dimension based on which characteristic might best describe you right now by placing an x on the dotted line. At the end of this workbook we will re-evaluate and see where you might have changed. For example, if you are more moody than stable put an x on the line as shown.

Moody……………………………………………………….. Stable
Friendly…………………………………………………….. Unfriendly
Courteous………………………………………………….. Rude
Argumentative…………………………………………….. Peacemaker
Composed………………………………………………….. Scattered
Expressive…………………………………………………. Closed
Hostile……………………………………………………....Empathetic
Peaceful……………………………………………………. Quarrelsome
Defensive…………………………………………………...Transparent
Kind-hearted……………………………………………….Mean
Vulgar………………………………………………………Tactful
Accepting…………………………………………………...Contemptuous
Critical……………………………………………………...Non-judgmental
Complaining……………………………………………….Complimentary

Embracing Consistency in Identity and Boundaries

Consistency in our beliefs, values, and goals is essential for setting boundaries that shield us from negative influences and experiences. Such boundaries enable us to focus on our objectives and protect us from external pressures that may lead us away from our goals and values. This self-imposed regulation is achieved by establishing personal boundaries, which are crucial for safeguarding our core values and aspirations.

Effective boundaries preserve our personal values and goals empower us to define our identity, beliefs, and what we find significant. We compromise our boundaries when we commit to a value but then engage in actions that contradict it. Similarly, we let others breach our boundaries when we allow their behavior to sway our decisions away from our stated values and goals, whether they pertain to emotional, social, intellectual, spiritual, or physical domains.

Being accountable for adhering to our values and goals signifies a deep sense of responsibility for our life and actions. Integrity manifests when we align our behavior with our identified values, set goals, and uphold boundaries, thus embodying them in our actions. Successfully achieving these goals enhances self-worth and fortifies a sense of control over our lives, demonstrating self-regulation.

Respecting Boundaries: A Key to Mutual Respect and Personal Growth

Establishing boundaries is not about diminishing the value or importance of others in our lives. On the contrary, setting appropriate boundaries is an expression of deep respect. Recognizing, accepting, and allowing others to be as they are, while expecting the same consideration in return, lays a foundation of mutual respect, appreciation, deference, and trust. It's a mutual understanding that both parties will treat each other with respect, and acceptance, fostering a healthy relationship environment where both individuals can flourish.

Healthy boundaries are also crucial for self-discovery and understanding our place in the world. They encourage mindfulness of our unique perspectives and the right to express and explore them, provided they do not harm others or infringe upon their boundaries. The result is a journey toward self-realization, finding one's place and purpose in the world, and cultivating inner peace and wisdom through self-awareness and understanding. Respecting our own and others' physical, intellectual, social, emotional, and spiritual boundaries creates a safe and nurturing internal environment, promoting personal growth and maturity.

Consider the analogy of a newborn's personality to the blank white walls of a freshly painted room, devoid of preconceived notions about oneself or the world. The individual's personality, identity, and potential are vast and open to personal shaping and creation.

If a child's early experiences are protective, warm, and accepting, with appropriate boundaries and coping strategies taught by parents, the child is likely to grow up with a positive and distinct sense of self and their place in the world. However, adverse early experiences, such as abuse, neglect, or trauma, can lead to poor boundaries and negative beliefs about oneself and the world. This could result in a perception of the world as unsafe, people as untrustworthy, love as conditional, self-doubt, and a reliance on others' approval for happiness.

For instance, consider Melissa's story. Raised by a violent father and a passive mother, Melissa experienced physical and emotional abuse. She learned to survive by avoiding conflict, remaining quiet, and trying to be invisible, constantly vigilant of her father's unpredictable moods. Despite her mother's love, Melissa understood she could not rely on her for protection. Melissa's upbringing profoundly impacted her sense of boundaries and self-perception, illustrating the critical role of early life experiences in shaping one's identity and understanding of interpersonal boundaries.

Empowering Self Through Strong Boundaries

Melissa's efforts to appease her father through diligence in chores and academic excellence were her strategies for maintaining peace. However, these tactics were not always successful, and her worldview became shaped by a pattern of either defensiveness or withdrawal in the face of perceived danger. This affected her ability to trust and form close relationships, leading to a lack of intimacy with her husband, doubts about her children's affection, and general anxiety when facing disapproval. Melissa found solace in substance use, feeling disconnected and unhappy with her life, marriage, and prospects. Is Melissa doomed by her past experience? Absolutely not! However, awareness of her weak boundaries is an important place to start the change process.

Weak boundaries often signal a propensity to prioritize others' opinions and needs over our own, compromising our self-protection. Such porous boundaries mean our self-definition is easily swayed by external disapproval, making our sense of well-being susceptible to fear and external influences.

With uncertain or ambivalent boundaries, we struggle to set limits and assert our needs, undermining our confidence in self-determination. Our identity and the strength of our boundaries are interlinked, each influencing the other positively or negatively.

Our brains are designed to learn from experiences, a critical survival mechanism. Yet, when our experiences have been marked by chaos, unpredictability, toxicity, or neglect, as in Melissa's case, we develop belief systems mirroring these adverse environments. Our coping strategies and interactions often become defensive, reflecting a need to protect ourselves from a seemingly hostile world.

However, as we grow in awareness of our need for self-definition and the benefits of healthy boundaries, we can consciously choose to establish and uphold boundaries aligned with our values. This healing process and resetting our boundary systems enables us to engage in healthier relationships moving forward.

This discussion circles back to aligning values, goals, and action steps with firm boundaries. Our sense of purpose and well-being is jeopardized when our boundaries are breached. Establishing and maintaining strong boundaries is not just about self-protection; it's about honoring our innermost values and aspirations, ensuring our personal growth and fulfillment.

Unlocking Potential Through Skills, Interests, and Abilities

The journey toward recognizing and embracing one's potential and future possibilities often begins by nurturing personal skills and abilities. This development is intrinsically linked to our values, goals, and actions, and plays a crucial role in career planning and academic success. When we engage in activities that captivate and mean something to us, we start uncovering our strengths and interests. Childhood pursuits, whether staging plays for the neighborhood or striving to win a school science fair, may seem trivial at the time, but they often lay the foundation for future accomplishments. These early endeavors can guide us towards acquiring the necessary training or education, steering us towards a career or field that permeates our adult lives with meaning and purpose.

It's important to note that this is a general perspective and may not align with everyone's experiences. Nevertheless, it highlights how our skills and abilities often stem from our passions and interests. Whether these interests lead to specialized skills or academic achievements is secondary to the realization that they form an integral part of our identity. Mindfully aware of our interests, skills, and abilities is crucial as we contemplate the trajectory of our life's journey. If there is a disconnect between our pursuits and interests, we might find ourselves in a struggle, feeling misaligned with our actions, direction, or methods. This misalignment can deprive us of the sense of well-being and mastery over our artistic selves that we aspire to achieve.

If you find yourself at a crossroads, uncertain if your current path aligns with your true interests, recall your Journey Map from Chapter 5. This map will focus on defining values, setting goals, and planning actionable steps towards realizing your aspirations. Remember, it's never too late to redirect your course. Each step towards living out your vision is a part of crafting a masterpiece that is continually evolving.

Integrating Self-Understanding

As we delve into the next reflective exercise, we pose a series of thought-provoking questions. Your answers to these aren't immediate solutions for crafting your identity but steppingstones guiding you towards understanding your core self. The deeper your insight into your unique persona, the more zeal, adeptness, and innovation you inject into every facet of your life.

In the upcoming reflection titled "How Do I Define Who I Am?" you will explore various aspects of your identity: your self-perception, life's meaning and direction, personal values, and goals, along with your skills and abilities. Contemplating these questions can illuminate your self-image and areas that might require more focus.

The subsequent reflection, "Activity Review," prompts you to examine how you allocate your time and energy. **The MindView Compass chart for this exercise can be found at the end of this chapter.**

Here's a guide for this introspective exercise:

1. List your activities within each section of the MindView Compass. For instance, if family interactions dominate your social life, note "family" under the "Social MindView domain. Extend

lines from the circle's center to incorporate as many activities as possible for each MindView Domain, adding extra lines where necessary. This visual representation will help you assess the balance of activities across different aspects of your life.

2. Mark the activities that resonate with your identity, creativity, and enjoyment. These are the pursuits that embody your true self and bring personal satisfaction.

3. Highlight the activities that align with your values and hold significance for you, even if they don't necessarily provide joy or a sense of well-being. Recognizing these commitments is essential in understanding the trade-offs and responsibilities that shape your life.

4. Identify and highlight any activities that don't align with your values, don't contribute meaningfully to your life, or detract from your well-being. Acknowledging these can be critical in reorienting your focus and energies towards more fulfilling and value-driven activities.

Through this process, you'll understand how your daily life reflects (or contrasts with) your inner identity, enabling you to make adjustments that steer you closer to your envisioned Artfully Lived Life.

^Pause & Reflect – Activity Review^

Reflective Exploration: Unveiling the Essence of Self: The upcoming reflective segment, "How Do I Define Who I Am?" prompts a deep dive into the core elements of your identity. This exploration is an opportunity to distill the essence of your being into distinct facets. Ponder these dimensions with thoughtful introspection: (You may want to revisit your Journey Map in Chapter 5 and reserve several pages in your journal for your responses.)

Journal Lines

___
___
___
___
___
___
___
___
___
___
___
___
___
___

^Pause & Reflect: How Do I Define Who I Am?^

How Do I Define Who I Am?

Articulating Your Identity
- Identify three adjectives that encapsulate your essence.
- Reflect on your top three personal strengths.
- Contemplate what distinguishes you from others - what's your unique edge?
- How would you encapsulate your identity in a brief introduction?

Meaning & Direction – Your Life's Compass
- What philosophy steers your life?
- Identify the principles you staunchly support and those you oppose.
- What aspects of life hold the highest value for you?

Personal Control – Goal Setting and Resilience
- Assess your ability to set and pursue goals.
- When faced with challenges, do you persist or recede?
- Is there a guiding motto that keeps you aligned with your goals?
- Are there impulsive actions or habits that hinder your progress?

Consistency in Life – Aligning Actions with Values
- Reflect on the congruence between your actions and your beliefs and values.
- How do you realign when your actions deviate from your values?
- Do your actions transparently reflect your values to others?

Developing Personal Skills and Abilities
- What accomplishments required your utmost dedication?
- Trace your journey to your current standing. What were the pivotal milestones?
- Identify your three most proficient skills and their development path.

_____
_____
_____

Summary – Integrating Insights. Consider how your responses to these inquiries paint a portrait of your identity. Do they reveal your core values, aspirations, and talents? Summarize your newfound insights. How have these reflections deepened your understanding of your intrinsic self?

Creating Art Wherever We Are. What have you learned about yourself as you completed these two exercises? Did any insights or new information jump out at you? When we look at our inner self, what is important to us, and how we spend our time, we can ask ourselves important questions about who we are, such as, are my interests, values, and behaviors congruent? Do they all tell the same story about who I am? Or is it a rather messy picture? Does my personality make sense to me? If not, what seems out of place? Am I doing what I am doing out of guilt, obligation, or remorse, or because I choose to? How do I express the wonder of my inner self to others? And if I don't see it, which of my MindView Domains might be blocking my view? What can I do about that?

One way we can think about the insecurity that can sometimes be so debilitating is that it is a subconscious signal to us that our personality, values, goals, action steps, and behaviors are out of sync. In other words, our behaviors are incongruent with who we are.

For example, consider a person with a deep desire to be an artist, but does not see a way to make a living out of art, so they accept a position as a scientist. It may meet his or her physical needs or even her thinking needs, but the emotional, spiritual, and social needs are completely hidden away. Her ability to express her inherent giftedness would be lost to her if she didn't find some other way to express her talent.

Similarly, insecurity can be triggered by engaging in negative self-talk. When we withhold important, positive information or knowledge from ourselves, it can have an impact on our ability to self-regulate, to be consistent with our values, and to masterfully use our personal skills and abilities as we make decisions about our future.

Understanding and embracing the needs of our inner core self or our nature will bring us much closer to living The Artfully Lived Life. Honestly honoring the amazing person that already exists within you will create immense joy as you master and apply The Artist's Tools, as well as the skills and strategies we will discuss in following chapters. With the necessary tools and skills, we can create art – or well-being – wherever we are.

Exploring Your Core Identity: A Meditative Journey

The Quest to understand oneself often entails pondering fundamental questions: "What sets me apart?" "How do I relate to my surroundings?" "What is my purpose?" "What direction is my life taking?" and "What strategies will lead me there?" These inquiries may seem daunting, as they often require a lifetime of introspection and self-discovery. Nevertheless, there exists a systematic approach to this exploration.

The journey begins with a deep dive into introspection, where you become an observer of your thoughts, acknowledging them without forming attachments. This process involves pondering the ultimate destination you desire in life. Once this is established, the next step is strategizing the pathway to reach that destination, which necessitates identifying viable routes and equipping yourself with the essential skills and resources.

The subsequent query, "What obstacles might I encounter?" also leans heavily on problem-solving abilities. Life's unpredictability means we can't foresee every challenge that may arise. However, this is precisely where our acquired tools prove invaluable, aiding us in navigating through unforeseen hurdles and staying aligned with one's true identity.

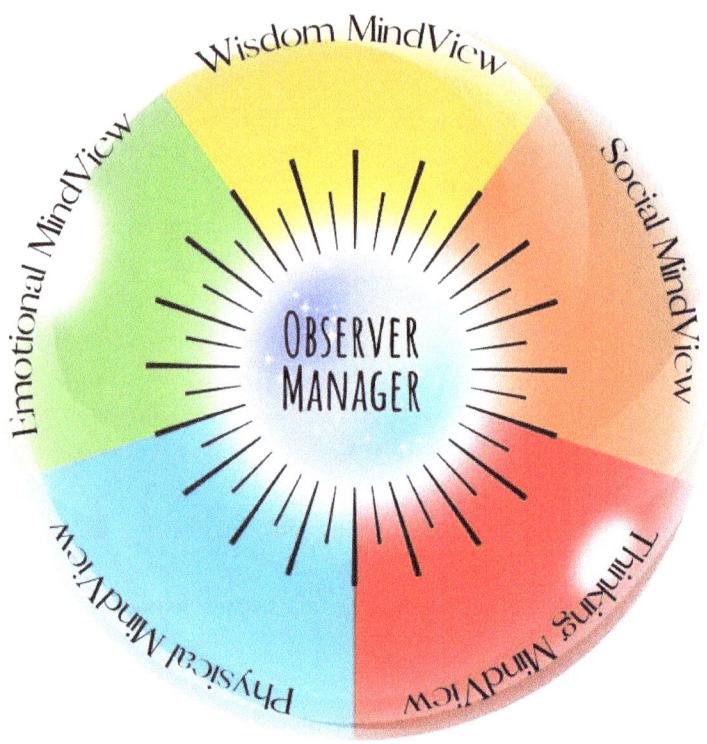

MindView Compass: How Do I Define Who I Am? Are my actions and behaviors consistent with my values?

Guided Meditation ~ Chapter Six: Identity Work

Boundaries protect us when we are vulnerable, and forgiveness, compassion, and gratitude motivate and inspire us to keep going, even when it gets tough. Your values and action steps act like a journey map and help guide your choices. Finally, it is the development of your skills and abilities, as well as your ability to remain consistent in your vision that will help you to consolidate a sense of direction.

Another thing to keep in mind is that most negative thoughts and emotions tend to appear when you are fatigued, over-stressed, overwhelmed, or vulnerable – the times you usually have the most difficulty coping. However, if you take time to meditate, and listen within, and if you take time to take care of yourself, you will be much more successful at screening out the muck that doesn't belong.

Workshop. The Guided Meditation for this chapter is focused on returning to your workshop where you can begin to create something new in your life. Your skills as well as your ability to remain consistent in your vision will help to consolidate a sense of direction and allow you to avoid the difficulties you might face as you follow your chosen life path.

GM Journaling Ch. 6: Identity Work	Journal Space
☙ What have your choices taught you about what is most meaningful to you? _____	
☙ Have your choices taken you in directions that have helped you to discover a sense of purpose and direction or have they interfered? _____	
☙ Do your values, goals, and choices seem to be in line with each other? If not, where are they out of sync? _____	
☙ Do you see these goals and choices moving you toward or away from the inner Masterpiece that you envisioned? _____	
☙ How would you describe yourself as you are right now? _____	

Guided Meditation ~ Chapter 6: My Workshop

The workshop will be a place where you can begin your healing work. This will be a place where you can try new things, think new thoughts, and feel completely safe. Your workshop can be elaborate or simple. It can be a cabin, a tent, or a beautiful bungalow surrounded by foliage. It can be any size or shape you choose. What would you like your private retreat to be like? Would it be in the mountains? Or in a field of flowers? Or on the beach somewhere private and unknown to strangers? Whatever kind of workshop you create, it will be a place that is familiar to you, where you are surrounded by the memories that have made you feel most loved and valued. You will feel at home and safe.

My Workshop

Lie down, get comfortable and close your eyes. Place your hand on the spot that rises and falls the most when you inhale. If this spot is on your chest, you are not using your full lung capacity. Put your hand on your stomach and take deep full breaths. Breaths that make your stomach rise more than your chest. Continue breathing slowly and deeply into your stomach. See your breath as a pure white cloud. Coming in through the top of your head. As it swirls down through your body, it picks up all the impurities, the tension, the fatigue, the pain, or the problems of the day. As you exhale, imagine the impurities exiting out through your toes; and disappearing out into space. The white cloud flows down through your head and face, carrying away the tension, down through your neck and shoulders, your arms, your hands, and then your fingers, carrying away the tensions and the worries. Down through your chest and into your stomach and abdomen. Down through your legs, into your ankles and feet, and carrying away the tension, worry, pain, or fear. Out through your toes. See these impurities exiting out through your toes and away. And now imagine that the cloud of oxygen turns a beautiful blue color. Calming, soothing, feel the color cleansing your body, your mind. Lighter with each breath, almost as if you are floating. Just floating.

In our first guided meditation, we helped you to create this beautiful garden space where you could begin to see and experience the best of who you are. You were good enough the day you were born.

In the second guided meditation, we introduced you to your inner world – your MindView Council – your Emotional, Social, Physical, Thinking, and Spiritual MindView spaces, as well as your Observer-Manager. Embracing all aspects of who you are and treating yourself with kindness, gentleness, and compassion will release all the good that is waiting to be realized.

In the third guided meditation, you were introduced to the tools you will need for creating your inner masterpiece: Acceptance, forgiveness, self-compassion, commitment, and gratitude. In combination with the gifts of the MindView Council, you can create whatever masterpiece you choose.

In the fourth guided meditation, you finally designed and planted the garden that you had been preparing. You practiced the tools of acceptance, forgiveness, and gratitude as you focused on healing.

Now you are here. Hold in your mind what you have discovered about your identity. What is most meaningful to you? Is that reflected in your choices? Use your imagination now to visualize yourself feeling empowered as an individual. See confidence and strength in your body and in the way you hold yourself. Your head is high. Shoulders back.

Now step back and observe this beautiful garden you have created. Allow yourself to enjoy this beautiful place. Notice the trees and flowers. You can hear the wind as it blows through the tops of the branches. You can feel the warmth of the sun on your face and the thick grass beneath your feet. This is a reflection of who you are.

Now take a moment to locate a welcoming space for a workshop. It can be a builder's workshop, an artists' workshop, or a hobbyist's workshop. It can be anything you choose. The workshop you create will be a place where you can begin your healing work. This will be a place where you can try new things, think new thoughts, and feel completely safe.

Your workshop can be elaborate or simple. It can be a cabin, a tent, or a beautiful bungalow surrounded by foliage. It can be any size or shape you choose. What would you like your private retreat to be like? Would it be in the mountains? Or in a field of flowers? Or on the beach somewhere private and unknown to strangers?

Whatever kind of workshop you create, it will be a place that is familiar to you, where you are surrounded by the memories that have made you feel most loved and valued. You will feel at home and safe here. When it feels complete simply say hello and feel the warmth of this retreat being radiated back to you.

When you have your workshop completed, step back and admire it for a moment. Is anything missing? Envision yourself bringing that to what you have created, as well. And know that this workshop will be waiting for you when next you need it.

And now it is time to come back. Say goodbye for now and take a deep breath. And, when you are ready, open your eyes.

Chapter 7 – Life Strategies and Enhancing Boundaries for the Brain and Body

"In times of stress, the best thing we can do for each other is to listen with our ears and our hearts and to be assured that our questions are just as important as our answers."
~Unknown

In a previous chapter, you used the Journey Map to define your values, set goals and action steps, and identify potential obstacles like impulsive behaviors and habitual patterns. With these insights, your path may seem clearer, but challenges like impulsive actions or entrenched habits might still create roadblocks. In this chapter we will dive into the impact of stress and offer strategies for managing impulsive behaviors that can affect each aspect of your MindView Council (Thinking, Emotional, Physical, Social, Spiritual, and Observer-Manager).

A critical and often challenging area in our lives is managing stress and regulating our behavior. The MindView council concept taught us that we operate as a system of interconnected parts working together towards our goals. Self-regulation involves setting goals, initiating actions towards these goals, and monitoring our progress. Effective self-regulation is evident when we identify a goal with rewarding outcomes and employ the necessary skills to achieve these rewards. When we lack resources to achieve our goals but possess the skills to acquire these resources, we engage in problem-solving and skill activation to reach our goals. The brain excels at problem-solving; however, when our efforts may be thwarted due to resource shortages or other barriers, and we can't find a workaround, we may experience a range of negative emotions, from frustration and anger to sadness or inadequacy.

It's important to acknowledge that distress can't always be avoided, as we are not always equipped in advance for every challenge we might encounter. However, confronting our problems head-on, enhances our ability to learn from mistakes and apply new strategies and skills. While even the best coping strategies can't shield us from distress in all situations, they can offer valuable methods for transitioning from dysregulation to effective self-regulation and from distress to improved stress management.

"Dysregulation" happens when our skills or resources fall short, preventing a return to equilibrium. This imbalance can manifest as a series of negative reactions affecting our emotional, physical, social, spiritual, or intellectual well-being. Reflecting on how you've handled past challenges can inform your approach to current problems. Developing self-awareness around problem-solving can lead to establishing a consistent, reliable method for addressing life events. Implementing strategic and skillful solutions saves time, effort, money, and emotional strain. Adopting a consistent problem-solving approach can empower and boost your confidence when facing life's challenges, ultimately reducing daily stress and the anxiety associated with encountering new obstacles.

Understanding Stress and Its Impact on Well-Being

Hans Selye, a prominent stress researcher, once noted that it's not stress itself that is harmful, but our reaction to it. Often, our responses to stress involve lifestyle choices that seem to alleviate stress temporarily but ultimately have long-term negative consequences. These choices can include poor dietary habits, insufficient sleep, smoking or vaping, excessive alcohol consumption, substance abuse, and lack of physical activity. As identified in the Journey Map exercise, these choices, often impulsive and misaligned with our values, can hinder our progress towards achieving our goals. Not only do they impede our efforts, but they also harm our physical and mental well-being.

Diverse Forms of Dysregulation: This chapter explores various forms of dysregulation that can derail success in achieving goals, along with potential strategies for management:

1. **Unmanaged stress leading to distress:** Understanding how unmanaged stress can escalate into distress, and learning strategies to cope effectively can help us de-stress, and establish our boundaries..

2. **Boundaries in personal and interpersonal contexts:** Discussing the importance of maintaining boundaries in social, emotional, physical, spiritual, and thinking dimensions,

3. **The relationship between brain health and physical health:** Highlighting that a healthy brain is fundamental to overall physical well-being, is critical for understanding the mind-body connection.

4. **Emotional dysregulation and mastering emotional regulation:** Exploring how to manage and regulate emotions effectively can significantly reduce stress.

5. **The concept of Emotional Intelligence (EQ):** Delving into the understanding and application of emotional intelligence is also important for our overall well-being.

Understanding Stress and Its Impact on Daily Life

Stress is an inherent part of life, arising from various sources and even positive life changes. For instance, a job promotion, generally seen as positive, can be stressful if perceived as overly demanding. Whether an event becomes a source of stress or distress largely depends on our coping resources.

Consider your immediate surroundings and identify potential stressors. From the start of your day to its end, life can seem like an unending sequence of stressful situations. Are environmental factors like temperature discomfort or a long list of pending tasks adding to your stress? Stress can stem from numerous sources, ranging from minor discomforts to significant life events.

Environmental stressors like pollution, traffic, and noise, which are often beyond our control, can significantly impact our stress levels. Physical factors such as illness or allergies also contribute to stress, which, in turn, can worsen our physical health. Social and emotional stressors might include challenging dynamics with family, friends, or colleagues. Balancing responsibilities like parenting, work, and education simultaneously can feel overwhelming. Unmanaged stress is known to exacerbate pain, hinder healing, and lower pain tolerance.

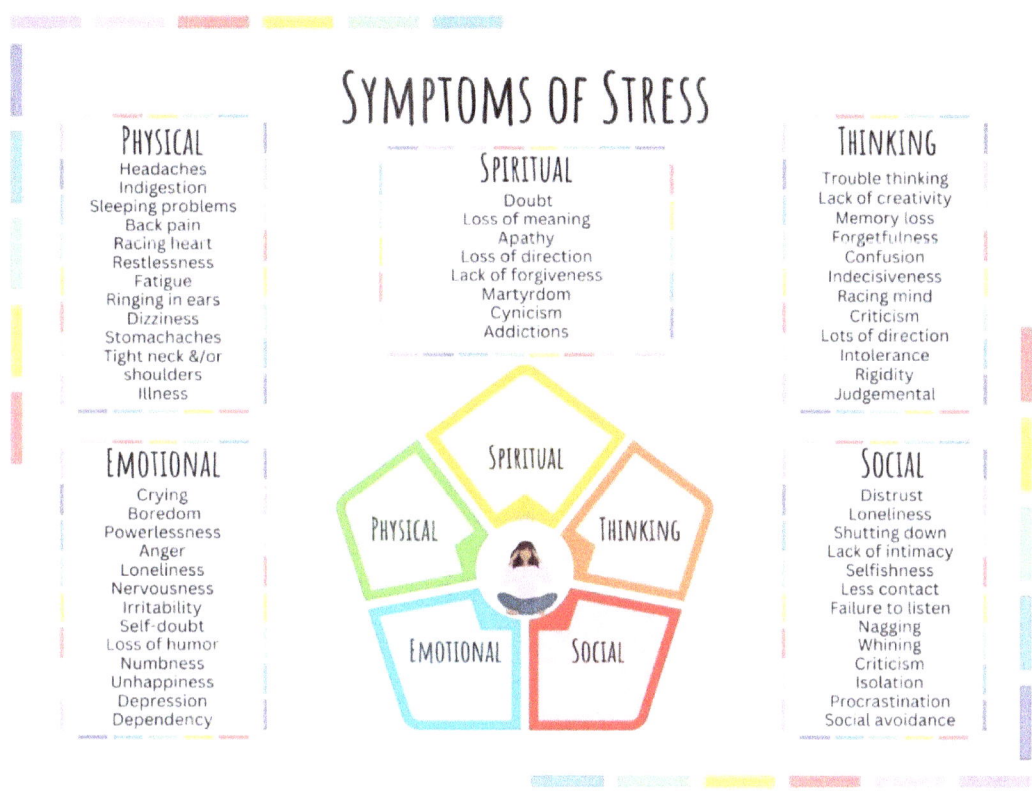

While much of our distress might stem from uncontrollable factors like weather or others' actions, our perception and response to these situations are within our control. The meaning we assign to events, shaped by our experiences, habitual responses, and self-talk, plays a crucial role in managing stress. Viewing problems from new perspectives can help alleviate distress. You might wonder how this applies practically in your life. The first step is recognizing how stress impacts you. We often notice stress symptoms more readily than the causes. While major life changes are easily identifiable as stressors, it's also important to acknowledge the cumulative effect of smaller stressors that we may encounter daily.

Exploring Stress and Its Impact on Well-Being. This section, delves into various events and their impact on well-being, categorized by the MindView Council domains. Understanding these influences can help craft effective strategies for a more balanced life.

Journal Lines

_____
_____
_____
_____

Event Impact Assessment: Below is a list of events. If any have occurred in the past two years, mark their impact on your life as mild, moderate, or difficult.

- Social: Changes in relationships with family, friends, peers, or coworkers. _____

- Emotional: Experiences of beginnings, losses, or struggles in relationships, living situations, or employment. _____

- Physical: Shifts or challenges in residence, finances, health, employment, relationships, or substance-related issues. _____

- Thinking: Variations or difficulties in education, employment, cognitive functioning, coping, or legal matters. _____

- Spiritual: Evolutions or challenges in spiritual beliefs, values, or coping strategies. _____

- Observer-Manager: Issues with decision-making, prioritizing, organizing, or applying skills. _____

Stress and Physical Health: The physical symptoms of stress vary widely. Although occasional occurrences of acute stress are not typically harmful to physical or psychological well-being, chronic stress can stretch our physical capabilities to their limits, leading to significant health issues. For instance, overexertion and lack of sleep can lead to dangerous situations like dozing off while driving, as reported by 36% in the National Sleep Foundation's Sleep in America Poll (www.sleepfoundation.org).

Research underscores the connection between psychological distress and severe health risks. A UK study linked psychological distress with a higher chance of stroke. The Neuroscience Behavior Review journal also detailed a clear association between psychological stress and cardiovascular diseases, including stroke, heart attack, and high blood pressure, as well as conditions like HIV/AIDS and depression.

Stress triggers hormonal changes that escalate heart rate, blood pressure, and muscle tension. Reflect on moments of high stress, like a near-miss car accident or walking alone on a dark street. You might recall symptoms such as a racing heart, tightened muscles, and heightened alertness to potential danger.

Understanding how stress affects various aspects of our health and well-being is crucial. In the following sections, we'll explore strategies for managing stress and enhancing our capacity to live a fulfilling life despite our challenges.

Understanding the Impact of Stress on Brain and Emotional Health

The "fight or flight" response is a fundamental human reaction, vital for survival in dangerous situations. Our ancestors relied on this instinct, but in modern times, its continuous activation can lead to adverse health effects.

Chronic Stress and Physical Health: Ongoing stress can seriously impair bodily functions. Studies indicate that prolonged activation of survival responses can lead to stress-related brain damage and serious health conditions like heart disease and cancer while also weakening the immune system (Amen, 2005). This constant stress resembles the overstretching of a rubber band, eventually leading to wear and tear in the body. The repeated production of stress hormones like adrenaline and cortisol can increase the risk of various health issues, including gastric ulcers, osteoporosis, diabetes, asthma, infections, strokes, and hypertension.

Addressing Stress in the Social and Spiritual MindViews

Impact on Social Relationships: Stress can significantly impact social dynamics, influencing how we interact with others personally and professionally. It can impair judgment, flexibility, and performance. Chronic stress might lead to increased negativity, intolerance, decision-making difficulties, and a rise in distrust and self-centered behavior. As stress levels climb, our ability to handle complex tasks diminishes, leaving us functioning well only in simple, undemanding situations. This is because managing psychological and physical stress consumes considerable energy, often at the cost of our social interactions.

Effects on Spiritual Well-being: Stress can profoundly affect spiritual wellness, potentially leading to feelings of hopelessness and a loss of direction, purpose, and confidence. This can result in confusion, despair, and a sense of meaninglessness, impairing our ability to navigate life's challenges effectively. A disrupted spiritual balance can echo through all facets of life, affecting physical health, thoughts, emotions, and relationships.

Harnessing Self-Awareness for Resilience: While we often overlook the process of surviving challenging events, understanding the "how" and "why" is crucial. Self-awareness about our problem-solving methods can help us establish a reliable approach to life's challenges, leading to peace and well-being. When our physical state, thoughts, emotions, and behaviors are in harmony, we experience greater a sense of tranquility.

^Pause & Reflect ~ Stress Responses^

> Think about how you manage stress. When you are under a lot of stress, does it tend to affect your diet, sleep, or exercise? In what way? _____
> _____
>
> If you smoke or vape, how does stress impact your tendency to use? _____
> _____
>
> How about alcohol or other types of recreational substances, does stress affect how you use those? In what way? _____
> _____
>
> Thinking about long term well-being, do you think recreational substance use is the best way to go, or is it possible your body and brain might appreciate a different approach? _____
> _____

Managing Stress with Mindfulness and Support: Beliefs about stress and our coping abilities play a significant role in managing its impact. Mindfulness meditation, which involves non-judgmental awareness of the present moment, is an effective tool in managing stress. This approach increases resilience and the ability to handle life's stressors more effectively.

Previous chapters have presented various strategies to combat stress, including breathing exercises, connecting with nature, and leveraging support systems like family and friends. However, the most effective strategies are those that you consistently apply in your daily life. Regular mindfulness practice and other stress-management techniques can profoundly influence your ability to navigate the complexities of social and spiritual well-being under stress.

Understanding Personal Boundaries

The Role of Boundaries in Well-being: Black & Ennes (1997), in their book "Better Boundaries: Owning and Treasuring Your Life," emphasize the importance of well-defined boundaries for safety, confidence, authentic expression, and healthy relationships. The extensive research on boundaries confirms that they bring order to life, foster respectful relationships, safeguard against harmful interactions, fulfill the need for personal acknowledgment, and are essential in pursuing one's life mission and purpose. Essentially, maintaining appropriate boundaries is vital for achieving personal goals.

^Pause & Reflect ~ Coping with Stress^

Describe a challenge from the past that was overwhelming to you—maybe the first time you used a computer or started a new job. It might have been a difficult relationship, or a health problem. Did you understand the purpose for having that experience in your life?

_____
_____
_____
_____

What motivated you to adapt? What made you decide it was better to overcome it rather than avoid, ignore, or run away from the problem?

_____
_____
_____

What made you believe you could adapt? What thoughts or beliefs gave you the confidence to tackle the problem?

_____
_____

Coping Strategies for Stress

Physical Exercise	Reduce Substance Use	Talk to family	Hot baths
Meditation	Healthy Diet	Reading	Tai Chi
Plan a solution	Get enough sleep	Walking in nature	Yoga
Breathing Exercises	Reduce thinking errors	Journaling	Stay busy
Resilience Exercises	Reach out to friends	Volunteer work	Take breaks

Think about the coping strategies listed above. Which of them have and do you use to help you cope? Which have been the most helpful for you? Do you have a system that works best for you? What else could you do? Can you think of any that are not on this list? Add them.

_____
_____
_____
_____

Boundaries can be seen as agreements within individual, community, and societal contexts, upholding the fundamental human right to a life of self-guidance, abundance, self-discovery, and personal development. Community-established rules, guidelines, and laws delineate and safeguard these rights. Typically, the foundations of sound boundaries are laid in childhood through teaching manners, morals, values, and appropriate behavioral etiquette. Social boundaries, for instance, are reflected in polite expressions like "please" and "thank you".

Emotional boundaries govern the treatment of oneself, children, and the emotionally vulnerable, extending to relationships with family and friends. They include the use of civil language, respecting individual rights, and use well managed responses that exclude intense emotional reactivity.

Spiritual and Intellectual Boundaries: Spiritual boundaries are often shaped by values, morals, and ethics, breaches of which can lead to severe social repercussions, including violent acts. Intellectual boundaries encompass rights such as those protected by copyright laws against plagiarism and intellectual property theft. They also include the right to privacy and personal decision-making.

Social and Physical Boundaries: Social boundaries refer to the right to dignity and respect in interpersonal interactions, with social norms guiding appropriate behavior. Physical boundaries protect our right to personal safety and property security. Laws predominantly defend these various personal rights, contributing to individual and community health and well-being.

In summary, personal boundaries are multifaceted, covering life's emotional, social, spiritual, intellectual, and physical aspects. They play a crucial role in defining our interactions with others and our approach to life's challenges, ultimately shaping our overall well-being.

Understanding Your Personal Bill of Rights

The Essence of Personal Rights: The "My Bill of Rights" section emphasizes the fundamental values and beliefs established by society to enable individuals to learn, grow, and reach their fullest potential. These rights encompass the social, emotional, cognitive, physical, and spiritual boundaries previously discussed, serving as a broad guideline. Notably, the treatment of children has evolved significantly over the past two decades. The shift from authoritative to more egalitarian parenting styles has shown to produce more trusting, creative, productive, and mature adults. This Bill of Rights, within safe and developmentally appropriate parenting guidelines, also extends to children.

The Role of Self-Regulation and Personal Accountability: Self-regulating relationships, underscored by personal accountability for our actions towards others, create a potent environment for fostering personal growth and well-being. Conversely, when rights are infringed due to a lack of self-regulation, it hinders our ability to define ourselves and exercise autonomy. Our identity is deeply intertwined with our capacity to maintain our boundaries. Violating our rights or those of others undermines the fundamental human need for self-regulation.

Responsibility for Boundaries: Acknowledging responsibility for our boundaries implies that we take charge of our well-being, recognize the variety of solutions available to meet our needs, and trust that others will do the same. Such an approach fosters a self-regulating society, where personal accountability and mutual respect for boundaries are paramount. However, it's crucial to adapt these personal rights to fit various environmental expectations, like those in employer-employee or parent-child relationships. The Bill of Rights provided here addresses those in positions of power in imbalanced relationships, advocating respect for the basic needs and rights of individuals to be expressive and self-determining adults.

^Pause & Reflect ~ My Bill of Rights^

1. I have the right to be happy.
2. I have the right to learn new things, to change, and to grow.
3. I have the right to say no when it's appropriate for me to do so.
4. I have the right and the responsibility to ask for what I want and need for my well-being.
5. I have the right to express my positive and negative feelings.
6. I have the right to make mistakes and to learn from them.
7. I have the right to be playful and silly.
8. I have the right to be exactly who I am without giving excuses or reasons for why I do what I do.
9. I have the right to be treated with respect and dignity by others and to treat myself the same way.
10. I have the right to ask for personal space and time.
11. I have the right to say "I don't know."
12. I have the right to change my mind if I need to for my well-being.
13. I have the right to be afraid, to express my fear, and to remove myself from any environment that feels unsafe to me.
14. I have the right to be healthy and to be in a non-abusive environment.
15. I have the right to ask for and expect honesty from others around me.
16. I have the right to be hurt or sad about, disappointed with, or angry at someone I care about.
17. I have the right to NOT take responsibility for others' feelings, behaviors, or problems.
18. I have the right to enjoy friendships and positive relationships with others and to end or distance myself from hurtful or unhealthy relationships.
19. I have the right to determine my own values, priorities, and standards.
20. I have the right to appreciate myself and my accomplishments.
21. I am in a state of constant change, and growth, AND I have the right to accept and love myself for who I am, as I am, right now.
22. I have the right to BE ME.

^Pause & Reflect ~ Protecting My Rights^

Think about **My Bill of Rights**. How might you have felt and experienced life differently if you and others around you had known about and respected personal rights and boundaries?
_____
_____

Do you see any rights that you allow others to violate in your life, and do you see any that you violate in the lives of others?
_____
_____

Which of the above mentioned rights strike the strongest chord within you?
_____
_____

Which of your rights still need protecting?
_____
_____

How can **My Bill of Rights** help you to better understand yourself as an individual?
_____
_____

Understanding Boundaries Between Individuals

The Function of Boundaries: Boundaries serve as demarcations between individual personalities and belief systems, providing guidelines for suitable interaction. They foster a sense of safety, independence, and self-respect and encourage acceptance and respect for the individual rights of others in social interactions.

Societal vs. Personal Boundaries: While society collectively decides on the rights and boundaries that govern community interactions, these boundaries are often overlooked or undervalued in personal relationships. Abuse, for instance, represents a significant violation of these boundaries. An example is a child being threatened for expressing emotions, such as being warned that their crying will lead to punishment. This demonstrates weak or unhealthy boundaries, signifying a lack of respect for personal autonomy.

Characteristics of Weak Boundaries: Individuals struggling with boundary issues may feel threatened by the individuality and autonomy of others. Their relationships often reflect problems such as dependency, submission, and behaviors aimed at ensuring complete loyalty and compliance. In such dynamics, any form of disagreement is seen as a threat to the relationship, leading to an environment where feelings, beliefs, and perceptions are intertwined and the individual feels constrained, frustrated, and fearful of expressing dissent.

Impact on Children: Children raised without effective boundaries learn to navigate life by avoiding errors and seeking approval, often forgoing necessary risks for personal growth. Their perception of life becomes binary – success or failure, all or nothing, acceptance or rejection – as defined by authoritative figures, including peers who may exhibit bullying behavior. These experiences can profoundly shape how these children grow into adults perceive and interact with the world.

Symptoms of Weak Boundaries: Weak boundaries in adults can manifest in various ways, including disproportionate emotional reactions, heightened sensitivity to criticism, feelings of insecurity or fear of abandonment, apprehension of aggression in various forms, defensiveness, and a general sense of distrust.

Effects of Unhealthy Boundaries on Childhood Development

Children who learn to seek validation and recognition from others often develop feelings of helplessness, anxiety, and fear of rejection or abandonment. This dependence on external approval hinders their interest in cultivating self-reliance and autonomy. They become overly attuned to the needs of others, often at the expense of their own development. This excessive focus on external validation can stifle their personal growth.

Consequences of Poor Boundary Development: Children who grow up without healthy boundaries are prone to developing similar issues as adults. They tend to view boundaries as unnecessary or bothersome and may consider it acceptable to overstep others' boundaries. This lack of healthy boundaries often leads them to engage in relationships where they are susceptible to harm or abuse, further perpetuating a cycle of boundary violations. As a result, these individuals struggle with self-awareness, self-direction, and acting in their best interests. The diagram demonstrates various types of interpersonal relationships and the importance of boundaries in protecting mental health and well-being. The absence of healthy boundaries in these relationships can lead to negative self-perception and a range of detrimental mental health impacts.

Identifying and Addressing Unhealthy Boundaries: The subsequent diagram lists and summarizes unhealthy boundaries, behaviors, and attitudes that contribute to distress. It's crucial to review and identify these aspects of one's life. Recognizing such patterns is the first step toward addressing and rectifying them. These broken boundaries often reflect a violation of basic human rights and can lead to

Well-Being: The Artfully Lived Life

host of negative emotions, including pain, fear, intolerance, insecurity, guilt, shame, and trauma. By identifying these unhealthy patterns, one can begin the process of establishing healthier boundaries and improving overall mental health and well-being.

^Pause & Reflect ~ Unhealthy Physical Boundaries^

> The first step in repairing destructive physical boundaries is to explore the source of the problem. Identify what is stopping you from setting healthy physical boundaries.
>
> What aspects of your life feel out of control? What are you telling yourself about the situation? _____
> _____
>
> How does it "help" you in your life to stay out of control?
> _____
> _____
>
> What do you believe this means about who you are? What could you do to regain control?_____
> _____
>
> How and when will you do that? _____
> _____
>
> Summarize some areas of your life that might benefit from stronger or more clearly defined physical boundaries. _____

Understanding and Implementing Healthy Boundaries

The concept of healthy boundaries is pivotal for self-growth and identity formation, influenced significantly by our early experiences and the subsequent beliefs we develop about ourselves and the world. Healthy boundaries enable us to honor our unique perspectives and expressions, provided they do not cause harm to others. They are essential for fostering a sense of safety, health, and freedom, crucial for personal growth. They contribute to peace, inner wisdom, and self-awareness, creating a supportive environment for personal development. Respecting boundaries across various domains – physical, intellectual (thinking), social, emotional, and spiritual – is key to nurturing a healthy inner environment that facilitates maturation and personal growth.

Healthy Boundaries Chart: The Healthy Boundaries chart outlines important aspects of healthy boundaries within the five MindView Domains. It serves as a guide to understanding and maintaining boundaries that promote well-being and self-respect.

^Pause & Reflect ~ Healthy Boundaries^

After reviewing the Healthy Boundaries chart, journal about potential changes you can implement to strengthen your boundaries. While this process may be challenging, the benefits of improved boundaries for your personal and interpersonal well-being are substantial.

(New Healthy Boundaries Chart)

HEALTHY BOUNDARIES

PHYSICAL
Health
Space
Freedom
Security
Safety
Respect
Growth
Protection
Shelter
Nourishment
Rest
Autonomy
Recreation

SPIRITUAL
Lying
Racism
Disrespect
Devaluation
Immorality
Unethical
Contempt
Dishonesty
Deception
Manipulation
Greed
Hatred
Control
Immaturity
Vulgarity
Intolerance

THINKING
Autonomy
Creativity
Resourcefulness
Problem-solving
Education
Competence
Profession
Discipline
Freedom
Vision
Negotiation
Responsibility

EMOTIONAL
Expression
Self-esteem
Self-respect
Identity
Appreciation
Instincts
Closeness
Intimacy
Nurturance
Validation
Compassion
Forgiveness
Responsibility

SOCIAL
Trust
Friendship
Support
Respect
Play
Understanding
Acceptance
Humor
Communication
Companionship
Loyalty
Forgiveness
Ethics

Central diagram: Five domains arranged as petals — SPIRITUAL (Peace, Wisdom), THINKING (Problem-solving, Growth), SOCIAL (Community, Belonging), EMOTIONAL (Acceptance, Maturity), PHYSICAL (Security, Health).

^Pause & Reflect ~ Healthy Boundaries^

Do your current choices and behaviors foster wellness in your life?
_____
_____

Think about your activities that may run counter to your health and wellness.
_____
_____

What changes do you need to make?
_____
_____

What do your choices and behaviors say about your boundaries?
_____
_____

How do you think better boundaries might help your sense of identity and/or self-image? _____
_____

Action Steps for Improvement

Consider the areas where your boundaries may be weak or non-existent. Reflect on how you can establish or reinforce these boundaries in a manner consistent with your values and beliefs. Think about strategies that will help you assert these boundaries respectfully and effectively in various aspects of your life. By understanding and implementing healthy boundaries, you embark on a journey of self-discovery and empowerment, paving the way for a more fulfilling and balanced life. For now, consider the following suggestions for maintaining a healthy brain and body.

Journal Lines

_____
_____
_____
_____
_____
_____
_____

Enhancing Brain and Body Health: A Comprehensive Approach

This section of the chapter delves into practical strategies for maintaining a healthy brain and body, emphasizing the need for a collaborative approach with healthcare professionals and self-care practices.

Medical Collaboration and Dietary Choices:
- Partner with your healthcare provider to effectively manage blood pressure, cholesterol levels, and essential nutrients like B12 and homocysteine.
- Incorporate a diet abundant in fruits and vegetables and consider nutritional supplements that are known to bolster memory function. Refer to the works of Dr. Amen (2006) and Dr. Fotuhi (2003) for detailed supplement recommendations.

Physical Protection and Lifestyle Habits:
- Prioritize brain safety by avoiding high-risk activities like boxing or soccer, always using seatbelts, and wearing protective headgear when necessary.
- Embrace regular exercise and ensure adequate sleep for optimal brain function.
- Engage in mentally stimulating activities that keep the brain active and challenged.

Social Engagement and Stress Management:
- Cultivate enriching relationships with family and friends and stay active in your community.
- Manage stress effectively by setting boundaries, saying no when overwhelmed, and avoiding over commitment.
- Address and treat conditions like depression and anxiety and participate in activities that provide emotional fulfillment.

Mindfulness and Relaxation Practices:
- Incorporate practices such as prayer, meditation, or relaxation exercises into your routine. Consider self-hypnosis as a tool for calming the brain.
- Add humor and laughter to your daily life to lighten the mood and reduce stress.

Proactive Health Measures:
- Educate yourself and seek early intervention for conditions like drug and alcohol abuse, cardiovascular diseases, diabetes, hormone imbalances, sleep apnea, and smoking.
- If you're experiencing chronic stress, depression, anxiety, trauma effects, or other Psychological disorders that hinder your daily functioning, consider psychotherapy as a means to regain balance and well-being.

By integrating these strategies into your life, you create a foundation for a healthy brain and body, enhancing your overall quality of life.

Brain Health Strategies and Benefits

1. Regular Exercise for Enhanced Brain Function:
• **Benefits:** Boosts concentration, prevents brain cell loss, stimulates new nerve cell growth, alters gene expression, and improves blood flow.
• **Suggestions:** Engage in activities like dancing, walking, gardening, or any form of exercise for at least 30 minutes daily.

2. Brain-Training Lifestyle for Cognitive Enhancement:
• **Benefits:** Optimizes brain power, necessitates healthy adaptation, improves memory, concentration, problem-solving, slows cognitive decline, and activates underused brain areas.
• **Suggestions:** Challenge your brain with new tasks, engage in memory training exercises like puzzles, and utilize all senses – taste, sight, smell, hearing, and touch.

3. Social Connection for Mental and Physical Health:
• **Benefits:** Extends lifespan, sharpens mental acuity, aids in pain management, reduces stress, maintains physical health, and enhances social bonds.
• **Suggestions:** Participate in community activities, clubs, travel, lectures, concerts, volunteering, attending educational courses, and considering adopting pets.

4. Brain-Healthy Diet for Memory and Health:
• **Benefits:** Slows memory decline, benefits heart health, protects brain cells, boosts short-term memory, improves balance, and lowers risks of dementia and cognitive dysfunction.
• **Suggestions:** Eat various colorful vegetables and fruits, foods rich in antioxidants, and omega-3 fatty acids. Include B vitamins and multivitamins in your diet.

5. Quality Sleep for Cognitive Functioning:
• **Benefits:** Enhances memory consolidation, reduces stress, increases alertness, and aids in pain management.
• **Suggestions:** Follow the sleep hygiene information provided earlier in this chapter.

6. Acceptance and Self-Compassion for Mental Wellness:
• **Benefits:** Bolsters overall brain health, improves relationships, increases personal control, enhances adaptability, enriches contribution to society, attracts positive experiences, and balances emotions.
• **Suggestions:** Practice accepting mistakes, be forgiving, show kindness and gentleness, cultivate gratitude, focus on solvable problems, remain committed to your values and goals, and incorporate laughter and humor into daily life.

Enhancing Brain Health: Practical Strategies and Their Benefits

This chapter section provides a detailed breakdown of various lifestyle interventions, highlighting their advantages for the brain and overall health, accompanied by practical suggestions to implement these strategies effectively.

These strategies offer a comprehensive approach to improving your brain and overall health, contributing to a fulfilling and healthy lifestyle. This chapter section presents a concise summary of the key strategies frequently cited for nurturing a healthy brain. Utilize this information as a guide to pinpoint and enact the necessary adjustments for enhancing your brain's capacity. Remember, it's crucial to consult a healthcare professional to exclude any underlying medical conditions before applying any of these recommendations.

Addressing Boundary Violations Effectively

Boundary violations, while not anyone's fault, are common experiences where people naturally react to relieve discomfort. This discomfort might prompt responses like blaming others, showing anger or aggression, or avoiding the situation altogether. The outcome of these automatic reactions often depends on the context. The crucial aspect of upholding physical boundaries is understanding that irrespective of others' responses, you are entirely responsible for your perceptions, thoughts, and actions. When the issue originates externally, it's likely that part of the problem belongs to someone else. While feeling victimized or responding with anger, judgment, or resentment might seem natural, these reactions are usually unproductive. Alternatively, imposing expectations or demands on others to change also crosses boundaries.

Consider a scenario where a roommate or partner comes home angry and behaves unpleasantly. Here are some possible approaches:

1. Feeling responsible, helpless, victimized, resentful, and unable to express your emotions is one option, though not particularly constructive.
2. Another option is to give them space to manage their mood and then have a conversation when they're more approachable. You could then assertively discuss their behavior, express your feelings, and request respectful treatment.
3. Alternatively, you might react with aggression, anger, or passive-aggressive behavior, such as refusing communication until an apology is offered, again, not particularly constructive.

Each choice reflects a different way of managing and asserting your boundaries.

Effective Strategies for Handling Boundary Violations

When dealing with boundary violations, it's essential to understand the implications of different response strategies:

1. Accepting responsibility for someone else's behavior and suppressing your feelings violates your own boundaries.
2. Recognizing and respecting both parties' boundaries involves acknowledging your rights and those of the other person.
3. Overstepping not just your boundaries but also those of the other person includes aggressive or confrontational reactions.

At any time, you can articulate both positive and negative emotions and remove yourself from uncomfortable situations. If faced with emotional abuse, it's crucial to establish boundaries for your emotional and physical safety and, if necessary, disengage from the situation. While it's reasonable to request changes in behavior, demanding them, criticizing, or verbally attacking the other person exceeds the bounds of healthy interaction. Your responsibility lies solely in managing your actions and deciding how to respond to harmful or inappropriate behavior.

In such scenarios, consider the following steps:

1. Utilize your Observer-Manager to safeguard the well-being of your MindView Domains. This involves recognizing your triggers and allowing yourself time to find a balanced state, enabling better reaction regulation and setting appropriate physical boundaries.
2. Apply Emotional IQ Skills to focus on the issue rather than the person, promoting a problem-centric rather than person-centric approach.
3. Employ Thinking IQ skills, including communication and problem-solving techniques, to establish boundaries and express your expectations for respectful treatment.
4. Utilize Social IQ Skills, like assertiveness, to articulate your perspective, needs, and preferences, and discuss a more favorable outcome for you.
5. Guided by your inner wisdom and the capabilities of your Observer-Manager, strive for a compassionate and respectful resolution for both involved parties.

Strategies for Enhancing Well-Being: Managing Stress and Establishing Physical Boundaries

This chapter has focused on equipping you with effective coping strategies to navigate daily stressors and activities, with particular emphasis on managing stress, optimizing physical and brain health, and establishing clear life boundaries.

Relaxation is often misunderstood or undervalued, yet it's essential for well-being. Your body and mind need regular care to prevent fatigue and breakdown. Excessive stress can exhaust both, but by tuning into your body's needs and releasing built-up tension, you restore mental clarity and perspective.

Meditation, for instance, encourages the brain to produce neurotransmitters and other chemicals crucial for rejuvenation. Extensive research shows that regular relaxation or meditation practices can significantly reduce distress, enhance physical and emotional health, improve focus, concentration, information absorption, and diminish negative emotions like anger. By mastering the skill of identifying and alleviating muscle tension, you develop self-mastery over your physical responses to stress, contributing to an overall sense of well being.

One key technique is Progressive Muscle Relaxation (PMR), specifically tailored to mitigate physical discomfort. Muscle tension is a natural defensive response to emotional, mental, and physical distress, preparing the body to counter potential threats. For instance, physical pain often leads to an automatic tightening of muscles in the affected area as a protective reaction. However, prolonged muscle tension can lead to adverse effects like increased heart problems, weakened immune response, and heightened physical pain. By progressively tensing and relaxing your body's major muscle groups, you can learn to identify and alleviate physical tension, thereby gaining control over your body's stress responses. Reflect on the Symptoms of Stress chart from earlier in the chapter. Did you identify any physical symptoms for yourself?

Summary

In this chapter, you have been learning coping strategies that will help you manage everyday stressors and activities, starting with stress, physical health, brain health, and life boundaries.

The "Progressive Muscle Relaxation" (PMR) exercise below is designed to help with physical distress. Muscle tension is one of the body's natural defense mechanisms. Body muscles tense up as a defense against emotional, mental, and physical distress. It prepares the body to defend itself and protect itself from internal or external threats. The experience of physical pain, for example, triggers a natural tendency to tighten up all of the muscles in the surrounding area as a means of self-protection against further harm.

Many people don't know how to relax and consider it a waste of time. However, consider the metaphor of a car. A car will operate only as long as it is maintained. This doesn't just mean gas; the tires need to be checked, the oil changed, the engine tuned, and the water and other fluid levels maintained. We all know that the better a car is cared for, the better it will operate.

Your body is no different. Your body and mind will become fatigued and break down when you experience too much stress. When you learn to tune in to your body and to release the tension as it builds, you also re-gain clarity and perspective as you go about your life. While you meditate, your brain releases neurotransmitters and other chemicals that are restorative and vitalizing for the mind and body. Years of research have suggested that those who relax or meditate daily experience less distress, fewer physical and emotional difficulties, and an increased ability to focus, concentrate, and absorb new information.

Relaxation also helps to decrease the intensity of negativity and anger and helps to improve one's overall emotional response to whatever may be going on.

As you learn to identify and release physical tension by progressively tightening and releasing major muscle groups throughout your body, you will gain a sense of self-mastery in your physical response to stress.

GM Journaling: Ch. 7~PMR

ଓ What did you experience as you did his guided meditation? What changes did you notice in your mind and body? _____

ଓ Recall the physical symptoms from the "Symptoms of Stress" table earlier in this chapter. Did you circle any of the physical symptoms of stress? What were they? _____

ଓ What did you notice about where you carry stress in your body? _____

ଓ How do you think this stress might Be affecting thoughts, feelings, and behavior in your life? _____

Journal any other experiences you may have noticed while doing this exercise.

Guided Meditation ~ Chapter 7: Progressive Muscle Relaxation (PMR) Exploration

Begin by centering your awareness on your breathing. Place your hand where the rise and fall of your breath is most pronounced. If your chest moves the most, you're not fully utilizing your lungs. Shift your hand to your abdomen, and draw in deep, comprehensive breaths. Visualize each inhalation as a white, purifying cloud entering through your heels, ascending along your spine, reaching the crown of your head as your lungs fill. This cloud gathers all internal impurities – tension, distraction, fatigue.

With each exhale, envision the cloud descending, sweeping down your front, gathering more impurities and exiting through your toes. Up the back, over the head, down the front, exiting through the toes. Feel your body growing lighter, clearer, rejuvenated with each cycle.

If your mind drifts, simply acknowledge it without judgment and refocus on your breath. There's no need for self-criticism; just breathe naturally, with ease.

Now, gently close your eyes. We'll embark on a journey of progressive muscle relaxation. Focus on different muscle groups, tense them, then release. Observe the feeling of relaxation post-tension. Let's start with your right hand. Clench it into a fist, feel the tension, then release. Breathe deeply, noticing the relaxation in your hand. Observe the contrast. Repeat the process, feeling the tension in your fist, wrist, and forearm, then let go. Embrace the ensuing relaxation.

Repeat with your left hand. Clench, feel the tension in your hand, wrist, and forearm. Then release. Feel the relaxation as it replaces the tension. Observe the feeling – heaviness, warmth, tingling.

Next, focus on your upper arms. Bend your arms at the elbows, tense them firmly, and then release. Feel relaxation seep into your arms. Repeat the tension and relaxation. Notice the sensation of relaxation coursing through your arms, wrists, and hands.

Shift your focus to your head. Wrinkle your forehead, cheeks, chin – creating a prune-like face. Hold this tension, then release. Visualize your forehead and scalp transforming, becoming smooth and relaxed. Repeat, wrinkling your forehead, cheeks, chin, and neck. Then release, letting your features flatten like a calm, still pool. Affirm to yourself that you are releasing all tension.

Now, deeply inhale, letting the breath invigorate you. Next, elevate your shoulders towards your ears, engaging the muscles there and along your upper arms. Feel this tension, holding it momentarily. Then, release, allowing your shoulders to fall gently. As they drop, a wave of relaxation cascades through your shoulders and neck. Offer your entire body this moment of tranquility. Breathe in fully, expanding your lungs to their capacity. Feel the tension in your chest as you hold this breath. Then exhale, letting a wave of relaxation envelop your chest. Inhale once more, deeply filling your lungs. Hold this breath, then exhale with a soft sigh, feeling relaxation drench your being.

Now, engage your stomach muscles as if partially sitting up. Direct your attention to the sensation in your abdomen. Hold this tension, then release. Observe the comforting feeling of relaxation as your muscles unwind. Let all tension dissipate. Inhale deeply, affirming within, "I am serene and increasingly peaceful."

Tighten the muscles in your buttocks and thighs. Engage these muscles, along with those at the back and front of your legs, as firmly as you can. Hold this tension briefly, then let it go. Feel the deep relaxation infusing your buttocks and thighs. Repeat this: tighten your buttocks and thighs, push your heels down strenuously, hold, feel the tension, then release. Savor the delightful sensation of releasing that tension.

Now, focus on your feet. Gradually curl your toes downward, tensing your calf muscles. Be mindful and ease off if you feel any cramping. With your toes curled, observe the muscle tension. Then, relax them. Next, pull your toes towards your head, engaging the muscles in your calves and shins. Hold this position, feeling the tension, then relax. Allow your toes to return to a comfortable position, whispering to yourself that the tension is dissipating.

In this state of profound calm and relaxation, imagine yourself journeying to a tranquil, safe haven. Take a deep breath, diving deeper within yourself, immersing yourself in the serenity and peace you've cultivated.

Picture yourself strolling along an idyllic, secluded beach. The sensation of fine, white sand under your bare feet is grounding as you walk beside the ocean. Attune your ears to the rhythmic cadence of the waves, their ebb and flow a soothing, hypnotic melody that deepens your relaxation. Gaze at the serene expanse of turquoise water, dotted with playful whitecaps where waves crest. The ocean's symphony lulls you into an even more profound calm state.

Inhale deeply, drawing in the crisp, salty aroma of the sea air. Feel the breeze caress your cheeks, playfully tousling your hair. In the distance, a small sailboat gracefully glides across the horizon. Watch as it approaches the shore, where a beloved figure - someone who cherishes you deeply - disembarks and strides toward you. As they draw nearer, discern whether they appear as a man, woman, or perhaps an animal companion. Observe their age, attire, and the emerging details of their visage. Welcome this guide warmly. Inquire their name and accept the first response that comes to mind. Introduce them to your tranquil sanctuary, exploring this wonderful place together.

Engage your guide in conversation. Ask for insights or whatever guidance they might offer. If your queries don't yield immediate answers, don't be disheartened; trust that understanding will find its way to you in due time. Enjoy the presence of this guide, a beacon of love and trust. When the visit feels complete, express gratitude, knowing they remain accessible whenever you seek clarity, support, or companionship.

Gradually refocus on your breathing. Observe each breath's natural, rhythmic ebb and flow, each breath, is the life force that animates you. Let your breaths be gentle and unforced. Now, conjure a word or phrase that embodies tranquility for you - perhaps "peace", "love", or "hope". This word will be your anchor, guiding you back to this sanctuary of relaxation and safety. Silently repeat your chosen word with each exhalation, allowing peace and security to permeate your being.

Whenever life's upheavals arise, let this word and your breath be your solace, leading you back to inner calm and safety. Now, as our meditation draws to a close, prepare to return to wakefulness. You emerge refreshed, rejuvenated, and empowered, carrying with you the healing and insights gained from this journey.

Chapter 8 - Life Strategies for Well-being – Emotional MindView Skills

"We can say what we need to say. We can gently, but assertively, speak our mind. We do not need to be judgmental, tactless, blaming or cruel when we speak our truths." ~Melody Beattie

Developing Emotional MindView Competencies

Emotional regulation refers to the capacity to manage and appropriately express intense emotions, a skill typically honed through life experiences beginning in infancy. If early life experiences disrupt the development of this skill, emotions can become overpowering and lead to dysfunctional behaviors.

Emotions play a critical role in focusing our attention and priming us for response. The nature of an emotion determines our course of action: fear may trigger fight, flight, or freeze responses, while affection or love encourages us to draw closer to the object of our feelings.

Consider emotions as tools for life management, helping to maintain balance and equilibrium. In the context of piloting a plane, if cognition (thought) is the pilot, emotion is the navigator. Cognition provides the know-how for problem-solving and response implementation, while emotion offers essential alerting information that guides these responses. Emotions like contempt, sadness, anger, or fear serve as alerts, signaling the need for self-protection. Conversely, positive emotions like love, pleasure, and passion indicate rewarding or satisfying aspects of our lives.

The Thinking MindView and Emotional MindView collaborate to maintain this balance, functioning optimally in harmonious alignment. Our emotional responses are shaped by our past experiences, and a deeper understanding of these experiences enhances our ability to monitor and manage our emotions effectively. Awareness of our emotional responses through our Observer-Manager is a vital first step in mastering emotional regulation.

Understanding Emotional Dysregulation

Emotional dysregulation, often referred to as "emotional hijacking", occurs when there's an imbalance between our rational thought processes and emotional responses. This can happen during a triggering event, where unbalanced emotions override rational thinking, leading to excessive or uncontrolled emotional reactions. These reactions can result in significant personal or interpersonal challenges and, in extreme cases, can contribute to societal issues like increased violence.

When our powerful emotional responses are unleashed without the guidance of self-regulation skills, the consequences can be severe, potentially wreaking havoc in various aspects of one's life. This lack of balance can also lead to physiological dysregulation, resulting in a breakdown of physical, emotional, social, and cognitive well-being.

Marsha Linehan (1993), a prominent psychologist, identified key characteristics of emotional dysregulation as:

    1. Distorted and exaggerated emotional evaluations that don't align with the situation.
    2. Intense physical and psychological unrest.
    3. Disruption in emotional, cognitive, and behavioral regulation.

The critical difference between normal stress response and pathological emotional reactivity is that the latter leads to ongoing dysfunction, often severely impacting interpersonal relationships. Nevertheless, it is important to note that strong emotional expression can range from inappropriate to overwhelmingly disruptive.

The fallout from emotional dysregulation can be extensive, including the development of affective disorders like generalized anxiety disorder or major depression, physical health issues such as cardiovascular diseases and digestive problems, weakened immune responses, and potentially, the onset of certain cancers.

^Pause & Reflect – Emotional Hijacking^

Do I see myself becoming emotionally over-reactive? _____

Do my emotions seem inappropriately intense for this situation? Yes   No _____

What happens to me behaviorally? What happens to me emotionally? Is this in the best interest of myself or my relationship? _____

What am I telling myself about this? _____

Am I allowing emotional hijacking to affect my life? What do I want right now? And how can I ask for it in a healthy way? _____

Enhancing Emotional Management Skills

Fortunately, emotional dysregulation is a manageable condition. Emotional wellness is dynamic, constantly changing, but with the right cognitive and emotional strategies, it's possible to mitigate the impact of triggers on emotional stability. Building resilience against emotional dysregulation involves integrating recovery strategies into daily life, providing a cushion against potential triggers.

Gaining emotional self-awareness—understanding what matters to us and recognizing our emotional triggers—is a vital step in communicating effectively with those around us. Here are some strategies that can be instrumental in managing emotions:

1. Cultivating and embracing positive emotions.
2. Learning to de-escalate intense emotions to prevent them from causing harm.
3. Employing self-comforting techniques like visualization and relaxation.
4. Balancing emotional reactions with cognitive strategies.
5. Establishing a routine of daily meditation practices.
6. Developing communication and problem-solving skills to facilitate conflict resolution.
7. Applying the stress management techniques outlined in Chapter 7.

The overarching aim of emotions management is to foster self-awareness that enables you to regain control over your emotional responses before reacting impulsively to triggers. This book's guided meditations and The Tools for the Artist Within are tailored to help you hone these skills. Achieving a state of inner calm is key to circumventing emotional hijacking, allowing you to respond to situations thoughtfully and effectively.

Understanding and Establishing Emotional Boundaries

The concept of emotional boundaries is crucial in relationships, particularly in the context of co-dependency (excessive emotional reliance on someone who requires support due to addiction). Difficulty in setting these boundaries often stems from fear - of disapproval, rejection, or abandonment. Recall our discussions on the inner critic, self-esteem, and identity: believing that your intrinsic value hinges on others' opinions or acceptance is akin to seeking satisfaction from a perpetually leaking cup or feeling satiated from a meal eaten by another. Your self-worth and value are deeply personal constructs shaped by your thoughts and early life experiences.

Many people grow up feeling powerless or undervalued, leading to a belief that external validation is the key to repairing these feelings. However, true self-worth must be realized from within, not sought from external sources. Our need to compensate for low self-worth may develop into wounded narcissistic or bullying tendencies.

Effective communication of our emotional, social, physical, spiritual, and intellectual needs is a personal responsibility. By assertively conveying our needs, we open the door to requests, compromises, and potentially harmonious resolutions using The Tools for the Artist Within. While it is important to be aware of our own emotional needs, resorting to abusive language or punitive actions to induce change in others is unhealthy and counterproductive. In disagreements, the optimal strategy is to focus on refining our boundaries while respecting the boundaries of others. By employing boundary-related tools, we strive for resolutions that respect both parties' needs. Examine the listed qualities and characteristics of impaired emotional boundaries. Reflect on your relationships – do you recognize any of these unhealthy patterns.

^Pause & Reflect ~ Inner Listening^

Think about your general emotional tone right now. Do any of the following feeling words describe how it feels to be in your skin? Check those that apply. Also, underline the words that describe how you felt the last time you were emotionally overwhelmed. Add additional ideas or feelings you may have felt that are not listed.

Hopeful	Anxious	Happy	Cheerful
Regretful	Excited	Withdrawn	Contemplative
Peaceful	Envious	Bored	Apprehensive
Indifferent	Interested	Depressed	Irritable
_____	_____	_____	_____
_____	_____	_____	_____

Think about the qualities you've already developed in your life and check those that apply.

Even-tempered	Approachable	Blissful	Joyful
Optimistic	Sympathetic	Accepting	Strong
Directed	Supportive	Acceptable	Worthy
Interested	Confident	Curious	Caring
_____	_____	_____	_____

Establishing Robust Emotional Boundaries

To cultivate healthy emotional boundaries, embrace The Tools for the Artist Within: acceptance, forgiveness, self-compassion, commitment, and gratitude. These tools foster internal healing more profoundly than any external love or validation.

Engage in journaling and meditation to reflect on your strengths, talents, and accomplishments. Document these attributes and achievements in your journal. Then, craft several affirmations highlighting your successes. Revisit these affirmations frequently throughout the day, allowing yourself to fully absorb these positive acknowledgments.

Empower yourself by acquiring and honing essential life skills. Focus on learning and practicing assertiveness, problem-solving, and effective communication, as outlined in the upcoming chapter. Advocate for yourself with confidence and determination. Remember, you possess the unique power to affirmatively consent or refuse. The more adept you become at setting and maintaining boundaries, the more joy and vitality you can share with others.

Regularly refer to "My Bill of Rights" to guide you in establishing suitable boundaries for yourself and others. Keep a copy handy as a constant reminder. Respect for others' boundaries is a mutual process, fostering an environment where you can confidently exercise your rights.

A central aim of living an "Artfully Lived Life" is to nurture well-being and to foster a supportive, loving worldview. Healthy emotional boundaries are key in creating a tranquil space where you can thrive and unveil your inner masterpiece. Remember, you have every right to distance yourself from anything that hinders this journey. Sometimes, the most empowering word you can use is "no".

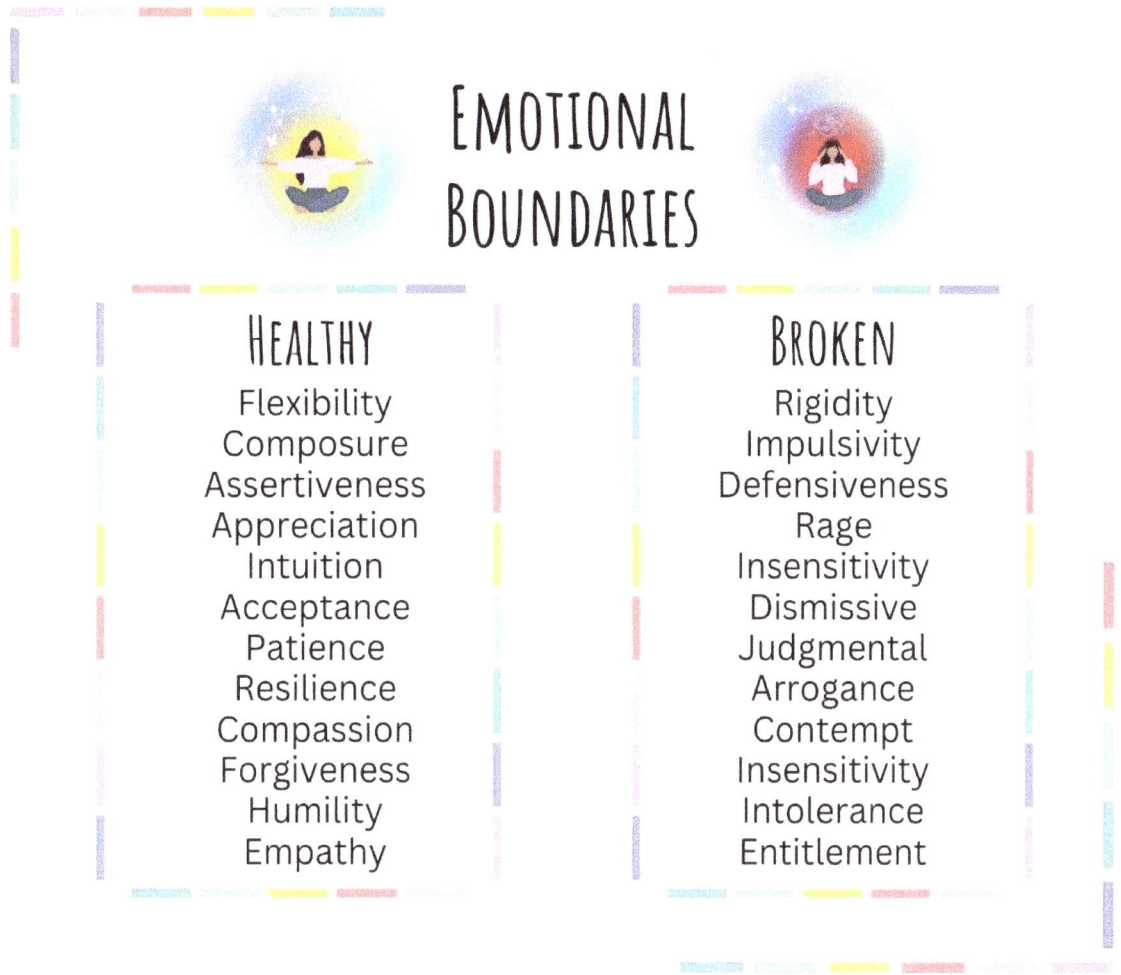

Emotional Recovery and Conflict Resolution

Emotional reactions are a natural and necessary part of life, serving as indicators and guides through our experiences. Yet, when emotions are mismanaged, they can be harmful, to ourselves and others.

Intense emotional experiences, especially those associated with pain, can linger in our minds, resurfacing in various forms like nightmares, heightened suspicion, concentration issues, and symptoms of depression or anxiety. Sometimes, these emotions persist even when the details of the triggering event fade, leaving us with unexplained feelings of pain or fear. This phenomenon, where our body retains the emotional impact but loses specific memories, can be bewildering and overwhelming.

Creating Healthy Emotional Boundaries

Develop and practice The Tools for the Artist Within: acceptance, forgiveness, self-compassion, commitment, and gratitude. These tools will help you heal in unexpected ways that the love and validation of someone external to you never could.

Through journaling and meditation, consider your strengths, talents, and abilities. Journal about all of these as well as your accomplishments. Then write several affirmations that remind you of what you have accomplished. Review these affirmations multiple times a day. Allow yourself to receive those affirmations of success and competence and any others that you need to hear.

Identify and learn the skills you need to intervene on your own behalf. Learn and practice assertiveness, problem-solving, and communication skills that we cover in the next chapter. Be your own advocate and champion. You are the only one who can assertively use your power to say yes or no. The more successful you are at appropriately setting and keeping boundaries, the more joy and energy you will have to share with others around you.

Practice using "My Bill of Rights". Keep a copy of it with you. Use it to help you set appropriate boundaries as needed for yourself and others around you. Remember, this is a reciprocal process; your respect for others' boundaries will contribute to a healthy environment in which you have the opportunity to exercise your own.

An important goal of creating an Artfully Live Life is to create well-being, as well as a healthy, loving, supportive worldview. Establishing healthy emotional boundaries will help you to create an environment in which you experience peace and the opportunity to reveal your own inner masterpiece. You have the right to ignore, avoid, and/or disengage from anything that interferes with this process. Just say no!

^Pause & Reflect ~ Emotional Boundaries^

Consider what you've learned about your own and others' emotional boundaries to this point. What's working for you and what's not? _____
_____

Think about the people in your life that you rely on for affirmation and reassurance regarding your worth and value. How can you develop an internal source of self-assurance? _____
_____
_____

What strengths and weaknesses do you see in your boundaries as they are now?
_____

What would you like to improve? _____
_____

To heal emotionally, it's crucial to become aware of these lingering feelings. Utilizing The Tools for the Artist Within - acceptance, forgiveness, and self-compassion - you can begin to process and heal these emotions. The strategies and exercises presented in this program, especially in chapters 9, 10, and 11, are designed to aid in this healing process. Guided meditations, reflective exercises, and content on addressing the Inner Critic and grief can assist in finding equilibrium among the six MindView Domains.

For those carrying significant emotional burdens from past events that continue to affect their personality or well-being, professional evaluation and therapy for potential residual trauma are highly recommended.

In situations of emotional conflict with others, our initial reaction often involves assigning blame rather than acknowledging our emotional responses. We try to change external circumstances, which may not always be within our control, and we often find that blaming others is ineffective. The first step in addressing conflict is to take a timeout, allowing emotions to cool and reflecting on the positive aspects of the relationship.

When both parties are ready, engage in a calm discussion to clarify the issue, seeking understanding rather than vindication of your perspective.

Reflect on the following questions to gain insight into the situation and your feelings:

1. What emotions am I experiencing in this conflict?
2. How might my past experiences influence my reaction?
3. What aspects of this situation can I control, and what must I accept?
4. How can I communicate my feelings and needs respectfully and effectively?
5. What positive qualities do I value in this relationship?

By approaching conflicts focusing on understanding and managing your emotional responses, you can work towards resolving issues constructively and maintaining healthy, supportive relationships.

Addressing Emotional Conflict and Learning to Let Go

When faced with emotional conflicts, it's natural to consider the strong emotions of the other person involved. Remember, their emotions are their responsibility, just as your responses are yours. If your boundaries or theirs are crossed, it's crucial to address these issues calmly and constructively once the immediate situation is resolved.

Journal Lines

Managing Emotional Conflicts

1. **Self-Reflection:** After experiencing strong emotions in a conflict, take time to reflect. Ask yourself key questions about your reactions, the triggers, and the underlying reasons for your emotional response. Ensure that you are calm and centered before attempting to resolve the issue.
2. **Seeking Support:** Discuss the conflict with a trusted individual who can help you process your feelings and provide a different perspective. This step is crucial for gaining clarity and preparing to address the issue directly with the person involved.
3. **Repeated Processing:** If similar painful emotions resurface, repeat the process of self-reflection and seeking support. Utilize the questions from the following Social/Emotional Conflict Pause and Reflect exercise to deepen your understanding of the situation.
4. **Professional Help:** If you find yourself repeatedly embroiled in similar conflicts or emotional responses, consider seeking the assistance of a therapist. They can offer guidance and support in processing your feelings and understanding the deeper issues at play.
5. **Letting Go:** The final step in the healing process is to consciously decide to release the emotional burdens you've been carrying. Letting go is a personal choice made for your well-being and is not about surrendering or accepting victimhood. If you're struggling with anger or resentment, spend more time exploring these emotions through journaling or other reflective practices before letting go. It's important to recognize that holding onto internal negativity often does more harm than good, affecting trust, self-esteem, and overall happiness.
6. **Guided Meditation for Letting Go:** At the end of this chapter, you'll find a guided meditation specifically designed to help you in the process of letting go. This meditation can be a powerful tool in your journey toward emotional freedom and well-being.

Remember, the aim is not to ignore important issues but to address them in a way that doesn't perpetuate negative emotions and harm your mental health. Letting go is about choosing to live without the constant burden of negative thoughts and feelings, thereby opening yourself to a more peaceful and fulfilling life.

Journal Lines

^Pause & Reflect ~ Social/Emotional Conflicts^

> **When you feel very strong emotions, consider the following questions:**
>
> What am I most upset about right now? _____
>
> What was the trigger for this feeling? _____
>
> What would I call this feeling? _____
>
> Is there something about this experience that is like what I have gone through before? When was that? Where was that? With whom? _____
>
> What are my interpretations of, or assumptions about, this person's intentions? Is this person trying to hurt me? _____
>
> Could there be a different motive for what they are saying and doing than I am seeing right now? _____
>
> I might not agree with what is going on, but might I feel or act the same way if I were in their shoes? _____
>
> If I put my own emotions, assumptions, and interpretations aside for the moment could I see this person's point of view? _____
>
> What is my deal-breaker in this problem? What do I need from this negotiation? _____

Understanding Emotional Intelligence

The concept of "Emotional Intelligence" (EI) was introduced by researchers in 1990 and later popularized by Daniel Goleman (1995) in his book titled "Emotional Intelligence". Goleman portrayed emotions as invaluable and insightful guides in our lives.

To revisit our airplane analogy: if cognition (thought process) is the pilot, navigating the plane with logic and precise strategies, then emotion is the navigator, alerting us to potential challenges, dangers, or obstacles along the journey. This comparison aptly illustrates the relationship between the Emotional MindView (the navigator) and the Thinking MindView (the pilot). Together, they synergize to ensure a successful journey to our desired destinations. This combination of skills and awareness is what we refer to as emotional intelligence. Goleman outlined emotional intelligence through five key components:

1. Self-Awareness: This involves recognizing and understanding our own emotions.

2. Mood Management: This is the capacity to regulate and adapt our emotional responses. It involves handling our emotions in a flexible manner, particularly in stressful situations.

3. Self-Directed Behavior: This pertains to directing our emotions and actions towards achieving specific goals. It's about using our emotional energy in a focused and purposeful way.

4. Social Awareness: This involves understanding the emotions, needs, and concerns of others. It's about recognizing and responding to social cues and functioning effectively in social settings. This aspect will be explored in greater detail in the chapter focusing on Social MindView Skills.

5. Relationship Management: This skill is about handling interpersonal relations judiciously and empathetically. It includes managing conflicts and building strong, healthy relationships, which will be discussed further in a later chapter.

By enhancing these aspects of emotional intelligence, we can improve our ability to navigate life's emotional complexities, both within ourselves and in our interactions with others. Developing emotional intelligence is crucial for personal growth, effective communication, and building strong, meaningful relationships.

Emotional Intelligence: Understanding and Application

Self-Awareness: Emotionally intelligent individuals possess a deep understanding of their feelings and can express them openly. They are adept at considering others' perspectives, know their personal rights and boundaries, and assertively uphold their integrity. Socially intelligent people, meanwhile, can connect effectively with others, excel in negotiations, and maintain emotional control in challenging situations. Those with high emotional intelligence also typically find satisfaction in their skills and adapt with ease to changing circumstances.

These skills lay a solid foundation for personal and social competencies in managing discomfort, conflict, or stress. Extensive research and literature support the notion that higher emotional intelligence correlates with reduced aggression, enhanced academic performance, and better adaptability in various environments. This chapter has covered self-awareness and mood management, while social awareness, relationship management, and "Social Intelligence" will be elaborated in the next chapter. The aspects related to self-directed behavior will be thoroughly explored in discussions about the Observer-Manager.

Emotional Self-Awareness involves the ability to internally identify and understand one's emotions in the present context. Recognizing our feelings enables us to express and manage our emotional states, connect with others, and resolve problems effectively, marking emotional intelligence traits.

Lower emotional intelligence is often observed in individuals who avoid responsibility for their mistakes, blame others, or make excuses. This is attributed to a lack of self-compassion and difficulty in accepting personal errors, viewing them instead as personal failures. In contrast, those with higher emotional intelligence are more likely to acknowledge their mistakes, apologize, and move forward. They are attentive listeners, open-minded and can discern essential details from extra information. High emotional intelligence individuals can attentively listen without being overwhelmed by their own emotions, ensuring full presence for the speaker. They are also truthful, even in difficult conversations, and possess the tact to convey hard truths with minimal distress.

The following table encapsulates various skills associated with emotional self-awareness. Assess own skills by circling "Yes" or "No" for each attribute. You can then set goals and go on to address those responses you would like to change.

Take a moment to review two significant relationships in your life and answer the following questions.

^Pause & Reflect ~ My Relationships^

Mindfulness and Emotional Self-Awareness	
Relationship 1:	**Relationship 2:**
Name: _____	Name: _____
Three things I appreciate and would like to remain the same are: _____ _____ _____	Three things I appreciate and would like to remain the same are: _____ _____ _____
Three things I'd like to see less of are: _____ _____ _____	Three things I'd like to see less of are: _____ _____ _____
Three things I'd like to see more of are: _____ _____ _____	Three things I'd like to see more of are: _____ _____ _____
Using the skills I have learned, I can support these changes by: _____ _____ _____	Using the skills I have learned, I can support these changes by: _____ _____ _____

^Pause & Reflect ~ Emotional Self-Awareness^

Yes No	Are you able to stay in touch with your emotions? (Can you tell what you're feeling and when you're feeling it?)
Yes No	Are you able to stay in tune with your physical body? Do you recognize the physical signals of emotional distress?
Yes No	Are you able to recognize the most important triggers for your emotional Responses?
Yes No	Are you able to acknowledge and accept your feelings without judging or condemning yourself for having them?
Yes No	Are you familiar with your emotional strengths and limitations?
Yes No	Do you have the ability to address your emotions by talking about them or managing them, rather than ignoring them or avoiding them?
Yes No	Are you able to question your emotional beliefs and test them for accuracy?
Yes No	Are you able to recognize the appropriateness of timing before addressing negative emotions with another person?
Yes No	Are you able to recognize the negative thought patterns that impact your ability to manage your emotions?
Yes No	Are you able to recognize/understand situations in which you tend to lose control?
Yes No	Are you able to step back from a situation to regain emotional control before allowing your emotions to escalate?
Yes No	Are you able to develop and nurture your own self-esteem and, at the same time, identify appropriate strategies for overcoming any limitations?

Dr. Jon Kabat-Zinn, a prominent figure in Mindfulness research, emphasizes emotional self-awareness as a crucial aspect of Mindfulness practice. Mindfulness involves a significant shift from a state of constant doing to a state of simply being. This transition is not just about taking a break; it's about cultivating an environment of inner peace, self-acceptance, and self-compassion. By intentionally setting aside time for personal reflection and tranquility, individuals create an essential space for themselves. This space becomes fertile ground for nurturing the skills vital for emotional well-being.

In this practice, the focus is on the present moment and the current emotional state. It's about acknowledging feelings without judgment and understanding their nature and impact. This process of mindful awareness fosters a deeper connection with one's emotional landscape, facilitating a more profound understanding and management of emotions. Such awareness is key to emotional intelligence, contributing significantly to overall mental health and resilience.

Core Concepts for Nurturing Emotional Awareness

In this chapter, the focus has been on cultivating acceptance, openness, and an awareness of the present moment as key strategies to navigate emotional challenges, particularly our inclination toward self-criticism. Embracing the present moment and accepting our emotions and thoughts, even when distressing, creates a conducive environment for personal growth and self-appreciation. This approach involves learning to coexist with uncomfortable feelings and beliefs, rather than trying to suppress or avoid them. It emphasizes the importance of maintaining focus and a non-judgmental attitude in our interactions and experiences.

The essence of these principles is recognizing and validating our internal experiences without letting them overpower or define us. By practicing detachment from negative emotions and beliefs we enhance our capacity to stay grounded and composed. The upcoming Pause & Reflect questionnaire is designed to guide you through a self-assessment of these guiding principles, helping you understand how well you're integrating these concepts into your Emotional MindView.

Fostering Emotional Balance: Present Focus and Values-Guided Responses

Embracing the present moment intentionally, with acceptance and openness, paves the way for a peaceful internal state and emotionally healthy interactions. This mindset is crucial for nurturing autonomy and well-being essential for effectively pursuing personal aspirations and goals.

In this chapter, we delved into emotional obstacles that can hinder goal achievement, particularly when our choices and actions aren't aligned with our values. Emotional dysregulation and unhealthy emotional boundaries can lead to a spectrum of issues - psychological, physical, and relational. Adverse experiences at any stage of life can lead to emotionally unstable coping mechanisms, varying from intense and erratic emotional responses to more complex issues like personality disorders, anxiety, and depression.

Through reflective exercises, you have examined your reactions to intense emotions and triggers, learning to apply emotional management techniques like de-escalation, self-soothing, effective communication, and problem-solving. You also discovered how the Emotional MindView and your Observer-Manager can assist in overcoming emotional dysregulation.

Next, we introduce a guided meditation designed for personal healing. Regardless of the type of pain – physical or emotional – employing The Artist's Tools of acceptance, forgiveness, compassion, commitment, and gratitude will aid in finding solace and recovery. While meditation guidance is broadly applicable, your journey will be uniquely personal, allowing you to explore and heal your inner self as needed.

Begin by identifying any pain you may feel in your body. This pain could be of any nature - physical, spiritual, or emotional - sharp or dull, long-standing, or recent. Gently place your hands over the area of discomfort. If the pain isn't specific, rest your hands on the center of your chest. If you have multiple points of pain, address each one in turn with this meditation, sensing the pain's gradual release. The more you practice this meditation, the more profound the healing effect will be.

^Pause & Reflect ~ Emotional MindView at a Glance^

1) I have very strong emotional reactions, sometimes so strong that I can't control them.

Disagree —O—O—O—O—O—O—O—O— Agree

2) If things don't go the way I expect, I often become quite upset.

Disagree —O—O—O—O—O—O—O—O— Agree

3) My emotions tend to control my life.

Disagree —O—O—O—O—O—O—O—O— Agree

4) I strive for a cognitive and emotional balance where they both enhance my life.

Disagree —O—O—O—O—O—O—O—O— Agree

5) I rely on my other internal resources such as my spiritual beliefs, my intellectual skills, my social support system, my physical activities, and inner strength when I feel overwhelmed or challenged beyond my emotional skill set.

Disagree —O—O—O—O—O—O—O—O— Agree

6) Gratitude and appreciation are what keep me going during difficult times.

Disagree —O—O—O—O—O—O—O—O— Agree

7) I try not to take myself too seriously. When I face my problems with humor, I feel like I have better control over them rather than the other way around.

Disagree —O—O—O—O—O—O—O—O— Agree

8) I am able to regulate my emotions so they guide what's important, and I am able to communicate those feelings without dominating the situation.

Disagree —O—O—O—O—O—O—O—O— Agree

9) My emotional life has been rich and satisfying.

Disagree —O—O—O—O—O—O—O—O— Agree
           1 2 3 4 5 6 7 8

Journaling
If I could change one thing about my emotional life, it would be _____
_____
_____

Journal Lines

_____
_____
_____
_____
_____
_____
_____
_____

Journal Space

GM Journaling: Ch. 8 ~ Choosing to Heal

✽ What did you experience as you did this meditation?

✽ What have your choices taught you about what is most meaningful to you?

✽ What did you learn about emotional Hijacking and Emotions management? Can you see how emotional boundaries can be helpful to you in your relationships with others?

✽ Did this chapter help you understand yourself a little be better?

✽ How would you describe your Emotional MindView as it is right now?

Guided Meditation ~ Chapter Eight: Emotional MindView Skills

In this chapter, you learned about and worked on some of the emotional problems that keep you from achieving your goals through value-based choices and behaviors. Emotional dysregulation and unhealthy emotional boundaries can result in psychological, physical, and relational problems. Chaotic and abusive experiences in childhood, youth, and adult life can result in emotionally dysregulated coping styles that range from exaggerated, intense, and inconsistent emotional reactivity to various personality disorders as well as anxiety and depression.

Through Pause & Reflect exercises, you explored how you respond to strong emotions and reactive triggers and how to apply emotional management skills, such as de-escalation, self-comforting, communication, and problem-solving skills. You also learned how your Emotional MindView domain, as well as your Observer-Manager, can help you heal your struggles with emotional dysregulation.

What follows is a guided meditation that will allow you to become your own source of healing. Whether you have experienced physical pain, emotional pain, or both, by using your artist's tools (acceptance, forgiveness, compassion, commitment, and gratitude), you will find relief and healing. Although the guided meditation text and recording are general, your experience can be very personal. You can visit your inner landscape whenever you feel the need.

Guided Meditation ~ Chapter 8: Choosing to Heal

Now, let's engage in controlled breathing. Inhale deeply for a count of four, hold your breath for another four counts, and then exhale smoothly for four counts, and then hold for four counts. We will repeat this pattern twice more.

Begin now. Inhale...2...3...4...hold...2...3...4...exhale...2...3...4...and hold...2...3...4. Repeat: Inhale...2...3...4...hold...2...3...4...exhale...2...3...4...hold...2...3...4. Once more, inhale...2...3...4... .hold...2...3...4...and exhale...2...3...4...and hold for four counts. Now, let your breathing return to its natural rhythm.

With your hands still over the area of pain, acknowledge it out loud, "I feel the hurt right here". Whisper to yourself, "I am open to the lessons this pain brings". Listen attentively for any insights or messages that may arise from this internal dialogue. Is there an underlying message or need?

We have a subtle yet powerful communication channel between our conscious and unconscious mind, often unnoticed. By quieting our minds and focusing on our breath, we create space to hear the wisdom of our deeper self and open ourselves to receive guidance. The Tools for the Artist Within - acceptance, self-compassion, and gratitude - are integral to your healing process. Often, our pain stems from a lack of integration of these tools at our core. It's time to embrace them.

With your hands still placed over the area of pain, channel the energy of acceptance, self-compassion, and gratitude into this space. Reflect on how this pain has contributed to your growth how it has reshaped your thoughts and being. Contemplate the lessons learned, the ways you've evolved into a more empathetic, compassionate person.

Embrace the gifts of acceptance, forgiveness, self-compassion, commitment, and gratitude as part of your healing journey. This pain has been a teacher, revealing deeper aspects of your relationships - with others and yourself. It has been a catalyst for empathy, compassion, and understanding. So, wholeheartedly receive these gifts as acknowledgments of your experiences and resilience.

Now, delve into the depths of your being, to your very core. Here, you may discover that the roots of your pain are intertwined with sadness and fear. Sadness stemming from a perceived lack of acceptance, and fear anchored in the belief that you were not enough due to this absence of acceptance. These are imprints from early life, formed before you had the boundaries necessary to shield yourself.

It's time to confront these feelings of sadness and fear and recognize them for what they truly are: misconceptions. These are not reflections of your true worth or inherent beauty, which are not dependent on external validation. You have the power to retain or release these old beliefs. To release them, acknowledge their presence and their falsehood. Visualize erasing them from your mind, as you would erase a chalkboard. Replace these erased messages with affirmations of your worth: "I am worthy. I am a wonder."

Picture yourself being filled with a pure, bright light. Feel this luminous energy entering from the top of your head, filling you, from your feet to your head. Embrace your worthiness, your beauty, and your inner brilliance. Visualize the light that emanates from within you, a radiant glow that is an integral part of your being. Carry this light with you always, a constant companion symbolizing your inherent worth and the unique wonder that is you.

Now, address your pain with a message of release and gratitude: "I embraced you, acknowledging you as a crucial presence in my life. But now, it's time for your release. Thank you for the lessons you've taught me."

Feel free to continue this dialogue with your pain at a later time. Express whatever brings you comfort and aids in your healing. When old thoughts resurface, or you find yourself doubting your worth, consider affirming your journey with these statements:

- *"I recognize that my healing and well-being are my responsibility. I have the power to hold onto suffering or to let go of this emotional pain. I choose to release it."*
- *"With a heart full of compassion, forgiveness, and gratitude, I choose to let go of past hurts."*
- *"I choose to cultivate more love and kindness towards myself starting now."*
- *"I accept my imperfections and flaws. I embrace myself as I am."*
- *"I choose to recognize and appreciate my own beauty, independent of external validation."*
- *"I commit to loving myself unconditionally. I embrace unconditional love for my life and for who I am, with profound gratitude."*
- *"Finally, I am prepared to embark on my healing journey with a fresh perspective, embracing the world with the curiosity and openness of a beginner's mind. Thank you for this opportunity."*

Use these affirmations as a guiding light, steering you towards a path of self-love, acceptance, and a renewed sense of purpose. And, when you are ready, return to this room.

Chapter 9 - Life Strategies for Well-being ~ Thinking MindView Skills

"Don't believe every worried thought you have. Worried thoughts are notoriously inaccurate." ~Renee Jain

Our previous discussion, delved into emotional aspects such as emotional boundaries, management skills, and emotional intelligence. This chapter shifts the focus to our cognitive realms by exploring thinking boundaries, communication abilities, and problem-solving techniques, along with addressing complex challenges within our Thinking MindView.

Cognition, or thought, encompasses our beliefs, expectations, aspirations, and the focus of our attention. Typically, our thoughts guide our actions and harbor recurring themes. The human brain is a prodigious thought generator, producing upwards of 60,000 thoughts daily, akin to the heart's relentless pumping of blood. A critical issue arises when we mistake these thoughts for absolute truth, leading to unintended emotional responses and behaviors. Often, we remain oblivious to our thought patterns and their overarching themes, which hampers our ability to control our emotions and actions effectively.

To mitigate response errors, it's crucial to align our internal theories with external reality. This process mirrors the scientific method: we start with a hypothesis, pose questions, conduct tests, analyze results, and confirm or adjust our initial hypothesis. In cognitive processes, however, there's a tendency to accept our conclusions without proper scrutiny. The fundamental principle of behavior is the interconnectedness of thoughts, feelings, and actions. Misunderstanding this triad can lead to actions that fail to yield constructive results. Thus, recognizing and managing the interaction between thoughts, feelings, and actions, is vital for achieving desired outcomes.

Understanding Self-Talk

Our internal dialogue, or self-talk, can adopt a positive, neutral, or negative tone. Generally, without conscious effort to direct it, self-talk skews toward negativity. This kind of talk often operates below our conscious awareness, subtly influencing our emotions and behaviors. Notably, if you've endured an overwhelmingly negative experience in the past that left you feeling powerless, this sentiment may re-emerge in similar contexts, perpetuated by your self-talk.

Consider a scenario where your boss reprimands you harshly. This might trigger feelings of helplessness, confusion, and resentment, particularly if you perceive the issue as beyond your control. You may start rationalizing why your boss is mistaken, convinced that the fault lies elsewhere and that you're being unjustly targeted. Subsequently, these thoughts evolve into beliefs and expectations, so any future criticism, however minor, is filtered through this lens. If events unfold as anticipated, you might feel a mix of negative emotions and oddly vindicated because your expectations were met. This reaffirmation of your worldview, albeit negative, lends a sense of predictability to your environment. This phenomenon is often labeled as "self-defeating behavior", particularly when the trigger is within your control, like tardiness for an important meeting.

The crux of the issue lies in recognizing how your perception shapes outcomes. By not understanding this dynamic, you inadvertently constrict your ability to alter future events positively. The real tragedy in such a cycle of negativity is the propensity to continually deflect blame onto others, like the boss, sidestepping personal accountability. This evasion denies you the opportunity to acknowledge and rectify the root causes of these negative cycles. When we cannot take responsibility for our mistakes, we lose the opportunity to learn and improve.

Recognizing Dominant Thought Patterns

Reflecting on Acceptance and Commitment Therapy (ACT), it's crucial to understand that our thoughts and feelings are just that: thoughts and feelings. They don't define us. Awareness gives us a choice. We can either let all of our thoughts, even the ones that are not factual shape our identity and actions (like losing motivation, avoiding confrontations, or feeling inadequate as a parent) or we can reevaluate these thoughts and choose a path of committed constructive action. This involves learning from our experiences and shifting the nature of our internal dialogue.

Our minds often play out negative scripts and repetitive thought patterns that frame our perceptions of ourselves and the world. Edmund Bourne (2010) identified four personality subtypes and their associated negative self-talk: The Worrier, the Critic, the Victim, and the Perfectionist. To some degree, we all exhibit these patterns. The key is recognizing and managing them.

The Worrier is constantly anxious about potential disasters, fixating on the worst-case scenarios despite their improbability. Their self-talk often starts with "what if…" and usually explores the worst outcomes. The Critic is the internal voice that relentlessly judges and condemns our actions, and often the actions of others. This self-talk damages self-esteem and confidence, often including harsh personal critiques and negative assessments of daily activities. It typically begins with "You are so…" The Victim feels trapped in helplessness and hopelessness, seeing situations in extremes of black or white. Their self-talk revolves around feelings of impossibility and inadequacy, and is characterized by despair.

The Perfectionist is never satisfied and always striving for more, often thinking in terms of "shoulds" and "musts". Their self-worth is externally driven, based on perceived external judgments. This mindset often leads to feelings of guilt, distress, and burnout. You might recognize these patterns in your thinking. Maybe one resonates more than the others. Remember, we have the power to respond to our self-talk. Again, we can dismiss these automatic thoughts and align our actions with our values, a topic which we will continue to explore further in the next section.

Aligning Thinking with Values Rather than Self-Talk and Expectations

Expectations can be both advantageous and detrimental, depending on their application. They help us prepare and protect ourselves, guiding us in fulfilling our needs. Our thoughts, beliefs, and self-talk, including our creativity, can either bolster or undermine these expectations. Positive self-talk and expectations can offer a framework for our aspirations, while negative self-talk and expectations often reinforce each other, leading to distress.

It's a common belief that anticipating the worst prepares us for potential outcomes. This mindset might be beneficial for professionals in safety or disaster planning, but it's not typically constructive for most of us.

According to Wellbeing: The Artfully Lived Life, one effective approach to counterproductive thinking is to accept what we can't change and engage in thought processes aligned with our values. This strategy enables us to manage day-to-day life while progressing towards our most significant goals. Thus, even challenging and uncomfortable situations can be navigated using The Artist's Tools, along with our emotional and cognitive MindView skills.

To effectively manage problems, we first calm emotional reactions by mindfully contemplating the issue. Then, we acknowledge and accept the emotional aspects that hinder our objectives, without labeling them as good or bad. Finally, we select responses that are solution-focused and adaptable.

Applying this thought process to the values identified in your Journey Map, the steps might look like this:

1. Journey Map Value: "I see myself as a valuable person destined for success."
2. You encounter a setback that previously would have led to self-criticism and diminished self-esteem.
3. You apply The Artist's Tools by: a) Forgiving the error, b) Accepting that mistakes are a part of life, c) Offering self-compassion for any resulting sadness or disappointment, d) Reaffirming your commitment to your goals with renewed determination, e) Expressing gratitude for the chance to pursue worthiness, even in failure, and f) Recognizing that this setback is a step closer to achieving your goal.
4. Success is already in motion because of your commitment and re-engagement with your values, and because you are persistently affirming your worth through your efforts rather than your outcomes.

Understanding Your Identity as a Thinker

Ron Miguel Ruiz, in his book "The Four Agreements", highlights the immense power of our thoughts and the words we use to express them. These thoughts and words shape our internal perceptions and how we interact with the external world. However, many of our thoughts are often remnants of past scripts or coping mechanisms that may have been useful previously but are counterproductive in our current lives.

Constantly engaging in self-critical or demeaning thoughts about ourselves or others fosters a profoundly negative view of ourselves and our surroundings. Our mind, influenced by these thoughts, works to realize them, acting under the belief that they are true because we've told it so (we accepted our negative evaluation as a fact.). It doesn't automatically dismiss these thoughts; instead, it trusts and follows the direction we provide. Moreover, the negativity from such thoughts consumes a significant amount of energy that could otherwise be channeled into positive growth, creativity, and transformation. In short, negative self-talk squanders our potential, time, and energy, impeding our progress and development.

^**Pause & Reflect ~ Affirming Self-Talk**^

Awareness ~ Knowing that negative self-talk only has the power that you give it.	Allow without Judgment~ Use The Artist's Tools to manage negative self-talk.	Affirm ~ Use statements of positive support for your efforts
<u>Focus</u> on your breathing. <u>Go</u> to your Garden or Workshop. <u>Shift</u> your thinking through self-reassurance. <u>Embrace</u> the possibilities rather than resist the particulars.	-Forgive ourselves for our mistakes. -Accept ourselves for who we are -Allow ourselves to feel what we feel. -Commit to observe and allow. -Allowing what hurts along with what doesn't. -Asking, "Is this what hurts?" without judgment of good or bad. -Simplifying – "this applies to one thing not all." -Questioning to understand the facts, without judgment of good or bad. -Feelings are not facts. -Thoughts are not always facts.	Peace is my choice. I am calm as I work through this. I am more effective when I solve problems using the skills I have learned. I have a goal to solve problems ~ not to fight with them. Each choice is my Own.

Enhancing Self-Awareness and Cognitive Boundaries

The development of self-awareness and establishing firm mental boundaries are vital for shaping and realizing a healthy and authentic self. It's essential to stay anchored in the present moment, consistently mindful of your learning, your achievements, and the skills you have practiced. It's crucial to understand that thoughts are mere mental events, not concrete facts. We aren't obliged to accept them as truths or allow them to define our identity. If they contradict our values and aspirations, we can disregard them.

In some chapters, you've been prompted to select words describing your current self. It's possible these choices may reflect longstanding beliefs and thoughts about yourself, stored in your mind, more than they represent who you truly are now. Often, these aged beliefs remain unchallenged and persistent. While relinquishing these ingrained notions and beliefs can be challenging, even in the face of strong evidence, it is a crucial step towards being true to yourself and your personal boundaries. Changing these entrenched mental patterns demands dedicated effort and might be tough, but it's necessary endeavor.

The term "Esteem Needs" encompasses our desire for experiences that reinforce our sense of self-worth, societal recognition, and achievements. "Esteem" pertains to our internal self-perception and how we believe others perceive us. We may find self-worth intrinsically, through our own internal standards, or at times, extrinsically, seeking validation and esteem from others and judging ourselves based on perceived external opinions.

This interplay between our self-concept and our perceptions of external appraisal is significant. It can influence every decision we make, our openness to new experiences, and our readiness to take risks. When we perceive the world as a positive and safe environment, we are more inclined to explore, learn, and spend time understanding our true selves and our place in the world. Conversely, perceiving the world as intimidating or threatening can significantly hinder our willingness to step out of our comfort zone and discover our full potential. Even though at some time in your life, the world may have been an unsafe or unfriendly place, your current efforts to develop your Artfully Lived Life suggest that you now have greater control over your environment.

Establishing Cognitive Boundaries

Our brain is a wellspring of creativity, innovation, and imagination, that steer our actions, thoughts, emotions, and desires. When the brain utilizes its capabilities to fulfill our needs constructively, it becomes a formidable ally in crafting a successful and fulfilling life. Conversely, if we channel our cognitive and emotional resources in ways that infringe upon others' boundaries, our journey toward psychological wellness becomes hindered.

Cognitive boundaries safeguard our right to independent thought, belief, and decision-making. They defend our liberty to explore our life paths creatively without undue influence. Actions that lead to the reduction of our own or others' dignity represent breaches of these boundaries. Manipulation, unjust criticism, anger, irrational reasoning, and domineering or aggressive actions are examples of how the brain might inappropriately adapt to its environment in the absence of boundaries.

The challenge lies in finding a balance that meets our needs while respecting appropriate boundaries. This quest can be intricate, time-consuming, and sometimes intimidating as we strive to understand ourselves without overstepping boundaries. Being responsible for our thoughts is akin to pioneering a new path, where following others' trails won't lead us to our unique destination. Instead, we must delve into understanding how our brain functions—how our thoughts impact us, our beliefs, and how these beliefs shape our behaviors and life paths. When we come to understand how our thoughts and beliefs impact our lives, we can envision and attain a higher level of freedom and empowerment in our behaviors.

^Pause & Reflect ~Thinking & Identity^

Think about how your negative self-talk has damaged your understanding of who you are, your potential as an individual, and how you fit into the world. Try to identify ways that negative thinking about yourself has affected the way you think about others as well.

_____
_____
_____

How has your negative self-talk affected the way you behave around others?

_____
_____
_____

What would you like to change about those behaviors?

_____
_____
_____

What are you noticing about the connections between your thoughts and your behaviors?

_____
_____
_____

Cognitive Boundary Violations: Cognitive boundary violations often stem from a pessimistic worldview. Identity theorists indicate that individuals with overwhelmingly negative worldviews often perceive themselves and others in a derogatory light, viewing themselves as incompetent, powerless, or unworthy. They may see the world as chaotic, untrustworthy, or malevolent. Most cognitive boundary violations are linked to intense emotions, beliefs, and behaviors, which can become deeply ingrained.

The list below outlines common cognitive boundary violations and suggests appropriate alternative responses. While it may seem extensive, it's not uncommon for people to occasionally breach some of these boundaries. However, being aware of our actions allows us to address and rectify them. The Artist's Tools ~ Acceptance, Forgiveness, Self-compassion, Commitment, and Gratitude – are crucial to substituting these detrimental cognitive boundaries with healthier ones.

Thinking Boundaries

Healthy	Broken
Autonomy	Manipulation
Creativity	Forgetfulness
Resourcefulness	Irrational thinking
Problem solving	Dominance
Education	Ignorance
Competence	Criticism
Profession	Toxic beliefs
Discipline	Stubbornness
Freedom	Irresponsibility
Vision	Lack of discipline
Negotiation	Belittling/Mocking
Responsibility	Defensiveness

- **Choosing Self-Reliance Over Dependency:** Depending on others for essential aspects like safety, purpose, identity, worthiness, or self-esteem can be counterproductive. People are fallible, and inevitably, they may disappoint you. When this happens, the effort spent seeking their approval may seem futile, leaving you feeling betrayed or exploited. A more effective approach is to build your own support system. This is similar to the airline safety instruction of securing your oxygen mask first before assisting others. This self-reliance can be fostered through the identity development exercises provided in this workbook.

- **Challenging "Prove-It-to-Me" Thinking:** This thought pattern involves making silent conclusions about others' actions, often interpreting them as evidence of their feelings or intentions towards you. For instance, if your teenager scowls at you rather than greeting you, it's unproductive to immediately interpret this as disrespect or a lack of affection. Instead, it could be unrelated issues like personal discomfort or a challenging day. "Prove-It-to-Me" thinking often leads to personalizing and generalizing situations inaccurately, overlooking the possibility that others have their reasons unrelated to you.

- **Embrace Disagreement:** Perceiving disagreement as a personal attack can lead to feelings of insecurity and the fear of rejection. When someone's opinions differ from yours, you might feel compelled to argue until they align with your perspective to alleviate your fears. However, it's important to recognize that disagreement is a natural aspect of human interaction and not a reflection of your worth or the validity of your opinions. Embracing diverse viewpoints without feeling threatened can lead to richer, more nuanced understanding and relationships.

- **Overcome the Need to Always Be Right:** This behavior often stems from an ego-driven fear of being wrong. When you insist on being right, it can lead to invalidating others' opinions through emotional or verbal aggression, such as using insults or intimidation. It's important to recognize that insisting on being right often arises from insecurity and can damage relationships.

- **Avoid Unfair Fighting Tactics:** Engaging in "dirty fighting" strategies like bringing up past mistakes to win an argument (gunny sacking) or making hurtful remarks is detrimental. Other harmful tactics include sarcasm, playing the victim, refusing apologies, using guilt, creating no-win scenarios, and manipulating information. These tactics harm relationships and hinder effective communication.

- **Steer Clear of Controlling Behaviors:** Trying to control how others express themselves, whether through dress, speech, or behavior, crosses cognitive boundaries. It's crucial to understand that personal discomfort doesn't justify actions that belittle or undermine others.

- **Rethink Unwanted Opinions and Advice:** Offering unsolicited advice or criticism often implies that the other person is incapable of solving their problems. Even when well-intentioned, this can lead to negative feelings like fear, shame, or lack of confidence. It's important to respect others' autonomy and their right to learn from their own experiences.

- **Address Justifications and Rationalizations:** Justifying, excusing, and rationalizing behaviors are ways of avoiding accountability. These mental gymnastics often lead to repeated harmful patterns and violate both personal boundaries and those of others involved.

- **Recognize "Twisty Tricks":** This term refers to tactics where individuals deflect responsibility by shifting the blame or focus onto someone else. It's crucial to recognize and take responsibility for one's actions instead of resorting to blame-shifting.

Reframing and Respecting Boundaries

When individuals struggle with low self-esteem and poor cognitive boundaries, they may feel justified in critiquing or dissecting others' thoughts and behaviors. Instead of seeking understanding and connection through respectful inquiry, they might attack or criticize ideas that differ from their own. It is crucial to realize that attempts to "correct ", "fix", or "change" someone else's thinking is a boundary violation and can severely harm relationships.

Every person's way of thinking is unique and doesn't have to align with ours. Our role is to accept and respect their right to their beliefs and thoughts. If we find ourselves in a relationship with incompatible views, we have three options:
- Address the issue and request change, acknowledging their right to remain unchanged.
- Adapt our perspectives to better align with theirs.
- If the differences are insurmountable and compromise is not possible, consider ending the relationship.

Tactics that violate cognitive boundaries, though sometimes effective in prompting change, can be mentally and emotionally damaging for both parties. These behaviors can lead to significant consequences, such as the loss of jobs and relationships, and disruptions in life goals. They undermine the essential right of individuals to be self-determining.

Cognitive boundary violations are often employed in emotionally charged situations. However, rather than resolving conflict, they tend to create more confusion and chaos, obstructing effective communication and problem-solving. Recognizing and avoiding these behaviors is crucial for maintaining healthy, respectful, and supportive relationships.

^Pause & Reflect ~ Boundary Errors^

The above types of thinking boundary violations are listed below. Think about each of them and consider whether they might be a problem in your life.

Dependency Thinking	Prove-it-to-me Thinking
The Need for Agreement	The Need to be Right
Dirty Fighting Strategies	The Need to Control
Opinions, Advice, or Criticism	Justifying, Excusing, Rationalizing
Twisty Tricks	Over-Analyzing

_____
_____
_____
_____

Overcoming Social Challenges through Effective Interactive Problem-Solving

In life, a "problem" often refers to a situation where there's a complication, disagreement, illness, or obstacle that hinders our progress toward a goal. Problems are an inevitable part of existence, varying in intensity from minor setbacks to significant crises, depending on how crucial the goal is to us. For instance, health is a fundamental goal, and illness represents a significant disruption. It is crucial to acknowledge that in problem-solving, particularly with others, there may not be a perfect solution that satisfies everyone completely. Compromise is often necessary, meaning you might have to let go of certain aspects of your ideal resolution. Success in problem-solving is more likely when cooperation and finding a mutually acceptable solution are prioritized over winning or being right.

To successfully navigate through problems, especially those that could lead to emotional distress, it's essential to use effective problem-solving strategies. Challenges in this process can include:
- A lack of effective problem-solving skills.
- Unmanaged stress.
- Pervasive negative self-talk.
- Issues with self-esteem.
- Emotional overreactions (emotional hijacking).
- Violating cognitive boundaries.

By remaining calm and concentrating on effective problem-solving techniques, most challenges can be approached constructively, minimizing emotional and interpersonal harm. This approach involves understanding the problem, brainstorming solutions, evaluating the options, and implementing the most viable solution while being open to adjustment and feedback. The following strategies for problem-solving can help to streamline the communication process and produce positive outcomes. It is referred to as the OLIVE Process.

Journal Lines

_____
_____
_____
_____
_____
_____
_____
_____
_____
_____
_____
_____

OLIVE PROCESS

1. **Outline the Problem and Desired Outcome:** Start by clearly defining the problem and what a successful resolution would look like. If the problem involves others, express your perspective and listen to theirs. Focus on one issue at a time, avoiding the temptation to drift into other related problems.
2. **List Possible Solutions**: Create a list of potential solutions without dismissing any prematurely. Write down each alternative and assess them, ranking from the most to least effective. Consider the possible outcomes of each solution, choosing the best one to try first.
3. **Implement the Chosen Solution**: With the top solutions identified, negotiate and compromise to determine the best course of action. Be mindful of cognitive boundary issues like irrational thinking or needing control, which can derail the process. If such issues arise, take a break and reset. Implement the chosen solution, setting a reasonable timeframe to assess its effectiveness.
4. **View and Evaluate the Outcome:** Observe any changes that result from the implemented solution. Often, the first attempt might not be perfect but could lead you in the right direction. Patience is key in this experimental process.
5. **Evaluate and Adjust:** If the initial solution doesn't yield the desired outcome, revisit the problem. Look at the solutions you've tried and consider if they need adjustment. Adjust the changes as necessary and reapply. This iterative process, while sometimes lengthy, reduces the likelihood of error or confusion and helps avoid conflict.

OLIVE Process Simplified

O	–Outline the nature of the problem and the outcome you desire.
L	–List the alternatives, then negotiate and compromise on the best two.
I	–Implement the first and best compromise.
V	–View the outcome.
E	–Evaluate your results, then return and implement the second-best compromise if the first was unsuccessful.

Remember, the OLIVE process is about structured, thoughtful problem-solving. It's not just about finding a quick fix rather it's about developing a systematic approach that reduces misunderstandings and fosters collaborative resolution.

Flexibility in Problem-Solving: Balancing Individual Needs

When facing a negotiation or problem-solving scenario, rigidly clinging to every detail of your position can set you up for failure. Instead, identifying what's essential in your position while being open to compromise on less critical aspects significantly increases the chances of finding a resolution.

Consider a scenario where one partner desires more social time with friends, while the other yearns for more intimate couple time. A practical approach would first quantify each partner's ideal time allocation. Then, examine the total available free time and explore ways to balance both sets of needs. If they demand all five available hours per week for their interests, it's a recipe for disappointment. However, a willingness to be adaptable opens doors to solutions like alternating preferences every other week or dividing the five hours weekly to cater to both desires. This might also lead to brainstorming other innovative compromises.

It's natural to prioritize our needs and view our perspective as the most valid. Yet, this approach often leads to competition rather than cooperation, which is crucial for harmonious relationships and peaceful coexistence.

Ultimately, the success of problem-solving lies not just in following a structured process but in fostering a spirit of cooperation and mutual respect. This collaborative approach not only resolves the immediate issue but also builds trust and strengthens the relationship overall.

Social Problem-Solving: Integrating Cognitive and Emotional Perspectives

Social problem-solving, which lies at the intersection of our emotional and cognitive realms, necessitates a willingness from all parties involved to make sacrifices for a fair solution. This process hinges on understanding the distinction between deeply held values and transient emotions. When a core value is central to negotiation, particularly a value shared with someone important to us, the negotiation transcends mere emotional engagement and becomes a cognitive imperative. The emotional investment in the issue reinforces the effectiveness of cognitive problem-solving strategies. In this way, finding solutions becomes a powerful tool that intertwines the Emotional, Thinking, and Social MindView domains. It is the alignment with core values that gives problem-solving its potency.

Employing specific problem-solving skills fulfills the requirements of these MindView domains. This approach is overseen by the Observer-Manager, who utilizes these skills to effectively navigate challenges in life. Building a strong sense of identity, self-esteem, and self-confidence is rooted in knowing your values, possessing the tools to create opportunities for achieving those values, and deploying those skills to actualize your goals. Mastering this approach epitomizes the concept of an "Artfully Lived Life", where cognitive, emotional, and social aspects harmoniously combine to guide decisions and actions.

^Pause & Reflect ~ Olive Process^

Look for a problem that needs to be solved and give yourself an opportunity to practice what you have learned about problem-solving.
Outline the nature of the problem and the goals you would like to achieve.
_____
_____

List the alternatives, then look for commonalities that you can agree on and negotiate the rest.
_____
_____

Pick an alternative you can both agree to try **Implement** it.
_____
_____

View the outcome. What do you notice?
_____
_____

Evaluate the results to decide whether you achieved your goals.
_____
_____

Optimist or a Pessimist?

1) Optimism is an attitude that the future will be bright and things will work out. Are you an Optimist or a Pessimist? Why? _____
_____
_____
_____

2) Things that get in the way of my being an effective problem solver and communicator are _____
_____
_____
_____

> **^Pause & Reflect ~ <u>Thinking MindView</u> at a Glance^**
>
> **Thinking MindView**
>
> 1) When I have a problem, I often ask myself, "How else can I think about this?"
>   Disagree ──○──○──○──○──○──○──○──○── Agree
>
> 2) I generally take things at face value. I don't always wait for the facts.
>   Disagree ──○──○──○──○──○──○──○──○── Agree
>
> 3) I often jump to conclusions and react as if my conclusions are true.
>   Disagree ──○──○──○──○──○──○──○──○── Agree
>
> 4) I often think life is getting more and more difficult.
>   Disagree ──○──○──○──○──○──○──○──○── Agree
>
> 5) I try to stay focused and open with what is happening right now.
>   Disagree ──○──○──○──○──○──○──○──○── Agree
>
> 6) I am a pretty good problem solver. I enjoy looking at problems as challenges.
>   Disagree ──○──○──○──○──○──○──○──○── Agree
>
> 7) When I solve problems with my partner, I consider and discuss all sides and angles equally before making a decision.
>   Disagree ──○──○──○──○──○──○──○──○── Agree
>
> 8) I find it is better to focus on problems I can solve rather than those I can't.
>   Disagree ──○──○──○──○──○──○──○──○── Agree
>
> 9) I don't MindView making mistakes because I learn from them and apply what I learn the next time I try.
>   Disagree ──○──○──○──○──○──○──○──○── Agree
>
> 10) I try to be flexible when problem-solving rather than being stuck on one right answer.
>   Disagree ──○──○──○──○──○──○──○──○── Agree
>
> 11) When I have negative thoughts, rather than just believing my thoughts, I ask myself to find the evidence or whether or not these thoughts are helpful.
>   Disagree ──○──○──○──○──○──○──○──○── Agree
>   1 2 3 4 5 6 7 8

Foundations of Cognitive Wellness in the Thinking MindView

Throughout this chapter, we've delved into the concept of "Cognitive Wellness", a state characterized by openness to fresh insights while critically assessing their relevance, significance, and factual accuracy, all within the framework of psychological and emotional limits. A key aspect of fostering cognitive wellness is becoming conscious of our tendency for negative self-talk and the common mistakes we make regarding cognitive boundaries. This heightened awareness is crucial for making sound decisions and forging and sustaining healthy relationships.

To enhance our cognitive wellness, we can utilize the "Artist's Tools", which offer a range of strategies for emotional and intellectual growth. Additionally, employing effective problem-solving techniques is essential as we strive to achieve our objectives. The OLIVE process, introduced in this chapter, stands as a powerful methodology for realizing the life we envision. By integrating these principles and techniques, we equip ourselves with the means to effectively navigate our thoughts and actions toward a fulfilling and well-balanced life.

GM Journaling: Ch. 9 ~ Thinking Mindview

- What did you experience as you did this meditation?

- What have your choices taught you about what is most meaningful to you?

- What did you learn about problem solving and communication?

- What do you think about the Olive Process? How and with whom might this strategy be helpful to you?

- Did this chapter help you understand your thought processes a little better?

- How would you describe your Thinking MindView as it is right now?

Meditation- Guided Meditation for Mindful Thought Processing

Begin this meditation session with a deep, measured breath. Inhale slowly, counting to four, hold that breath for another count of four, gently exhale to the count of four, then hold for a count of four. Repeat this cycle twice more, maintaining a rhythm that feels natural and calming.

Inhale... 2... 3... 4... hold... 2... 3... 4... exhale... 2... 3... 4... and hold... 2... 3... 4. Again, inhale deeply... 2... 3... 4... hold your breath... 2... 3... 4... exhale slowly... 2... 3... 4...and hold 2... 3... 4... Finally, one last time, breathe in... 2... 3... 4... hold... 2... 3... 4...and exhale... 2... 3... 4. Now, let your breathing return to its natural rhythm.

Reflect on the previous chapter, where we delved into the Emotional MindView. We understood that sometimes our emotions might lead us to discomfort, and we learned techniques to soothe our MindViews, seeking insights or messages necessary for our healing. Through this process, we have cultivated kindness and compassion. We have also integrated The Artist's Tools - acceptance, forgiveness, self-compassion, commitment, and gratitude - deep within ourselves. We chose to let go of the belief that our self-worth is determined by others, and instead embraced more self-love and self-care.

In this chapter, we focused on cultivating healthier, more affirming self-talk. We explored the concept of unhealthy thinking boundaries and learned effective problem-solving skills. As we continue this guided meditation, let's concentrate on releasing lingering thoughts of inadequacy.

Revisit the healing workshop you envisioned in a previous meditation. Remember its location, in the mountains, a serene field, or along a tranquil beach. As you enter this familiar, safe space, notice the comforting ambiance – the lighting, the sounds, the temperature, and even the scents. This workshop is your sanctuary for practicing new skills, a place of safety and non-judgment.

As you step inside, observe a mirror on the wall to your left. Look into it and see yourself. What do you notice about the person looking back at you?

Now, moving deeper into your workshop, feel the sense of peace enveloping the space. Notice the table, the comfortable chair, and the whiteboard. This is your haven for growth and exploration, free from judgment and with potential for positive change. Focus on the whiteboard in your workshop. Two words prominently displayed catch your eye: "Acceptance" and "Compassion", key components of The Artist's Tools. Below these words is an empowering affirmation: "I am enough! I accept myself for who I am. I can show compassion to myself and others."

Take a moment to internalize this message. Repeat to yourself: "I am enough! I accept myself for who I am. I can show compassion to myself and others." As you do so, notice a small, dark cloud materializing in one corner of the board, symbolizing a negative emotion or memory – perhaps a recent mistake at work. This cloud is enveloped in negative self-talk: "You are not good enough, your boss thinks you are incompetent, your coworkers could do your job better." These thoughts, attempting to cling to you, can be rejected. They are not facts but scripts, narratives from the past that you've come to believe.

Recognize that you have a choice. These negative thoughts are not an immutable part of you; they are transient, like passing clouds. Imagine wearing a Teflon suit, allowing these thoughts to slide off you effortlessly. Remember, it's not about ceasing to have negative thoughts; it's about not allowing them to define you.

Once centered again, shift your focus inward. Bring to MindView loving memories of people who care about you and those you've positively influenced. Reflect on your personal growth and the knowledge you've gained about yourself.

A new message appears on the whiteboard: "I am enough, just the way I am." Understand that your worth and value are intrinsic, not based on external achievements or accomplishments. You are a work in progress, continually learning and growing. You've practiced reducing emotional reactivity through mindfulness and have learned to step back to see the broader context around your emotions and self-critical narratives. These skills will aid you in staying solution-focused and adaptable in your daily life.

As you prepare to leave this meditation, a final message emerges: "Love is at the center of the universe. You are loved." Embrace this truth for your well-being.

Return your focus to your breath. Inhale for a count of four, hold for four and exhale for four. Gently bring yourself back to the present moment, carrying with you the affirmation "I have always been enough."

As you exit your workshop, remember that this space is always open to you, a sanctuary of safety and growth. Take a final look at the serene landscape you've created in your mind, then re-engage with your day, renewed with a sense of self-worth, dignity, and hope.

Chapter 10 ~ Life Strategies for Well-Being: Social MindView Skills

"It is only with the heart that one can see rightly ~
What is essential is invisible to the eye." ~The Little Prince

In our journey through this book, we have explored challenges like low self-esteem and the complexities of interpersonal relationships. Now, in this chapter, we shift our focus to enhancing social awareness, establishing firm social boundaries, and creating enriching social connections while navigating common social challenges. These issues typically stem from problematic interpersonal or social boundaries.

Our brains are hardwired to constantly engage with those around us, a concept Daniel Goleman (2006) likened to a "neural Wi-Fi". This means that as we interact, our brains engage in a rapid, reciprocal communication process. This exchange is not limited to verbal communication; it includes facial expressions, vocal tone, and body language. Both parties in an interaction interpret these cues in the context of their own experiences and emotions, forming expectations and predictions about the unfolding interaction.

This intricate exchange of cues and responses between two brains occurs almost instantaneously and is laden with emotional undercurrents. The process starts even before a single word is spoken. Understanding the neurological, emotional, and cognitive facets of communication is crucial for two reasons. Firstly, it allows us to recognize and correct ineffective or erroneous perceptions and interpretations that may disrupt a relationship. Secondly, it enables us to devise new, more effective strategies for enhancing our interpersonal connections.

Conflicts in relationships often arise from miscommunications during this complex exchange. Misinterpreting or inaccurately responding to the blend of emotional, behavioral, and cognitive signals can easily lead to misunderstandings. Therefore, mastering the art of interpersonal communication is key to overcoming these common relational hurdles.

Enhancing Communication and Strengthening Relationships

Navigating the complexities of interpersonal communication and enhancing our relationships can be challenging. However, there are several strategies we can employ to facilitate smoother interactions and build stronger connections.

Strategies for Enhancing Relationships

1. **Effective Communication Skills:** Mastering communication skills is crucial for preventing misunderstandings. This includes listening, articulating thoughts clearly, and empathetically responding to others. Even in situations where we share similar views, effective communication plays a vital role in maintaining clarity and understanding.
2. **Understanding Personal Boundaries:** Recognizing and respecting personal boundaries is essential. Boundaries act as a safeguard, providing a sense of security during the intricate communication process. They help us define how much we are willing to share and receive in interactions, preventing overstepping and discomfort.
3. **Stress Management Techniques:** Effective stress management is key in handling our physical responses to emotionally charged interactions. Techniques such as deep breathing, mindfulness, and taking breaks can help in maintaining composure during challenging conversations.
4. **Emotional Regulation Skills:** These skills are vital in reducing the intensity of emotional responses, which can sometimes overshadow rational thought. By managing our emotions effectively, we can prevent them from taking control of the conversation, allowing for more reasoned and balanced exchanges.
5. **Cognitive Skills for Communication:** Developing cognitive skills helps in challenging and changing erroneous beliefs that may hinder assertive communication and effective problem-solving. This involves recognizing unhelpful thought patterns and replacing them with more constructive and realistic ones.

By integrating these strategies into our daily interactions, we can significantly improve our communication skills, leading to healthier and more fulfilling relationships.

Deepening Social Connections Through Communication

The foundation laid in previous chapters about Physical, Emotional, and Thinking MindViews sets the stage for this chapter, which delves into the Social MindView. Here, we focus on enhancing tools and skills for enriching interpersonal relationships. This chapter aims to refine communication skills for effectively conveying ideas, exchanging information, clarifying misunderstandings, and resolving conflicts.

Extensive research underscores the pivotal role of healthy, loving, and supportive relationships in promoting longevity.

Key aspects that facilitate connecting with others include:

1. **Understanding Social Boundaries:** Recognizing and respecting social boundaries is fundamental. It helps in navigating relationships without overstepping or under-engaging, thus maintaining healthy interactions.
2. **Refined Listening Skills:** Active listening involves fully engaging with the speaker, understanding their perspective, and responding thoughtfully. It forms the basis of effective communication and mutual understanding.
3. **Skills in Acknowledgment and Validation:** Validating others' feelings and experiences and acknowledging their perspectives fosters deeper connections and trust.
4. **Advanced Communication Skills:** Beyond basic conversation, these skills involve expressing oneself clearly, interpreting others accurately, and engaging in meaningful dialogues.
5. **Problem-Solving Abilities:** Effectively addressing and resolving conflicts or disagreements in relationships is key to their longevity and health.
6. **Emotion Management:** Managing one's own emotions in social interactions is essential for maintaining harmony and understanding.
7. **Negotiation Skills:** The ability to negotiate reflects a balance of giving and taking, crucial for sustaining equitable relationships.
8. **Interdependence Versus Independence or Co-dependence:** Cultivating interdependence allows for mutual support and growth in relationships, as opposed to the isolation of independence or the unhealthy reliance of co-dependence.

At our core, the instinctual need for belonging, alongside self-preservation, guides our social interactions. Our brains, fundamentally wired for survival, recognize that being part of a community is essential for this survival. This chapter aims to harness these instincts and enhance our social skills for more fulfilling and lasting relationships.

Exploring the Impact of Social Interactions on Well-being

Daniel Goleman's work in "Social Intelligence" (2006) illuminates the intricate links between social interactions and neurological functions. Research in this field reveals how our relationships influence various aspects of our physical health, from brain activities and organ functions to biochemical processes, immune system responses, and even genetic expressions. These insights underscore the profound impact of interpersonal relationships on our overall health.

Positive, nurturing relationships can significantly bolster our body's health and resilience. Conversely, relationships characterized by negativity and toxicity can adversely affect our physical well-being. To understand the influence of your personal relationships on your health, consider two pivotal relationships in your life. Reflect on the following questions to gain insight into their impact:

1. Nature of Interaction: How do these relationships make you feel on a day-to-day basis? Are they sources of comfort and support, or do they often lead to stress and discomfort?
2. Communication Patterns: Do these relationships involve open, honest communication, or are there frequent misunderstandings and conflicts?
3. Emotional Influence: Do these relationships uplift and energize you, or do they leave you drained and stressed?
4. Physical Response: Have you noticed any physical reactions, such as relaxation or tension, when interacting with these individuals?
5. Long-term Effects: How have these relationships shaped your outlook on life, your self-esteem, and your sense of well-being over time?
6. Support Systems: Do these relationships provide a sense of security and understanding, or do they often lead to feelings of isolation and loneliness?
7. Growth and Development: Have these relationships contributed to your personal growth, or have they hindered your development in some ways?

Reflecting on these questions can provide valuable insights into the role these relationships play in your life and their impact on your physical and emotional health.

Journal Lines

_____
_____
_____
_____
_____
_____
_____
_____
_____
_____
_____
_____

^Pause & Reflect ~ My Social MindView^

Take a moment to consider who you are, who you always have been, and who you want to be by completing the following exercise.

As a social being, even as a little child, I have always felt
_____

My social self has made it possible in my life to
_____

I love and appreciate my social self for
_____

My greatest strength as a social being is
_____

My greatest passion in life is
_____

What creates the most meaning for me as a social being is
_____

If I could do anything in the world without any holds, blocks, or barriers, it would be
_____

The things that are stopping me from achieving my hopes, dreams, and wishes are
_____

Can I choose to let them go? When?
_____

Enhancing Social and Emotional Skills for Better Interactions

This chapter delves into two key concepts from Daniel Goleman's work on Emotional Intelligence (1995), which are closely intertwined with his ideas on Social Intelligence. These concepts are crucial for understanding and improving social interactions. We'll explore two primary skill categories: Social Awareness and Social Facility.

Social Awareness involves a set of abilities that are fundamental to healthy and effective social interactions:

1. <u>Attunement:</u> This skill refers to the ability to genuinely tune in to another person, going beyond mere surface-level engagement to truly understand their perspective and emotions.
2. <u>Empathy:</u> This is the capacity to sense and understand others' needs and feelings. It's about recognizing and responding to the emotional states of others, which can be observed through their facial expressions, body language, and tone of voice.
3. <u>Rapport Building:</u> This involves developing a connection with others through both emotional and behavioral responses. It's about creating a sense of understanding and mutual respect in interactions.
4. <u>Empathic Accuracy and Social Cognition:</u> These skills relate to accurately interpreting another person's communicated thoughts, feelings, and intentions. They encompass a broader understanding of the dynamics of social interactions.
5. <u>Full Attention:</u> Providing undivided attention is crucial in social interactions. It conveys two essential messages to the other person: "You are important," and "I am fully engaged in understanding you."

To gauge your proficiency in these areas, reflect on the following:

- How well do you feel you attune to others in conversations?
- Are you able to sense and respond appropriately to the emotions of those around you?
- How effective are you at building rapport in various social settings?
- Do you find it easy to understand the intentions and feelings behind what others communicate?
- How often do you offer your full attention in interactions, and what impact does it have?

If you're in a relationship, it might be enlightening to compare your self-assessment with your partner's perceptions. This can offer insights into how well you understand and engage with each other on a social and emotional level.

Social Facility and Its Components

Social Facility is a key aspect of Social IQ, building upon social awareness to enhance one's ability to interact effectively and smoothly. This skill set includes:

1. Synchrony: This involves the nonverbal exchange of emotional information. In conversations where synchrony is present, participants often mirror each other's expressions and gestures, intuitively responding to unspoken cues. This creates a natural rapport and connection as if the conversation is perfectly timed.

2. Self-Presentation: This skill is about adapting to the social and emotional context of a situation, rather than being solely focused on one's inner feelings. It includes the ability to build confidence, trust, and intimacy in social interactions. A person with good self-presentation, like a charismatic individual, knows how to capture others' attention and interest by timing their actions to suit the social environment.

3. Influence: The ability to empathetically and tactfully gain cooperation from others. This requires managing cognitive, emotional, and behavioral responses, especially in challenging situations. Influence involves significant self-discipline and the ability to control impulsive reactions. A crucial part of influencing is active listening, which fosters trust and open communication, essential for emotional closeness.

4. Concern: Acting with care and consideration for the needs of others. This aspect of social facility is about being genuinely attentive to what others need and responding accordingly.

Each of these components plays a vital role in effective social interactions. Mastering them enhances one's ability to connect with others in meaningful and productive ways.

^Pause & Reflect ~ Social Facility^

Yes	No	Are you able to use body language, voice intonations, and facial expressions to show people you're paying attention to what they're communicating?
Yes	No	Are you able to observe and accurately interpret nonverbal social cues such as facial expressions, tone of voice, eye contact, and social gestures and respond to them appropriately?
Yes	No	Are you able to accurately assess the social setting and demonstrate an appropriate mix of self-restraint and emotional discretion for the situation?
Yes	No	Are you able to experience compassion and concern for others' distress and then act on the desire to help through service or humanitarian efforts?
Yes	No	Are you able to express yourself in such a way that you invite a specific social response to achieve the desired goal?
Yes	No	Are you receptive to information and feedback from the social environment?

To enhance healthy connections with important people in your life, it's essential to invest physically, emotionally, and thoughtfully in these relationships. This investment involves dedicating time and effort to build, improve, and sustain them. Relationships don't automatically thrive; they require active involvement. Think of it like flying an airplane: even though computers do a lot, a pilot and a navigation system are still crucial. If your time and energy are consumed by other goals, it's vital to communicate and align these priorities with the other person. When both parties share these values, time spent apart can be seen as contributing to the relationship's future, not as a lack of commitment.

The upcoming sections will delve into the skills crucial for nurturing healthy interpersonal relationships. We'll focus primarily on intimate relationships due to their complexity, but the principles apply to all types of relationships, including those with friends, children, siblings, extended family, coworkers, and bosses.

^Pause & Reflect: Essential Elements^

> To form positive interpersonal connections, several key elements are necessary:
> - **Time:** Devoting sufficient time is fundamental.
> - **Attention:** Being attentively present in interactions.
> - **Focus:** Concentrating on the relationship and the other person.
> - **Positive Intention:** Approaching the relationship with good will.
> - **Appropriate Prioritization:** Placing the relationship high on your list of priorities.
> - **Absence of Distractions or Interruptions:** Minimizing external disruptions.
>
> Effective tools for fostering interpersonal connections include:
> - **Active Listening:** Fully engaging and understanding the other person.
> - **Maintaining Appropriate Boundaries:** Respecting personal limits within the relationship.
> - **Problem-Centered "Damage Control" Skills:** Addressing issues directly and constructively when they arise.

Prioritizing Time for Relationships and Refining Communication Skills

Understanding the importance of dedicating time to foster and sustain healthy relationships. Ignoring a relationship is a major factor leading to its breakdown. The challenges of daily life can easily disrupt even strong relationships. Opportunities for quality time together often require deliberate planning and effort. A relationship needs this dedicated time and effort to develop and maintain a strong emotional bond.

If it's hard to find these moments spontaneously, make them a priority in your schedule. Plan regular times to connect with your partner. Use this scheduled time to discuss important matters, make plans, solve problems, or strengthen your bond. And if there are no pressing issues, use this time to deepen your existing connection and enjoy each other's presence.

Developing Effective Communication Skills

Expressing your thoughts and feelings without considering their impact can harm a relationship. For a healthy interpersonal connection, certain skills are necessary. The goal of skilled listening is to create a bridge of understanding. Empathy, awareness, and a real connection can't happen without them. Active listening is essential for creating this bridge.

There are two crucial aspects of active listening:

1. Genuine Understanding: Merely saying "I understand" isn't enough. Your perception might differ from what the speaker intends to convey. Avoid assuming you understand and seek to clarify.
2. Communication as a Process: Communication isn't just about exchanging information; it's a continuous process. The true value in communication lies in the expressions of love, care, and commitment, which come from respecting and valuing your relationship.

The Role of Active Listening. Active listening involves paraphrasing, which means summarizing in your own words what the speaker just said. It shows you've understood both the content and the emotions involved. This process indicates respect and appreciation for the speaker's effort, and your commitment to clear understanding. It also helps prevent misunderstandings and the potential escalation of conflicts. For example, responding with empathy and understanding to a concern about not being informed of late arrivals, rather than defensively, can prevent conflict.

Clarification is also a part of active listening. It involves asking questions until you fully comprehend the speaker's message. This is crucial before explaining your perspective.

Active listening requires openness. Without it, you're essentially dismissing the other person's words. Open listening means suspending judgment during the conversation. The focus is on understanding the speaker's thoughts, not on explaining your own viewpoint. Agreement is secondary at this stage and can be addressed once understanding is achieved.

The Five Steps of Effective Communication

Effective communication in relationships can be achieved by following these five steps:

Step 1: Initiating the Conversation: The partner who has an issue begins by expressing their feelings related to a specific event, using the format, "I felt _____ (emotion), _____ when _____ (event) _____." During this, the listener should be fully attentive, facing the speaker without distractions, open in posture, and maintaining comfortable eye contact.

Step 2: Expressing the Problem: The speaker details their problem, feelings, and thoughts. They should also suggest what they would like to happen differently and propose a solution. It's important to use "I feel" statements, focusing on one's feelings and perspective, rather than blaming the other person.

For example, saying "I'm so angry about being spoken to like that!" instead of "You made me so angry when you spoke to me like that!" which can sound accusatory.

Step 3: **Reflecting and Summarizing:** The listener's role is to reflect and summarize the speaker's problem and feelings from the speaker's point of view, using similar language. Reflecting means to repeat back what you heard and understood about what the speaker said. The listener should then ask for confirmation, like "Did I understand you correctly?" and "Did I leave anything out?" The listener should remain non-defensive and empathetic, continually reflecting and summarizing until the speaker feels fully heard and understood.

Step 4: **Validating and Acknowledging:** After the speaker has finished expressing their thoughts and feelings, the listener acknowledges and validates the speaker's right to feel and think as they do. The listener should remember that the speaker's message is about the speaker's experiences and feelings, not necessarily about the listener, even if it involves something the listener did.

Step 5: Proposing Solutions: The speaker, having fully expressed their issue, is responsible for suggesting a change or solution. If they are unable to propose one, they can continue the discussion and then refer to the OLIVE process (in a previous chapter) for joint solution-finding.

Throughout these steps, the listener's role is to understand and empathize without trying to correct or challenge the speaker. The goal is connection, not correction. The listener should let go of the need to be right and focus on understanding the speaker's perspective.

The Listeners' Role in Communication

Even if the listener's actions may have initiated the conversation, it's essential to understand that they are hearing the speaker's emotional reaction to these actions. The speaker is sharing their personal internal experience - thoughts and feelings - with the expectation that the listener will provide respectful and supportive attention. It's not necessary for the listener to agree with the speaker; what matters is listening to each other with trust, respect, and support. This practice is a fundamental part of any loving relationship, regardless of whether the message is positive or negative.

At this stage, the listener should express gratitude to the speaker for their trust in sharing their experiences. Then, the listener can ask if they may respond. However, this response should not be a counterargument or rebuttal.

The focus is on understanding and connecting, not winning an argument. This isn't an opportunity for a counterargument. Remember, the goal is not to "win" but to understand and connect.

Exchanging Communication Roles

The listener becomes the new speaker (Speaker 2), and the original speaker assumes the role of active listener (Listener 2). Before Speaker 2 starts, they should recap the initial speaker's concerns to ensure they have understood correctly. It's important to remember the conversation is centered on resolving the problem, not on personal differences, and is aimed at mutual support rather than winning a debate.

Speaker 2 then shares their perspective on the proposed changes, explaining why they may or may not be feasible. It's important to remember that this isn't Speaker 2's issue, so rehashing the problem isn't necessary. Speaker 2 then addresses whether the proposed solution is feasible, explaining their viewpoint. Since the problem originally belonged to the first speaker, Speaker 2 does not need to revisit the problem but can express their feelings and thoughts about the situation, following the same communication steps outlined earlier.

Once both individuals have shared their perspectives, they can use the OLIVE method from Chapter 9 to collaboratively work through the problem-solving process and reach a resolution. This method emphasizes cooperative problem-solving and aims to find a resolution that takes both parties' views into account.

In effective communication, it's crucial to recognize that while the listener may have inadvertently caused the "problem". The listener's role is to provide respect and support, understanding that agreement on the matter isn't necessary. Differing perspectives are natural, but the focus should be on listening with trust, respect, and support with the intention of finding a compromise or a resolution between them.

Enhancing Communication with Empathy and Assertiveness

Empathy is a cornerstone of active listening, enabling you to emotionally and cognitively connect with the speaker. It's a key skill in healing and repairing emotional, cognitive, or spiritual damage. When learning these communication steps, it's crucial for both the speaker and the listener to adhere closely to the guidelines. Pay attention to non-verbal cues like body language, facial expressions, and tone of voice. If these come across as condescending, judgmental, or sarcastic, this can trigger negative emotional responses, obstructing empathic and open communication.

It's important to remember that communication can be affected by intense emotions linked to past experiences. Feelings of vulnerability, insecurity, or fear may disrupt the ability to communicate effectively. If this happens, strategies from previous chapters, including the OLIVE strategy, can be helpful. These techniques, combined with guided meditations, can support empathic and reflective listening.

Recognizing that certain triggers or reactions stem from past experiences rather than the present can greatly enhance trust and intimacy in a relationship. Handling these together through empathic listening is beneficial. It's also helpful if partners can manage their negative responses while giving each other the benefit of the doubt. Engaging in artistic expression as a couple can be a powerful healing process, beneficial both individually and for the relationship.

Assertive communication is similar to active listening. It involves stating your wants, needs, and feelings. The goal isn't to hurt, win, or blame but to negotiate for change. The steps for assertive communication, especially useful in situations with high emotional intensity and low compromise willingness, are outlined in the following "Pause & Reflect" section. While less formal methods may suffice for simpler situations, adhering to these steps shows deep respect and concern for the other party and can improve the relationship.

^Pause & Reflect ~ Creating a Supportive Environment for Good Communication^

Guidelines
- Schedule a time and place that will accommodate both parties.
- Briefly inform the other individual of the general topic so they can feel ready to talk.
- Start by describing the problem, your thoughts and feelings, and your hopes and dreams surrounding the issue.
- Describe what the ideal situation would look like.
- Make a suggestion that might help improve the situation while remaining sensitive to the other person's needs.
- Describe how the changes will be helpful.
- Describe the likely outcome if changes are not made.
- Listen respectfully and openly to the thoughts and feelings of the other person.
- Discuss solutions that integrate both positions.
- Describe where you can compromise and where you cannot.
- Decide on an outcome that will benefit both parties.

Exercise
Think about a problem you are experiencing in your life right now and how you might handle it using the above guidelines. What is an outcome that will benefit all parties? What would be your compromise point? What would be your deal-breaker? What would be the likely outcome if changes are not made? Can you communicate all of these ideas respectfully, using your assertiveness skills?

_____
_____

^Pause & Reflect ~Assertive Communication^

The Three P's of Relational Communication

In relational communication, especially with couples who experience high emotions and conflicts, a straightforward strategy that both authors use in couples counseling, "The Three P" Method, can be particularly effective. This approach emphasizes staying as factual as possible and minimizing emotional content during discussions, which is crucial given that the conflict level in such relationships is often already high, with many potential triggers.

Implementing this method begins with following the initial steps of assertive communication. A person might request a conversation and schedule a specific date and time. It's also beneficial to set an agenda for the discussion, but it's important to focus on only one topic at a time.

On the agreed date and time, with all involved parties present, the speaker uses the format outlined in the Pause & Reflect section below. This structured approach helps manage the conversation effectively, ensuring that it remains focused and constructive, particularly in emotionally charged situations. By adhering to this format, couples and families can address their issues more calmly and productively.

1. **First P (Problem):** Begin by stating the issue as you see it. Focus on describing the problem and why it's a concern for you, but keep this description factual, without incorporating opinions or emotions.

2. **Second P (Preference):** Next, express what you would ideally like to happen. Outline your preferred outcome or the changes you wish to see. Keep this part concise and straightforward, avoiding complex explanations.

3. **Third P (Proposal):** Finally, propose a solution. Your suggestion should aim to resolve the issue in a way that works for everyone involved, not just for you. The objective is to simplify the problem and reach a consensus efficiently and effectively.

^Pause & Reflect ~The Three P's^

> **The problem we need to talk about is (summarize just the facts – no opinions or emotions):**
>
> **First P (Problem)** – This is the problem as I see it . . . (explain why this is a problem for you personally.
>
> **Second P (Preference)** – What I would prefer is . . . (explain the outcome or the difference you would prefer to see, but be sure to keep it very short and in simple terms. Nothing complex, no explaining).
>
> **Third P (Proposal)** – What I propose is . . . (offer a suggestion that you believe might work for everyone involved, not just you. The goal is to simplify the problem and gain consensus as quickly and easily as possible).

This structured approach allows for a focused discussion on the issue at hand, helping all parties understand the problem, the desired outcome, and the proposed solution without getting bogged down by emotional or complex explanations.

Understanding and Implementing Boundaries in Social Relationships

Boundaries play a crucial role in shaping the quality, longevity, and significance of our relationships, as discussed in Chapter 3, "Guiding Principles of the Artfully Lived Life". In our social interactions, we may sometimes establish healthy boundaries and at, other times, unhealthy ones.

The first step toward adopting healthier boundaries is to recognize and understand our current practices. We develop unhealthy boundaries for various reasons – they might have been behaviors we observed growing up, or ways we found to cope with low self-esteem by overstepping others' boundaries. However, we can choose boundaries that align more closely with our values and goals.

While it's often easier to spot these behaviors in others, real change starts within ourselves. We can only control and improve our own boundary-setting. When it comes to others, we can express our preferences for healthier boundaries and then decide how to engage in those relationships. This holds true even if others in our social circle are not receptive or able to maintain socially and emotionally healthy boundaries. Our role is to communicate our boundaries clearly, offer guidance if others are open to it, and then determine our level of involvement in the relationship based on these interactions.

Establishing and Maintaining Healthy Social Boundaries

Healthy social boundaries are foundational for respectful, trusting, and responsible relationships. When two people agree to the principles of "I take care of me", "you take care of you", and "we will ask for what we need". They are creating a mutual understanding of respectful boundaries. This agreement means that each person is responsible for their own thoughts, feelings, and actions while sharing their lives through common interests, values, and activities. Such guidelines foster honorable, respectful, and loving behavior in a relationship.

It's important to recognize that if you are hurt by someone else's actions, it doesn't necessarily mean it's their fault. Each person is responsible for communicating how they are affected and what they want like to see change. Healing emotional pain is a personal responsibility, as we are the only ones who can directly address our emotional hurts. While apologies and empathetic discussions are helpful, the primary responsibility for healing lies within us.

Social Circles

When considering personal boundaries, think about who should have access to your innermost self. Healthy relationships are characterized by safety, respect for individual needs and rights, and mutual accountability for well-being. These relationships, such as close friendships, intimate partnerships, or family ties, typically exhibit appropriate boundaries and enjoy deep social, emotional, spiritual, intellectual, and physical closeness.

Conversely, relationships that violate healthy boundaries and lead to toxic interactions should have limited access to your inner core. In such relationships, it's advisable to share less information and maintain a degree of emotional distance due to the lack of protective boundaries. Relationships with friends, acquaintances, coworkers, and bosses may require more caution and a "keep at arm's length" approach until safe and consistent boundaries are established.

Personal Boundary Choices

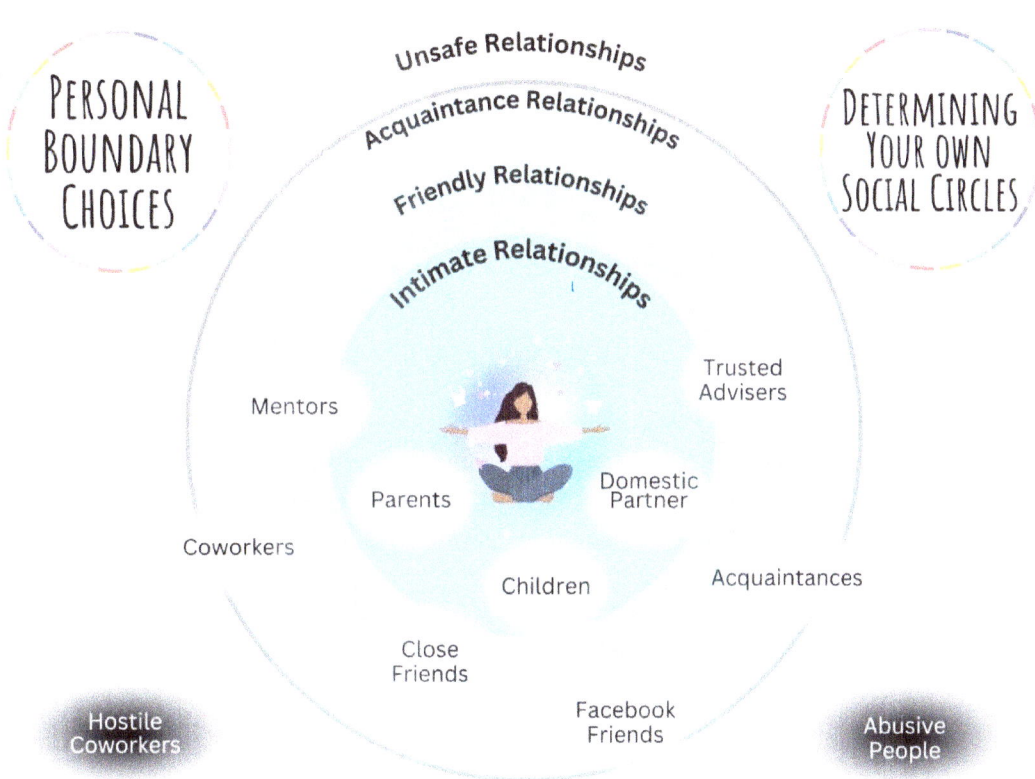

Navigating Early Intimacy and Maintaining Boundaries in Relationships

It's crucial to be cautious of relationships where closeness and intimacy are rapidly established soon after meeting. Such relationships often indicate poor emotional and social boundaries and can lead to hurt and emotional damage due to increasingly dysfunctional boundaries. Taking time to gradually get to know someone, sharing personal information slowly, allows you to preserve your identity while carefully monitoring and setting boundaries. This approach also makes it easier to adjust boundaries or end the relationship before significant harm occurs. Taking time to reveal your innermost self offers you the opportunity to see how the information will be used. For example, will it be used to discredit you in a moment of conflict? Or, will it be used to deepen the intimacy between you.

In cases of extremely destructive or emotionally dangerous relationships, it's best to maintain only a very distant or peripheral connection to your inner core self. Ideally, these relationships should be avoided. If avoidance is not possible, establish clear boundaries from the outset. The previous diagram illustrates healthy boundaries in relation to the proximity to your inner core self.

Social norms typically dictate appropriate boundaries for various types of relationships. For instance, in the provided illustration, the center area symbolizes the inner core self, akin to a personal sanctuary. Just as we wouldn't invite strangers into our homes or share personal details with unsafe individuals, the innermost part of our being is reserved for those closest to us—those who have consistently demonstrated trustworthiness.

Likewise, individuals who are emotionally or physically abusive should be allowed only minimal access to our emotional, physical, social, intellectual, or spiritual aspects. Maintaining this distance is essential for personal well-being and emotional safety.

Identifying and Addressing Unhealthy Social Boundaries

Unhealthy social boundaries can manifest in several ways. Signs of poor boundaries include oversharing personal information with just about anyone, engaging in intimate conversations upon first meeting, falling in love rapidly with someone new, or acting impulsively on sexual desires. Other indicators are touching someone without their consent, compromising personal values to appease others, engaging in sexual activities for your partner's sake rather than your own, and failing to recognize when someone violates your boundaries. These actions not only disrespect others but also compromise your own integrity and sense of self.

In family dynamics, verbal abuse often occurs unintentionally and isn't typically premeditated. Addressing abusive behaviors in families isn't about assigning blame but about fostering interactions that avoid causing unnecessary pain. Developing self-awareness and relationship skills, along with recognizing and upholding appropriate boundaries, is vital for creating a family environment conducive to personal growth and healthy relationships. This approach helps maintain a respectful and nurturing atmosphere where each family member can thrive.

Journal Lines

_____
_____
_____
_____
_____
_____
_____
_____
_____
_____

Social Competence, Forgiveness, and Emotional Health

Social competence is built upon a blend of skills and personal attributes that enhance interactions between individuals. Effective self-management and understanding of the world around us are deeply connected to emotional self-awareness. This involves the capacity to monitor, evaluate oneself, and organize information into practical action plans, a skill known as "social judgment."

The social reasoning skills explored in this chapter are crucial for engaging positively with others and building enduring social relationships. Our brains are inherently social, requiring emotionally supportive environments for optimal growth. Children deprived of emotional nurturing can develop into adults who are fearful, emotionally unstable, or even dangerous.

In life, we encounter various negative emotions like hurt, sadness, and disappointment, whether from our actions or others'. Humans are capable of extraordinary compassion and kindness but also of significant harm. While we might expect fair treatment, the reality is that people are imperfect and make mistakes, sometimes severe ones.

Forgiveness is often described as a paramount virtue, not a sign of weakness but strength and courage. It's important to understand that forgiveness is a choice. Forgiving too hastily can lead to deeper resentment, but not attempting to forgive can harm one's physical, mental, and emotional health.

Robert Enright, in his book "Forgiveness is a Choice", discusses common misconceptions about forgiveness. Forgiveness doesn't mean condoning, forgetting, or ignoring the offense. It's not a sign of weakness or self-disrespect. Forgiveness is a gradual process that involves decision-making, desire, and willingness to cultivate compassion and see the offender in a new light.

This challenging process of forgiveness can lead to a greater sense of freedom, healthier relationships, improved well-being, reduced anxiety and depression, and better physical health, including lower blood pressure and heart rate.

^Pause & Reflect ~ A Dangerous Relationship^

Noelle Nelson (1997) has identified a dangerous relationship as possessing the following seven warning signs:

A whirlwind beginning	Possessiveness
Emotional extremes	Blame
Verbal abuse	Insensitivity
Past or present violence	Gaslighting or mixed messages

Recognizing these warning signs is critical to the ability to avoid them. Every one of these qualities is characteristic of unhealthy boundaries. Abusive statements are those that define you in ways that you know are not true about who you are. These statements might involve what you feel, want, or believe. Verbal abuse is a lie that's being told to you or to others about you that would lead you to think you are less than or different than you really are. It can be verbal, such as in the statement, "You're just too sensitive," or behavioral, such as when someone uses a facial expression to discount you. Both types of responses convey a basic lack of respect for the person you are. Are you aware of any verbal abuse you have experienced in the past, or might be experiencing currently?

_____
_____
_____

How does this verbal abuse affect your life?
_____
_____

How might you begin setting boundaries that will improve your level of comfort, using the assertiveness tools you have learned thus far?
_____
_____
_____

In exchange for the hard work, you will experience a greater sense of freedom, healthier relationships, improved well-being, fewer anxious and depressive symptoms, and lower blood pressure and heart rate.

Chapter 10: Social MindView Skills ~ Guided Meditation: Forgiveness

Let's begin our meditation by engaging in a controlled breathing exercise. Inhale deeply for a count of four, hold that breath for another count of four, then exhale slowly over a four-count. We'll perform this breathing cycle three times.

Commence now: Inhale... 2... 3... 4... hold... 2... 3... 4... exhale... 2... 3... 4... hold... 2... 3... 4. Again, Inhale... 2... 3... 4... hold... 2... 3... 4... exhale... 2... 3... 4... hold... 2... 3... 4. One more time Inhale... 2... 3... 4... hold... 2... 3... 4... exhale... 2... 3... 4... hold... 2... 3... 4. Now, let your breathing return to its natural rhythm.

In the context of the Well-Being: The Artfully Lived Life program, we acknowledge that the challenges we encounter can be more successfully navigated by utilizing The Tools for the Artist Within. This meditation focuses on the concept of Forgiveness—a deliberate choice and an ongoing process. Embracing this process can lead to a profound sense of liberation and well-being.

Concentrate solely on your breathing. As you breathe in and out, visualize inhaling and exhaling a pure, cleansing light. Imagine this light gathering in your chest, radiating throughout your body, bringing relaxation and tranquility. With each breath, let this sensation of calm spread from your chest to every part of your body, leading you into a state of deep relaxation. Feel the soothing light circulating, creating an aura of peace. Allow this relaxation to ascend through your neck, face, and head, enveloping you in profound tranquility.

Now, envision yourself looking at the palm of your hand and discovering a beautiful, silvery sponge. This sponge, a gift from the universe or your higher self, is designed to absorb and eliminate any negative thoughts or feelings that hinder your progress toward realizing your full potential. Imagine all feelings of anger, hurt, resentment, and any other emotions associated with a lack of forgiveness flowing into your hand, being drawn into the sponge. Watch as the sponge, which once shone brightly, darkens with the absorbed negativity. But fear not; this sponge is crafted for this purpose—it neutralizes the negativity without being harmed.

Now it is time to release these negative feelings. Clench your hand tightly around the sponge, tighter still, and observe the dark essence draining from the sponge, seeping into the ground, where it dissipates harmlessly into the earth. Slowly unclench your hand and notice the sponge is now restored to its original silvery sheen, free of any negativity. Your mind and body are cleansed of these burdens.

Finally, take a deep, rejuvenating breath, filling your abdomen with air, then exhale completely. Visualize breathing in and out the purifying white light, feeling it spread relaxation, calmness, and healing throughout your body. Return to a state of peacefulness, fully relaxed, aware only of the steady, comforting rhythm of your breath.

As you breathe deeply, let's reaffirm the power of releasing negative emotions. Remember, any distressing feeling, including pain, resentment, and feelings of betrayal, can be released without harming the symbolic sponge or the earth. However, holding onto these feelings can harm you. When you're ready to release them, imagine them flowing into the sponge. Then, clench your hand into a fist, sending these negative emotions into the earth, away from your being.

The sponge in your mental imagery will always be there for you, ready to absorb any unsettling emotions. Visualize these emotions seeping into the sponge as you hold it in your hand. Squeeze your fist tightly, allowing the darkness and distress to leave the sponge and be absorbed by the earth, where they can cause no harm. This process is a cleansing ritual for both your mind and body. Inhale deeply, drawing in healing energy, and then exhale, visualizing each breath as a purifying light that infuses your body with relaxation, calmness, and healing. Embrace this peaceful state, deeply relaxed, and attuned to the steady rhythm of your breath.

Recognize that within you lies the ability to accomplish any task or overcome any obstacle. Your deeper, wiser self is there to guide and support you. As you listen to and trust the power of your mind, you'll find yourself growing in peacefulness, courage, and strength. These qualities are inherent within you, available for you to embrace as you take time to listen to your inner wisdom.

Now, focus on your breathing. Spend a few moments in this tranquil space, appreciating all you have experienced and learned during this meditation.

Reflect on Wayne Dyer's words, "We can choose to align ourselves with our desire to live peacefully in this world, regardless of external circumstances... We can maintain an inner peace even amidst external turmoil." Arthur Egendorf reminds us, "Each of us, individually and together, is responsible for creating joy in our lives, here and now." This requires that we detach from thoughts of hatred and negativity despite the challenges and darkness we may encounter in the world.

As we delve deeper into our meditation, we uncover our innate balance and potential for peace. Amidst the acts of chaos in the world, countless acts of love and peace prevail. The Serenity Prayer captures this essence: "Grant me the serenity to accept the things I cannot change; courage to change the things I can; and wisdom to know the difference." Resisting unchangeable adversity only amplifies its control over us. Therefore, the key is not to fight but to focus our energy on aspects within our control, primarily ourselves. By advocating for our beliefs and standing for peace, we reshape the world's narrative to one of harmony. We transform our experience of the world by altering our interaction with it.

Wisdom dictates that we must make choices. Accepting what we cannot change can empower us to focus on what we can influence. While others may choose a path of turmoil, we recognize their right to choose their journey, understanding that our energy is best spent on forging our path of peace and acceptance.

Now, gently bring your focus back to your breathing. We will transition out of this meditative state with a four-count breathing pattern. Let's begin.

Inhale... 2... 3... 4... hold... 2... 3... 4... exhale... 2... 3... 4... and hold... 2... 3... 4. Again, inhale... 2... 3... 4... hold... 2... 3... 4... exhale... 2... 3... 4... and hold... 2... 3... 4. And one last time, inhale... 2... 3... 4... hold... 2... 3... 4... exhale... 2... 3... 4 and hold... 2... 3... 4. Now, let your breathing return to its natural rhythm. When you feel ready, gently open your eyes, carrying with you the sense of peace and clarity gained from this meditation.

Chapter 11: Life Strategies for Well-being ~ Spiritual MindView Skills

"The quieter you are able to become, the more you are able to hear." ~Rumi

In therapy, one of the most common questions people ask is "Why?" They wonder why certain things are happening to them and if there's more to life than their current experiences. While these questions often lead to discussions about religion and religiosity, there's another perspective to consider, that is, the Spiritual MindView and its significance in our lives. As we've seen earlier in this book, the brain naturally seeks to understand the context of its existence. Answers to these existential questions can profoundly influence our life choices.

Why is recognizing the Spiritual MindView essential? Zohar and Marshall (2000) posed critical questions about the need for spiritual intelligence to find deeper meaning in life. They wondered whether the changing times, evolving human needs, or a new stage in the evolution of intelligence are driving this quest. We live in an era where traditional culture, customs, and social norms don't always provide the answers we seek. In the absence of clear understanding, many turn to ego-driven pursuits for fulfillment, such as materialism, substance abuse, anger, or promiscuity.

But what about those who are not religious? There are individuals worldwide who do not adhere to any religious beliefs. Yet, emerging research suggests that certain brain areas respond to what might be considered "spiritual" content. This observation highlights the importance of defining what we mean by a Spiritual MindView, especially for those who might not traditionally engage in religious practices or beliefs. Understanding this concept can offer a broader perspective on finding meaning and purpose in life beyond conventional religious frameworks.

Broadening the Definition of Spiritual Experience

Spiritual experiences aren't confined to religious practices; they can encompass everyday activities and sensations that you might not typically consider "spiritual". For instance, taking a moment to savor the scent of a rose, enjoying the flavors of a well-prepared meal, feeling the texture of your pet's fur or a loved one's hair, or listening to the sounds of nature like birdsong, waterfalls, or ocean waves. Spending time fully engaging with these sensory experiences can nurture the spiritual centers in your brain, often associated with the ventrolateral prefrontal cortex. These experiences may also provide a sense of meaning to one's life beyond routine, everyday experiences. As suggested by Christina Puchelski, MD, "Spirituality is the aspect of humanity that refers to the way individuals seek and express meaning and purpose and the way they experience their connectedness to the moment, to self, to others, to nature, and to the significant or sacred."

It's important to understand that one can be religious without being spiritual, and vice versa. Additionally, it's entirely possible to integrate spirituality within religious beliefs and practices. The concept of the Spiritual MindView focuses on exploring what is purposeful and meaningful in our lives, like striving to excel in our endeavors and comprehending our role in the broader human experience.

Previously, we described the Spiritual MindView as a quieter presence rather than other aspects of our mental council, often called as the "quiet inner voice". This aspect of our consciousness represents a deep sense of inner knowing, insight, and understanding about choices that serve our best interests. The Spiritual MindView, encompassing both conscious and unconscious elements, provides a wealth of information derived from life's experiences. The pursuit of our values-guided goals contributes to what we might call spiritual intelligence. This involves learning lessons about values and meaning as we work towards our objectives. While we might initially seek popularity, attention, or wealth, we often discover that achieving these goals doesn't necessarily increase our happiness. Conversely, when we direct our efforts towards meaningful endeavors, we frequently find that the journey itself is more rewarding than the result. The path to achieving something we deeply value can be more fulfilling than the ultimate reward.

Defining and Developing Spiritual Intelligence

The term Spiritual Intelligence (SQ) is relatively new, with various interpretations. In this context, we view spiritual intelligence as encompassing deep compassion, conscience, and commitment to human values, coupled with an awareness and concern for the well-being of ourselves and all beings in the universe. Danah Zohar and Ian Marshall (2000) describe Spiritual Intelligence as the intelligence we use to find meaning and value, to place our actions and lives in a broader, meaning-rich context, and to evaluate the significance of different life paths and actions. They propose that Spiritual Intelligence underpins both emotional and intellectual intelligence, terming it the "ultimate intelligence". They argue that while IQ is essential for effective thinking, Emotional Intelligence and Intellectual IQ alone cannot fully explain the complexity of human experience.

Cindy Wigglesworth defines spiritual intelligence as acting with wisdom and compassion while maintaining peace, regardless of circumstances. She further elucidates this concept through 21 skills, organized into nine steps towards achieving a "Higher Self". The progression begins with 1) articulating your belief system and 2) understanding your purpose in this life. The third step involves 3) choosing and comprehending your values. This is best achieved by becoming self-aware of the choices you're making. 4) She emphasizes the importance of recognizing who controls these decisions - your ego or a higher, wiser source. This source, whether internal or external, should transcend the ego. 5) This desire leads to viewing life with awe and wonder. Practicing this connection to something greater than ourselves involves 6) learning from diverse perspectives, 7) acknowledging our limitations, and 8) staying true to our inner perceptions or spiritual insights. As we endeavor to understand ourselves and others better, 9) we also seek to grasp the teachings and concepts from the spiritual realm.

These steps guide us in nurturing our spiritual intelligence, enhancing our understanding of life's profound dimensions and the interconnectedness of all things.

Core Competencies of Spiritual Intelligence

Spiritual intelligence can be viewed as a set of competencies or skills. Notable in this field, Robert A. Emmons (2000) identified five key abilities indicative of spiritual intelligence. According to Emmons, spiritually intelligent individuals typically demonstrate: (a) the capacity for transcendence beyond the immediate physical and psychological realities; (b) the ability to experience heightened spiritual states of consciousness; (c) the capability to imbue everyday activities, events, and relationships with a sense of the sacred; (d) the skill to use spiritual resources for problem-solving in life; and (e) the capacity for virtuous behavior, such as showing forgiveness, gratitude, humility, and compassion. These virtues align with The Artist's Tools mentioned earlier, including Acceptance, Forgiveness, Self-Compassion, Commitment, and Gratitude.

Emmons also proposed that spirituality might be considered a set of competencies within the broader definition of intelligence, which traditionally focuses on adaptive problem-solving. While spirituality's components are challenging to quantify in scientific research, its significance is growing as we deepen our understanding of brain physiology and the connection between a Spiritual MindView and brain structure. For instance, studies using Single Photon Emission Computed Tomography (SPECT) scans have shown increased activity in the right temporal lobes of the brain when individuals listen to peaceful music or engage in meditation. Daniel Amen's research using SPECT scans also found that these brain regions are active during moments of insight and problem-solving, often referred to as "Aha moments".

Our inherent human needs for love, safety, and acceptance shape our capacity for spiritual intelligence. When these needs are fulfilled, we attain the emotional liberty to delve into our inner knowing and understanding. When the noise of emotional drama and our often-obsessive inner critic drop away, this is when we can hear our quieter and wiser Spiritual MindView. It is important that we use our tools and skills to go there more often. The principles and core values we choose to live by then become integral to our decision-making processes, influencing all aspects of our lives and choices.

Interplay of Core Values and Spirituality in Decision-Making

Core values fundamentally shape our beliefs about our place in the universe and our understanding of life's purposes. They form the bedrock of our belief systems, steering our choices in significant and routine matters. For instance, a core value like honesty influences our decision to be truthful. Similarly, the value of integrity drives us to act with kindness, empathy, and respect consistently, not just when it's convenient or easy.

The way we incorporate these core values into our daily experiences hinges on the guiding principles that direct our actions and decisions. For example, if living addiction-free is a core value, the corresponding guiding principle could involve avoiding environments or associations that tempt addictive behaviors. Similarly, a core value of serving others might manifest in engaging with service-oriented organizations and demonstrating personal traits like selflessness, generosity, empathy, and respect for all human life.

Our core values clarify what matters most to us and inform the guiding principles that shape our choices. These choices lay the foundation of our lives, turning our behaviors and decisions into reflections of our values and the principles we uphold. When our actions, values, and principles are aligned, we often experience profound peace and joy. This inner peace guides our meaningful life choices and provides support during challenging times. Living in accordance with and sharing these values often gives our lives deeper meaning.

The following exercise is designed to assist you in identifying and understanding your own core values and principles, aiding in the alignment of your actions and beliefs.

Exploring the Impact of Spiritual MindView

Spirituality encompasses various interpretations, not all of which refer to a higher power. A common understanding of spirituality involves moving beyond the ego, seeking a deeper sense of self-awareness and purpose. Spirituality is also seen as an expression of creativity, the ability to love unconditionally, and a state of integration and self-actualization. Integration refers to the harmonious combination of elements to create a balanced whole, while self-actualization is the realization of one's potential and abilities. Additionally, spirituality can be viewed as a journey of continuous growth, personal meaning development through wisdom and maturity, mastery of personal responsibility, and adherence to moral choices. In some perspectives, spirituality also encompasses faith in a higher power or supreme being.

^Pause & Reflect ~ Your Core Values^

> Examples of core values might include honesty, generosity, courage, honor, freedom, and wisdom. How do you define right and wrong when it comes to:
> - How to treat other people? _____
> _____
> - A Sense of morality? _____
> _____
> - Can you describe a "credo," or a moral code, that you live by? _____
> _____
> - What is the most important thing in your life? _____
> _____
> _____
>
> Below are ways of expressing core values. Which of them apply to your life? Please circle.
> - Safety, security, money, fame, success, love, fun, relationships, approval, need, compassion, power, duty, faith, purity, recognition, fear, commitment, autonomy, sacrifice, obedience, honor, independence, selflessness, selfishness, hope, peace, kindness, vision.
> - Do your behaviors reflect your guiding principles? _____
> _____
> _____

These various interpretations of spirituality ultimately circle back to fundamental existential questions: "Why am I here?" "What is the meaning of life?" and "What is my purpose?" In our journey toward answering these questions for our own lives, developing our values and using The Artist's Tools to understand better and listen to our Spiritual MindView is an invaluable practice.

Mind/Body Studies and Spiritual Practices

Research has consistently shown that practices like meditation activate brain areas associated with the integration of information. Studies have found that individuals who identify a clear sense of purpose often experience inner peace, calmness, and satisfaction (Boudreaux, 2002). Additionally, numerous benefits have been attributed to regular practices of prayer and meditation, including:
- Reduced stress levels,
- Improved sleep quality,
- Decreased depression and anxiety,
- Fewer headaches,
- Enhanced relationships, and
- Increased longevity.

These findings underscore the significant impact that spiritual practices and a well-developed Spiritual MindView can have on both mental and physical health, contributing to an overall sense of well-being and fulfillment.

^Pause & Reflect ~ Spiritual Code^

What is your personal philosophy about spirituality? _____
_____
_____

Do you have a spiritual code that you live by? _____
_____
_____

What is it? _____
_____
_____

Do you exemplify a spiritual code in your life? How? _____
_____
_____

The Positive Effects of Spiritual Practices on Well-being

Survey studies have shown that individuals in North America and Australia often turn to spiritual practices as a method for coping with depression. Activities like meditation, prayer, and attending church services have been commonly reported among patients as coping strategies (Payman et al., 2008). Furthermore, for those dealing with significant medical issues and the accompanying anxiety, engaging in spiritual practices such as prayer and meditation has been linked to numerous positive outcomes. These benefits include enhanced overall well-being, increased feelings of resilience, and a reduction in symptoms (Boudreaux et al., 2002). A recent study by Antonietti et al. (2019) has shown that spirituality and religiosity are positive predictors of subjective well-being.

In conclusion, irrespective of the specific definition one adheres to, spiritual practices offer many benefits. These benefits span physical, emotional, social, and cognitive aspects, highlighting the value of understanding and incorporating spirituality to achieve overall well-being. This connection between spiritual practices and improved health and resilience underscores the potential advantages of embracing a spiritual perspective daily.

Cultivating Inner Peace through Spiritual MindView Practices

Achieving inner tranquility involves relaxing your body and mind and then introspectively observing your experiences. This calm state allows the brain to process and integrate psychological content, making it accessible and beneficial later. Without this period for integration, the brain might be unprepared for life's challenges, leading to feeling caught off guard, anxiety, or stress. Experiencing excessive or chronic stress or tension can indicate a lack of internal resources, strengths, or skills needed for daily life. However, this inner strength and consolidation can be regained through practices that foster inner quiet.

Activities like meditation, prayer, guided visualization, and journaling can help reestablish a sense of centeredness. This restoration of inner peace and quiet builds confidence and a sense of connectedness with your inner self – the part of you that is known to you but may not be visible or accessible to others. This connection fortifies confidence, self-awareness, and personal identity, which can sometimes become obscured in the hustle of daily life. Without this inner connection, there's a risk of losing your sense of self, identity, and direction.

Meditation and Mindfulness

Many contemplative traditions offer pathways to achieve balance, peace, and well-being. One such tradition, mindfulness, which was introduced in an earlier chapter has been adopted in Western society for both medical and mental health purposes.

The concepts of mindfulness have been incorporated into the guided meditations throughout this book. Additionally, adopting a regular mindfulness meditation practice can be greatly beneficial. There are numerous resources available, including books, CDs, and websites that teach the principles of mindfulness. Prominent practitioners in this field include Jon Kabat-Zinn, Jack Kornfield, Tara Brach, Thich Nhat Hanh, and Rick Hanson, whose works offer valuable insights into practicing mindfulness.

Enhancing Spiritual MindView through Meditation and Inner Guidance

As you've progressed through the guided meditations in previous chapters, you've had the chance to quieten your mind and turn inward. For optimal results, it's beneficial to find a peaceful place for meditation, perhaps starting in your mental "safe place" or engaging in a focused breathing exercise. While relaxing your mind, embrace the silence and concentrate on your breathing or a chosen mantra. If you find your thoughts wandering to daily tasks or concerns, gently acknowledge this by naming your thoughts, such as "thinking", "planning", "worrying", etc. and then redirect your attention back to your breathing or mantra. With continued practice, you'll gain clarity and find a method that suits you best.

Initiating your meditation with a prayer, spiritual reading, or inspirational music can also be effective. Concentrate on uplifting elements like music, art, color, or beautiful imagery. Visualize peaceful settings such as mountains, lakes, or the ocean. Begin by centering yourself by focusing on your breath and then listening to the inner silence. There's no strict duration for meditation to be effective. Even a few minutes can yield positive changes, though aiming for a 5 to 10-minute session initially is a good start. After meditating, pay attention to your body's sensations and any changes, accepting them openly. Another approach is to spend a few minutes observing your thoughts and feelings without judgment, embracing your inner experience as if listening to a close friend.

Seeking Inner Guidance

As you become more comfortable with meditation, focus on a question or issue needing clarification. In a state of acceptance, observe your inner responses. Experiment with verbalizing different solutions to your problem as if you've already chosen a path: "I think I will….". Then, listen for your body's response, particularly in the midsection. A positive answer might feel like expansion, warmth, or peace, while a negative one could feel like constriction or tension. If you receive no clear response, it may indicate that either option is suitable, or you might need more information before making a decision.

Alternatively, consider reviewing your options before sleep and seeking guidance upon waking. If you're still uncertain, reflect on past decisions - both successful and unsuccessful ones - to help identify the feelings associated with good and poor judgment. These exercises are valuable for cultivating your ability to recognize and trust your inner guidance, enhancing your judgment and decision-making process.

Remember that there is a central location in your brain for accessing, processing, and utilizing wisdom to observe and consider life's experiences on a deeper level. The more we access that area through practice, the better integrated, and the more effective we will be in finding wise solutions to our problems.

Understanding the Boundaries of Inner Wisdom

In prior chapters, we've explored healthy boundaries in physical, emotional, social, and intellectual aspects of our lives. Discussing healthy boundaries for the Spiritual MindView is equally crucial for The Artfully Lived Life process.

In their book "Boundaries", Cloud and Townsend (1992) address common misconceptions about the implications of setting personal boundaries. These myths include the belief that having firm boundaries is selfish, unloving, or disobedient and that boundaries result in harm to us or others. Other misconceptions are that boundaries signify anger, cause guilt, or damage relationships. However, when we see ourselves as stewards of our lives, our responsibilities become more evident. We are obliged to safeguard our spiritual and emotional growth from all forms of harm - verbal, physical, intellectual, social, or spiritual. Healthy boundaries are founded on love, honesty, and trust, emphasizing the equal importance and respect of everyone's best interests. The result of appropriate spiritual boundaries is an increase in safety, confidence, trust, integrity, and maturity.

The absence of boundaries equates to a lack of personal responsibility. The traits listed below indicate not just a deficiency in boundaries but also a failure to take responsibility for our inner experiences. These behaviors often lead to the violation of our own rights and those of others, promoting one individual's gain at another's expense.

The purpose of setting boundaries is twofold: to establish guidelines for healthy interactions and to enable us to take responsibility for what we can control—our thoughts, feelings, desires, and needs. It requires relinquishing control and manipulation over others' time, space, emotions, words, and truths and taking charge of our own.

Inner wisdom recognizes that our truths are personal to us. We can share our truth with others, given their consent, while respecting that they have their own truths. Synchrony between beliefs and emotions can be magical but rare in some relationships. It's vital to distinguish when our ego or arrogance is speaking instead of our inner wisdom and to respect the differences between ourselves and others. By responsibly maintaining wisdom boundaries, we not only foster personal growth and spiritual transformation but also deepen respect and intimacy in our relationships.

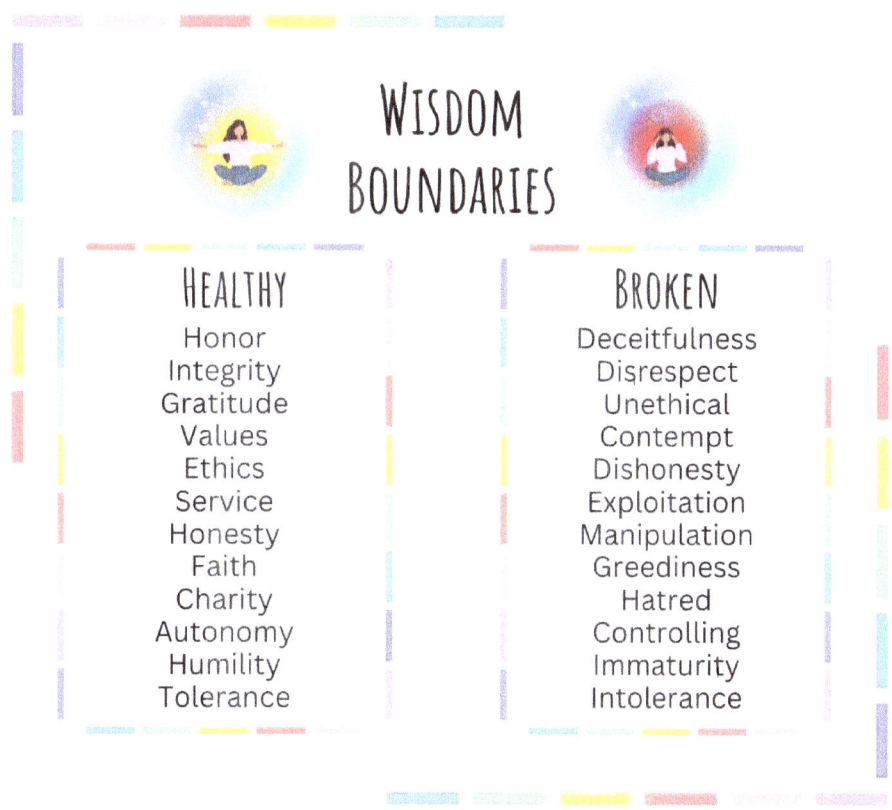

Exploring Wisdom Competencies and Their Impact

Recent research has established a strong correlation between certain wisdom traits and various aspects of well-being. These traits have been linked to physical and mental health, perceived well-being, resilience, and positive outlook during challenging times. In 2010, a panel of experts, led by Jeste et al., reached a consensus on the defining characteristics of wisdom.

Later, in 2019, Thomas and colleagues expanded this set of wisdom competencies to closely relate to physical health, mental health, and overall well-being. These competencies include:

1. <u>General Knowledge and Social Decision-Making</u>: This encompasses the ability to provide sound advice, knowledge, and life skills.
2. <u>Emotional Regulation:</u> This involves managing and controlling one's emotions effectively.
3. <u>Prosocial Behaviors:</u> Traits like empathy, compassion, altruism, and a sense of fairness fall under this category.
4. <u>Insight:</u> This is the capacity to deeply understand oneself and one's actions.
5. <u>Value Relativism:</u> This involves being tolerant of diverse values, non-judgmental, and accepting different value systems.
6. <u>Decisiveness:</u> The ability to make quick and effective decisions is a key component.
7. <u>Spirituality:</u> This refers to a sense of connectedness with oneself, nature, or a transcendent entity like the soul or God.

In a follow-up article (Thomas et al., 2019), they introduced a concise, 7-item wisdom assessment tool known as the Abbreviated San Diego Wisdom Scale (SD-WISE-7). The next Pause and Reflect section in this book provides an opportunity for you to evaluate your wisdom qualities. It invites you to consider which aspects are enhancing your well-being and which might be lacking, helping you understand the role of wisdom in your life more comprehensively.

^Pause & Reflect ~ SD-WISE-7^

Think about the following questions and answer yes or no. (Scoring is not provided as the purpose of this summary is to provide insight and understanding rather than clinical measurement.

1) Do you tend to postpone making decisions as long as you can?   Y N
2) Do you remain calm under pressure or are you easily triggered?   Y N
3) Do you engage in self-evaluation?   Y N
4) Do your spiritual beliefs increase your sense of inner strength?   Y N
5) Do you enjoy conversations that involve different points of view?   Y N
6) Do you avoid situations where your help may be needed?   Y N
7) Do you know what to say when others need your help?   Y N

Thomas et al., 2021. Adapted from the abbreviated San Diego Wisdom Scale (SD-WISE-7) and Jeste-Thomas Wisdom Index (JTWI)

Integrating MindViews for a Consistent Personal Wisdom System

In addition to the previously discussed characteristics, an essential aspect of the Spiritual MindView is the ability to harmonize the various MindViews into a consistent system within an individual's personality. Ultimately, you are the author of your values, desires, and behaviors. Nevertheless, discrepancies among the values, desires, and behaviors associated with different MindViews can lead to feelings of discomfort, insecurity, or confusion.

For instance, optimal functioning of the Emotional MindView focuses on emotional regulation, self control, and the capacities for compassion, empathy, and emotional connectedness with others. The Social MindView emphasizes social engagement, the development of effective social skills, and the rewards and fulfillment derived from relationships. The Thinking MindView is about engaging with the world through curiosity, a desire for understanding, and effectiveness in various life domains.

Emotions, thoughts, social connections, and physical well-being can all positively and negatively influence our behavior. Understanding these influences offers valuable insights into our feelings and actions. Inconsistencies between these aspects can lead to conflicts within an individual's personality.

The key to resolving these conflicts lies in trusting our deeper, wiser self and seeking guidance from our Spiritual MindView. Achieving congruence within the "MindView Council"—the collective of our emotional, social, thinking, and spiritual perspectives—enables us to make compassionate and wise decisions. These decisions enhance our life experiences, aligning our actions with deeper values and understanding. This integrative approach helps us navigate life with greater consistency and harmony between our inner values and outward actions.

Your inner guide is a resource for decision-making, offering clarity on problems and revealing solutions that might not be immediately apparent. It can provide insight into what is needed in certain situations and help determine if an action or decision aligns with your best interests. Like a sage counselor, your inner guide can aid in achieving your goals, quieting inner fears, and fostering a sense of calm confidence. The subtle, often quiet voice of this guide can, at times, be far more influential than the entirety of our emotional experiences.

By attuning to this inner voice, you can unlock significant achievements in your life. Listening and understanding your inner guide can be a powerful tool for personal growth and self-realization, guiding you toward fulfilling your potential and navigating life's challenges with greater wisdom and confidence.

The purpose of this guided meditation is to give you an opportunity to go within and identify what you might call an inner guide. An inner guide can be whatever feels right for you. It can represent your deeper, wiser MindView, or it can represent a supreme being as you understand it.

Your inner guide may at times help you to make decisions, to see problems more clearly, or to find solutions that might not otherwise have occurred to you. It can also help you to understand what might be needed for a situation or whether or not an action or decision is in your best interest. Just as any guide might be, your own inner guide can help you to reach goals, silence your inner fears, and replace those fears with calm confidence. The still small voice within each of us is sometimes a thousand times more powerful than all of our emotions combined. When we listen, we can accomplish great things in our lives.

^Pause & Reflect ~ My Spiritual MindView^

Take a moment to think about who you are, who you always have been, and who you want to be by completing the following statements.

- As a spiritual being, even as a little child, I have always felt . . .
- My spiritual self has made it possible to. . .
- My greatest strength as a Spiritual Being is. . .
- What creates the most meaning for me as a spiritual being is. . .
- If I could do anything in the world without any holds, blocks, or barriers, it would be. . .
- My hopes, dreams, and wishes for my spiritual self are. . .
- The things that are stopping me from achieving my hopes, dreams and wishes are. . .
- Can I choose to let them go?
- When?
- I am grateful to my spiritual self for. . .

Journal Lines

GM Journaling: Ch.11~ Inner Guide

☙ What did you experience as you did this meditation?

☙ How might this process help you to heal the painful memories in your life?

☙ How can knowing your inner guide help you to make better decisions?

☙ How can an inner companion help you to be kinder, gentler or more compassionate with yourself and others?

☙ How would you describe your inner guide?

Guided Meditation ~ Chapter Eleven: Inner Guide

Close your eyes and take slow deep breaths, allowing yourself to relax. Focus your attention on the rhythm of your breathing, acknowledging there's no right or wrong way to do this. Feel your lungs expand fully as you inhale and experience a sense of release as you exhale, letting go of any tightness and relaxing more deeply with each breath.

Visualize a small, golden light forming just above your head. As you relax further, this light grows brighter and larger, enveloping your entire body. Breathe deeply into your abdomen, feeling this golden light encompass you, bringing peace, quiet, and tranquility. Feel its energy as it surrounds you, creating a state of deep relaxation.

Now, turn your focus to your hands. As you inhale, clench them into tight fists; as you exhale, release and relax them. Imagine letting go of burdens you've been carrying for a long time - emotions, memories, disappointments, or fears - releasing them into the universe where they dissolve away.

Once again, concentrate on your hands. Open them as if receiving warmth and love from the universe. Feel the golden light traveling through your fingers, shoulders, neck, face, head, and down your body until you're completely engulfed in loving, golden energy. This energy merges with your own, blending into a feeling of being composed of pure, loving light.

Picture yourself as thousands of tiny sparkles on the ocean's surface, sitting peacefully on the beach. Feel the gentle breeze and acknowledge the comfort it brings. There's no place you'd rather be than here, immersed in the light within and around you. Pick up a stick or some stones nearby and write "Inner Guide" in the sand.

Trust your deeper, wiser, core self to lead you through this meditation. Whatever you experience is exactly what it's meant to be. Initially, it might be challenging, and it could take several attempts, but that's completely normal. Persist in your practice, and in time, your inner guide will manifest.

Now, look towards the ocean and notice a small boat or raft approaching, carrying a person who means you no harm. If you feel safe, consider inviting them to join you. Ask, "Are you my inner guide?" and listen for their response. If they aren't your guide, kindly request that they send your guide, and watch as they depart. When your guide arrives, whether human or animal, they will affirm their identity, saying, "Yes, I am your Inner Guide. Thank you for calling me.

When your guide appears, take a moment to greet them. If you're unfamiliar with who they are, you might even ask for a name. Spend time getting to know each other. Your guide is keenly interested in you—your passions, your challenges, and your life. You'll feel their warmth and affection, coupled with a profound sense of wisdom. There is so much to learn from your inner guide.

Now, engage in a conversation about whatever is on your mind. Ask for guidance or insight. Be open to the responses, whether they are direct answers, comfort, reassurance, or thought-provoking questions. Listen and accept whatever comes your way, free from expectations, to allow a natural flow of communication.

Your Inner Guide plays a crucial role in your healing journey. They may provide insights into your identity, life purpose, or the challenges you face. For a few moments, simply be present with your inner guide. Relish the peace and connection between you. Fill your surroundings with light, love, forgiveness, gratitude, and hope. Receive any messages from your inner guide by listening attentively to your experience.

As this meditation concludes, gently return to your physical space. Remember, your inner guide is always within you, accessible whenever you reach out for help, guidance, or advice. To connect with your guide, set aside your ego and heed their promptings. Listening to this quiet, inner voice can be incredibly powerful and insightful. This voice within holds the key to great accomplishments and deeper understanding.

Take some time now to reflect on this experience. Allow the insights and feelings to envelop you like a soothing, warm breeze. Feel peaceful, enlightened, and prepared to continue your journey of healing. Express gratitude to your inner guide and bid farewell, carrying with you the knowledge that you can connect with this guide any time in your life.

Now it is time to return to the space where you started your meditation – feeling peaceful, calm, and rejuvenated.

Chapter 12 ~ Understanding the Journey toward Resilience and Healing

"The whole is greater than the sum of its parts." ~Aristotle

In the first chapter, we discussed the story of the Golden Buddha and its significance. Similarly, there are many stories like it, each with its profound impact. To conclude our discussion on Well-Being: The Artfully Lived Life tools we have learned thus far and the MindView Council, let's explore Alice's story. This story is challenging but important, as it illustrates the power of the concepts we've explored in this workbook in the context of healing. Alice's journey, marked by faith, hope, and courage, is shared with the intention of inspiring. However, if you find Alice's story distressing, feel free to skip to the next section about The Artist's Tools and the MindView Council.

Alice was in her early 30s when her house caught fire. Her parents were visiting from the Netherlands, and along with her two-year-old son, they were all asleep when the fire alarms sounded. Alice managed to quickly evacuate her family, but the house and garage were already engulfed in flames. They barely escaped with bare feet and wrapped in blankets. The fire was eventually put out, but the next day Alice developed severe breathing difficulties and a persistent cough, prompting her to go to the hospital.

Her condition deteriorated rapidly in the emergency room. Her kidneys began to fail, and most of her organs began to shut down, including her heart. After reviving her, the doctors induced a coma and they placed her on heart and lung bypass to keep her alive.

When Alice awoke six weeks later, she found herself in immense pain, disoriented, and unable to move or speak. Her only means of communicating with her family and doctors was through eye blinks. She was diagnosed with a multi-system failure disorder, and she was paralyzed from the neck down.

During her long hospital stay, Alice made significant progress through physical therapy. She learned to transfer from her bed to her wheelchair using a sliding board and gradually regained some of her most basic physical abilities. Eventually, after 98 days in the hospital, Alice was discharged. Although she had lost her hair and a leg had to be amputated due to oxygen deprivation, she was overjoyed to be reunited with her family. She continued to struggle with immense physical pain, and she had difficulty caring for her young son. She was grateful to be alive, but she fell into a deep depression. Her recovery required two years of physical therapy, and multiple surgeries, but eventually Alice learned to walk with a prosthetic leg. Over the next five years, she became more independent and she was eventually able to return to work. However, the depression held on, and she experienced crushing grief over all that she had lost. She had begun to compare herself to others who were healthy physically, and able to enjoy all there was to enjoy in a family. She believed she would never again experience what she once had.

By then it had been 10 years since the fire, and she began to realize that no matter how many surgeries she had, her life would never be the same. Driving to work one day, however, she was contemplating her life, and she saw families out in their yards and children playing; it was a beautiful day. The wave of depression washed over her again, and she had thoughts about ending her life. But then she realized she had to make a choice. Either she could watch as life passed her by, or she could move with her life by beginning to make the best of each moment. She could stay stuck where she was, or she could begin to move forward. She also realized that whichever way she went, her life would continue along the same path, whether she chose to participate or not. She thought of her beautiful young son, her parents, her coworkers, and her patients, and decided she didn't want to give up. She wanted to move forward, with her life. She actively began to embrace her body as it was with compassion, gratitude, and forgiveness, and with the passage of time she began to thrive. Today she is married, and miraculously she was able to give birth to another child. She has become a testament to the amazing power of the human spirit for all those who know her.

Alice's Resilience and the Power of Inner Resources

Alice realized that what truly mattered was how she utilized her time and the person she chose to become marked a turning point in her recovery. She understood she would be okay, not because of her circumstances, but because of her inner resolve.

While Alice's experience was extraordinary, we all encounter moments in life that push us beyond what we think we can handle. It's during these times that our internal and external resources become invaluable.

Alice was lucky to have the support of friends and family, but not everyone has the benefit of such a strong support system. The most crucial resources, however, are those found within determination, courage, fortitude, hope, and faith. It's these internal strengths, some of which we may not even realize we possess, that enable us to navigate through life's most challenging moments.

Before her ordeal, Alice didn't know the depth of her resilience, a common sentiment many of us share until we face significant challenges. Stories like hers underscore the importance of cultivating faith in ourselves and recognizing our incredible capacities. They reflect the undiscovered masterpiece within us, waiting to be revealed in times of adversity.

Alice's Recovery and the Role of Our MindViews

Alice's journey of recovery after her hospital release provides a clear illustration of how the MindView concepts contribute to well-being, even in the face of severe challenges. Reflect on the last significant challenge you faced and how you navigated it. What did you learn about yourself? Like you, Alice discovered her inner strengths during her ordeal, which were instrumental in her healing process.

As a physician, Alice was already familiar with some of these principles, and they intuitively supported her through this incredibly tough phase of her life. Looking back, we can recognize the role each

MindView domain plays in our healing and the necessity of The Artist's Tools – acceptance, forgiveness, self-compassion, commitment, and gratitude – in our recovery.

The Physical MindView in Alice's case was deeply affected. As a young woman, newly divorced and looking forward to a new chapter, the fire upended her life. She lost her home and struggled with her physical and medical needs. Fortunately, her parents were able to support her and her son during her recovery. She fixated on walking as the key to reclaiming her lost life.

Emotionally, Alice's journey was as painful as her physical injuries. She struggled with feelings of isolation, believing no one could truly understand her experience. She battled discouragement, sadness, depression, and feelings of unworthiness. It wasn't until she accepted the new reality that she began to truly heal, both internally and externally. The reconstruction of her leg to fit a prosthesis became less about necessity and more about enhancing a life that already had purpose and meaning.

Socially, Alice's desire to reconnect with her family and career was a strong motivator. Initially, she equated being "whole" with having two legs. However, as time passed, she realized that her worth and ability to live a fulfilling life were not contingent on her physical condition. This realization was a profound turning point in her recovery.

Finally, Alice's Thinking MindView made the crucial leap. She had to choose between living in the past and building a new future. It was then that she truly grasped the importance of acceptance as the only real choice she had. This epiphany marked a significant step in her journey towards a renewed, purposeful life.

Alice's Renewed Perspective and Spiritual Growth

Alice's journey to acceptance marked the beginning of a transformative phase in her life. She shifted her focus from striving to be pain-free to actively engaging with the world. This change in perspective was like opening her eyes to a new reality, appreciating the things around her rather than lamenting what she no longer had. She learned to embrace the present moment, living fully in the "here and now".

Her Spiritual MindView also began to heal during this time. Alice started practicing gratitude, concentrating on what she still had rather than what she had lost. On difficult days, she reminded herself that each new day brought another opportunity to try again. She came to accept the limitations of her body, understanding that both good and bad days are transient and temporary.

Reflecting on her early recovery, particularly when she could only communicate through eye blinks and an alphabet board, Alice realized that she had already endured the worst. Now, equipped with psychological and emotional tools, she felt prepared to handle future challenges. This realization enabled her to maintain a broad perspective on life, keeping things in context, utilizing the tools she had acquired, and living according to her most cherished values.

Alice's experiences have endowed her with enhanced wisdom and compassion, particularly in her interactions with her patients. She remains mindful of the miraculous turnaround in her life, focusing on her abundance. Each day for Alice is now a fresh start, a new opportunity to embrace life's potential.

Six Council Members and Their Internal Personal Resources

MindView Domains

Thinking:
Curiosity, Teachability, Logic, Problem Solving, Decision Making, Planning, Impulse Control

Wisdom:
Moral and Ethical Behavior, Internal Compass, Awareness of Self and Others, Empathy, Compassion

Emotional:
Passion, Purpose, Interest, Drive, Survival, Avoidance, Guidance, Bonding, Memory

Social:
Sense of Belonging, Relatability to Others, Ability to Connect, Community Behavior

Observer & Manager:
Awareness, Perspective, Oversight, Connects Past, Present, and Future Experiences, Wise Mind, Internal Coach, Teacher

Skills & Strategies

Thinking Mindview:
OLIVE Problem-Solving; Values-Guided Thinking; Mindful Awareness; Thinking Errors are Disruptive; Self Talk is Related to Behavior

Spiritual/Wisdom Mindview:
Intelligent Wise Mind; Spiritual Principles as a Personal Stewardship; The Spiritual Journey is a Life that is Defined by Principles

Emotional Mindview:
Emotional IQ and Setting Boundaries; Strategies for Creating Inner Safety; Recognizing Triggers

Social Mindview:
Social IQ; Assertiveness & Social Boundaries; Attending, Speaking, & Listening Skills; Social Skills and Problem Solving

Physical Mindview:
Lifestyle choices that fit; Committed Action; Commitment to Wellness; It's the Brain and Body that Keeps Tally

Observer Manager:
Overseer of the Five MindViews; Executive Functioning; Dialectical Thinking; Meaningful perseverance; Mindfulness of the whole person

---

These tools were crucial in helping Alice reconstruct her life after the fire. She has resumed her role as a physician with a full practice, enjoys a fulfilling family life, and continues to integrate and learn from her experiences. Alice no longer defines herself by her physical limitations; instead, she acknowledges her strength, courage, and tenacity. Her newfound confidence and inner peace surpass anything she knew before. More equipped for life's uncertainties, she feels she offers more depth, wisdom, and compassion to relationships than ever. Alice has even expressed that she wouldn't trade her current self for the return of her leg, as it would not equate to the personal growth she has achieved. When Alice reflects on that period of her life, she doesn't see a victim but a testament to the resilience and power of the human spirit. She recognizes the inherent determination in all of us to live, survive, and flourish.

While not everyone may have a story as dramatic as Alice's, we all have our unique challenges and victories. These experiences shape us into beings of strength, intelligence, empathy, and insight, constantly striving to exceed our limits. In our most triumphant moments, we experience the bliss and magic of these qualities converging. Although we can't always predict when these moments will occur, our ability to be present and embrace them when they do define our journey.

Applying The Artist's Tools in Life – Alice's Example

Reflecting on Alice's story in the context of The Artist's Tools reinforces their significance in healing the mind, body, and spirit. These tools include:

- **Acceptance:** Embracing imperfections and mistakes while pursuing meaningful activities and goals.
- **Forgiveness:** Offering forgiveness to yourself and others for shortcomings and errors, staying fully engaged in the present.
- **Self-compassion:** Extending kindness and care to yourself and others while engaging in your abilities.
- **Commitment:** Demonstrating intention, focused action, and bravery, even during challenging times.
- **Gratitude:** Appreciating everything, including the lessons and growth opportunities from difficult experiences.

The Role of the Observer-Manager in the MindView Council

The concept of the Observer-Manager represents the final element of the MindView Council we've been exploring. This concept aligns with Aristotle's philosophy that "the whole is greater than the sum of its parts". Through Alice's story, we've witnessed the remarkable depth of the human spirit and the extensive capabilities we possess to manage our lives. Even in moments of perceived blankness or emptiness, we are far from being void of potential. With patience and self-trust, we can tap into a wealth of information, inspiration, creativity, and companionship. We are never truly alone.

In such moments, the brain is likely synthesizing thoughts, emotions, and physical experiences from different MindView perspectives. This synthesis allows the Observer-Manager to select an appropriate response. We often view our thoughts, feelings, and life events in a linear or concrete way, seeking a single solution to a problem, like solving a simple mathematical equation. But what if life's problems don't have a single answer?

Take the MindView Council, for instance. If one MindView overly dominates our response to a situation, especially in a reactionary manner, we may limit ourselves to a singular solution from an intellectual or emotional standpoint. However, considering our social, physical, and spiritual perspectives can open up a more complex range of solutions aligned with our values. This is where the concept of a personal dialectic comes into play. A dialectic is a method of exploring and understanding opposing ideas to discover the truth. A personal dialectic involves blending and synthesizing multiple perspectives, resulting in a rich and varied behavioral repertoire. The Observer-Manager's primary functions are to integrate experiences with knowledge and well-being across physical, emotional, spiritual, and social dimensions and to use these integrations as learning experiences. These experiences enhance decision-making and improve behavioral and emotional responses.

We all possess an Observer-Manager within us, but when we live reactively or without awareness, we lose the ability to maintain perspective and apply the skills needed for our best interests and those of our values and goals. By using your Observer-Manager you have been cultivating awareness and learning to harness these abilities. Let's move a little bit deeper into this by talking about dialectical thinking.

Dialectical Thinking and Effective Decision-Making

Dialectical thinking becomes crucial when we encounter various experiences from our environment, events, circumstances, or preferences. Sometimes, we don't have the luxury of time for our Observer Manager to thoroughly ponder a situation. That's where having "rules of thumb" – guidelines that align with our values – can be beneficial. Without such guidelines, our reactions might seem random and lead to chaos. Thoughtfully crafted rules of thumb can minimize negative outcomes and enhance positive ones. Would you want to create such guidelines for yourself?

Consider an example where a coworker or boss criticizes a project you've worked on for a long time. Your immediate reaction might be defensive or even retaliatory. A non-productive approach would be to react impulsively with anger or defensiveness, acknowledging your initial feelings as valid yet not considering the broader implications. Here lies the opportunity for a different response. You could slow down, contemplate the criticism, and assess whether or not there's any validity or potential benefit to it that could improve your performance. The guiding principle in this scenario is to respond in a way that aligns with your best interest. This concept may seem obvious, but it's often overlooked in the heat of the moment.

Frequently, our Emotional MindView reacts impulsively, bypassing the insights of the Thinking MindView, the wisdom of the Spiritual MindView, and the awareness of our Social and Emotional MindViews. When these MindViews collaborate dialectically, they enrich our interactions through the Observer Manager. In mere fractions of a second, the Observer Manager synthesizes information and skills from all five MindViews for a unified response.

Embracing dialectical thinking allows us to break away from linear or black-and-white thinking and explore a world of multifaceted and adaptable possibilities. When faced with challenging life events or feelings of fear and anxiety, our interpretation and expectations shape our problem-solving approach. Relying solely on linear thinking or seeing things in black-and-white terms limits our capacity to flexibly address and cope with problems, potentially exacerbating the situation. Understanding the value of dialectical thinking opens a broader perspective, enhancing our ability to navigate life's complexities effectively.

Dialectical Thinking and the Artfully Lived Life

Dialectical thinking encourages us to view situations in multifaceted and sometimes paradoxical ways. It involves understanding and valuing the presence of opposites in all aspects of life. For instance, to truly appreciate the absence of something we love, we must have experienced its presence. Similarly, to recognize the beauty of a wonderful day, we need to have endured a truly bad one. This perspective can guide us from despair to hope and joy. Consider Alice's story, where for years she believed happiness depended solely on her ability to walk on two legs. Eventually, she moved beyond this binary thinking to appreciate that each day brings new opportunities, regardless of her ability to walk. This shift in perspective allowed her to discover joy in unexpected places.

Dialectical thinking aids in letting go of negative and painful emotions, paving the way for recovery and healing. It teaches us that our lives are not a series of random events but a tapestry woven from carefully chosen skills and tools. These tools help us manage the conflicting thoughts, feelings, and demands we face.

The primary task of the Observer Manager is to creatively synthesize potential responses or solutions that align with our values and produce outcomes we can embrace. With The Artist's Tools – acceptance, forgiveness, self-compassion, commitment, and gratitude – we can formulate responses that not only address the problem at hand but also enhance and enrich our relationships with those involved. An Artfully Lived Life, therefore, is one where every decision and action is a deliberate choice, reflecting our deepest values and contributing to a fulfilling and meaningful existence.

Understanding and Enhancing Executive Functions

The Observer Manager oversees the executive functions of the brain, which play a crucial role in controlling, interpreting, and integrating our choices and behaviors. Executive functions are cognitive processes activated when we need to concentrate or pay attention. They require active engagement, in contrast with the "automatic pilot" mode many of us default to, where we rely on ingrained habits. However, not all habitual behaviors developed in our early or adult years serve our best interests.

Executive functions enable us to pause and think before acting impulsively, focus on tasks, and resist temptations, steering us away from automatic reactions that can lead to adverse outcomes. These functions also promote creative thinking and problem-solving abilities, helping us navigate unexpected challenges and plan and organize responses effectively. With consistent practice, utilizing executive functions becomes more natural and easier.

Research shows that our executive functioning improves in supportive communities, when we are engaged in tasks, and when not hindered by stress, sadness, or poor physical health. Under adverse conditions, we may struggle with memory, problem-solving, discipline, and self-control.

Core Executive Functions:

1. Inhibitory Control: This involves self-regulation and the ability to control our attention, behavior, thoughts, and emotions.
2. Working Memory: This refers to holding and manipulating information in the mind over short periods.

3. Cognitive Flexibility: This is the ability to switch perspectives or approaches to a problem and adapt to new situations.

These core functions are vital for everyday activities and are integral to the concepts presented within the MindView Council. Enhancing executive function involves maintaining good physical, mental, emotional, social, and spiritual health. Signs of successful executive functioning are evident in various life aspects, such as a fulfilling quality of life, successful relationships, academic achievement, and career success. For example, completing a college degree is a positive indicator of strong executive functioning. By understanding and nurturing these core functions, we can improve our ability to manage life's challenges and achieve personal goals more effectively.

Executive Functions – Inhibitory Control, Working Memory, and Cognitive Flexibility

Inhibitory Control: This executive function is crucial for suppressing the urge to act impulsively and instead, choosing behaviors that align with our best interests. It allows us to live within the boundaries discussed in previous chapters, focusing on tasks without distraction and completing demanding tasks by delaying gratification. A lack of inhibitory control can lead to underperformance across various life areas. Research indicates that without intervention, inhibitory control, whether it involves suppressing actions or focusing attention, remains consistent across one's lifetime. It's observed early in life, that children with better inhibitory control are less likely to engage in risky behaviors as teenagers, more likely to succeed academically, and as adults, they tend to have better health, fewer legal issues, and higher earnings.

Working memory is the capacity to hold and manipulate information. It comes in two forms: Verbal and Nonverbal (or visual-spatial). This ability is vital for processing information over time, such as maintaining the main point of a sentence over several paragraphs or keeping a goal in mind while considering various solutions. Working memory is essential for breaking down and creatively reorganizing problem components. It often works in tandem with inhibitory control, as highlighted by Adele Diamond (2014), who noted the need to inhibit distractions to maintain focus. Mindfulness meditation has been shown to enhance working memory and focus by training the mind to return to a focal point, like the breath, when distracted.

Cognitive Flexibility is a function is built upon both inhibitory control and working memory. It involves changing one's mind when presented with new, legitimate information, thus revising an initial opinion. This mental flexibility requires deactivating the original viewpoint and activating a new one. While this ability doesn't fully develop in children until ages 7 to 9, adults generally can hold and adjust multiple perspectives more easily. However, this ability can decline in older adults.

Each of these executive functions is integral to almost every decision we make. Understanding and enhancing these functions can significantly improve our capacity to navigate complex situations and make informed, thoughtful decisions in our daily lives.

The Role of the Observer in the MindView Council

The Observer is a key component of the MindView Council, enabling us to step back and introspectively examine our inner experiences. This involves gathering information about both our external surroundings and internal state, then synthesizing this information into a coherent and usable form. While the Observer Manager has been discussed as a singular entity, it also functions as two distinct parts, with the Observer acting like a radar, collecting external data and comparing it with existing internal knowledge. This process leads to the formation and storage of memories.

The Observer not only gathers information but also facilitates coordination among the other MindViews, aiding in decision-making and problem-solving. It is involved in self-reflection, emotional regulation, cognitive processing, and integrating the needs and values of the Spiritual, Physical, and Social MindViews.

Also, functioning somewhat like a "wise mind" as depicted in the Spiritual MindView, the Observer is integral to self-reflection. It involves understanding one's thoughts, motivations, and actions. Thomas et al. (2019) identifies additional components of wisdom that the Observer embodies, such as pro-social behaviors (empathy, compassion, altruism, a sense of fairness) and acceptance of diverse perspectives, indicating interest and respect for others' value systems.

The Observer also acts as a moderator among the five MindViews and serves as a link between these MindViews and the Manager. Within the framework of Well-Being: The Artfully Lived Life, the Observer's role is to monitor the internal and external functioning of our MindView Council members. It translates these observations to each of the other MindViews, enhancing our understanding of our thoughts, feelings, and behaviors in relation to our goals, values, and response options. The Observer provides feedback, ensuring balance and consistency across MindViews, and evaluates what strategies have contributed to our satisfaction and well-being in the past. This intricate process underscores the importance of the Observer in maintaining harmony within our mental and emotional landscape.

Navigating Complex Situations with the Help of the Observer Manager

Let's consider a scenario that many of us might encounter in our professional lives. Imagine you're at work, deeply focused on a significant project with an impending deadline. Suddenly, your boss drops by your office for a casual chat, even bringing you a morning coffee and seemingly expecting an invitation to sit and visit. This friendly gesture poses a dilemma because of your time-sensitive project, yet professional courtesy suggests you should welcome the interaction.

^Pause & Reflect ~ The Observer^

> As you have been learning about your own Observer Manager, think about times you have become aware of them operating in your life. It might have been regarding a big decision or a dilemma that you were facing. Perhaps your Observer was watching the situation and guiding you in an appropriate direction, but your preferences were to do something else.
>
> Think of a time when your deeper, wiser self prompted you with advice. Did you listen? What did you do? Summarize the situation briefly below: _____
> _____
>
> What were your choices? 1) _____
>
> 2) _____
>
> 3) _____
>
> How did you come to a decision? _____
>
> Do you remember being aware of an underlying tendency in a specific direction? Describe.
> _____
> _____
>
> Did you listen to your deeper wiser self? _____
>
> Are you able to recognize your Observer Manager when it is guiding you? _____
> _____
>
> If you didn't listen, what got in your way? _____
> _____

At this moment, you're faced with a decision that requires quick thinking and a balance of your personal and professional priorities. Your neurons are working rapidly; you need to be courteous but also mindful of your work commitments. You might find yourself contemplating your values and goals. What do you prioritize? And more importantly, how do you navigate this situation without offending your boss or compromising your project?

You have several options. You could politely excuse yourself to focus on your project, ensuring you meet the deadline. Alternatively, you could engage in the conversation, hoping to make up for the lost time later. Another option could be to extend an invitation to lunch at a nearby restaurant, allowing for both the meeting and sufficient time afterward to complete your project. Or you might decide to be upfront about your time constraints, expressing your inability to chat due to the urgency of your project.

The choice you make in this scenario will vary based on your specific circumstances and the professional dynamics at play. However, with the skills you've developed from previous chapters and an awareness of your Observer Manager functions, you are equipped to make a decision that aligns with your values and goals. This example illustrates how the Observer Manager aids in navigating complex situations, helping you to act in a manner consistent with your personal and professional ethos.

^Pause & Reflect ~ Observer-Manager^

> Think of a time in your life when you were facing a very difficult experience or decision, you felt torn between the different solutions, and you didn't know what to do.
> Summarize the situation briefly below: _____
> _____
>
> What were your choices?
> 1) _____
> 2) _____
> How did you come to a decision? _____
> Was your decision dialectical (a combination of more than one choice)? Describe.
> _____
>
> Are you more of a black and white thinker? Or a dialectical thinker? _____
> _____
> _____

The Manager's Role in Decision-Making and Well-Being

The Manager in our mental framework plays a pivotal role after gathering insights from the Observer and the five council members. It utilizes dialectical thinking to select the best skills and tools for an optimal response. By understanding and mastering skills like The Artist's Tools and recognizing the strengths of each MindView, the Manager has a well-equipped arsenal to address challenges. These resources are invaluable, especially during significant challenges, enhancing self-worth, satisfaction, and overall well-being.

When we face difficulties, our instincts often drive us toward familiar response patterns, but these may not always serve our best interests. Take Alice's story, for example. She focused on regaining her pre-fire life rather than adapting to her new circumstances. It took her 10 years to accept her situation and find a resolution she could live with. Initially, Alice was stuck in a non-dialectical mindset, convinced that her happiness hinged solely on her ability to walk. It was her fear of embracing new life possibilities that kept her trapped in this binary thinking.

Her breakthrough came when she realized that life could still be fulfilling and positive, regardless of her physical state. This moment of clarity marked a significant shift in her thinking, allowing her to apply dialectical reasoning effectively.

However, various factors can impede our executive functions, including unmanaged stress, insufficient sleep, inadequate exercise, and loneliness. These issues particularly affect the prefrontal cortex, leading to deficits in reasoning, problem-solving, memory, and self-control. Maintaining healthy boundaries in all life areas represented by the MindView Council is crucial. Neglecting these aspects can lead to a downward spiral of impaired executive function and poor lifestyle choices.

Conversely, adopting committed, values-guided behavior can transform this negative cycle into a positive one. Mindfulness meditation practices, as discussed in this workbook, have been shown to promote well-being through values-based thinking and actions. The skills and practices explored here are proven to enhance well-being, but it's essential to remember that they require commitment, and patience to be effective.

Synergy of the Observer-Manager in Personal Development

The Observer-Manager functions like a highly efficient management team, orchestrating our actions, thoughts, and speech. It plays the crucial role of a problem-solver, assisting the other MindViews in identifying and executing the most suitable actions for any given life situation. By gathering, consolidating, and organizing information, it guides us in optimally utilizing our acquired knowledge.

Becoming aware of this dynamic duo and its functions significantly contributes to our personal growth in various areas, including intrapersonal and interpersonal development, intellectual and spiritual progress, and social and emotional stability. The more attuned we are to the Observer-Manager, the more we can navigate life's challenges. Those who neglect this internal guidance face greater challenges in their external environment.

Reflecting on Alice's journey, her Emotional MindView initially posed an obstacle, with the belief she could never be happy in her new physical state. Her Social MindView deemed her changed body as socially unacceptable, her Thinking MindView struggled to envision a future so altered from her pre-fire life, and her Spiritual MindView grappled with questions about life's meaning and purpose. Her path from this low point to the commencement of her recovery is pivotal as it represents a significant shift from post-fire tragedy to her present daily recovery.

The Observer within Alice was the first to adapt, recognizing that time was moving forward regardless of her condition. This realization, when communicated to the Manager, manifested in transformative behavior. Alice initiated her private practice where she could work from a wheelchair, ceased pursuing surgical options, and sought trauma therapy. Her Emotional MindView gained from therapy, while her Thinking, Spiritual, and Social MindViews all benefited from her work. Her Physical MindView found new purpose and meaning. The Observer-Manager facilitated this shift by offering new perspectives and information, enabling Alice to move forward and reconnect with her life meaningfully.

The following diagram is a summary of the skills and strategies that we have discussed to this point. It is organized according to the MindView domain that the tools are designed for.

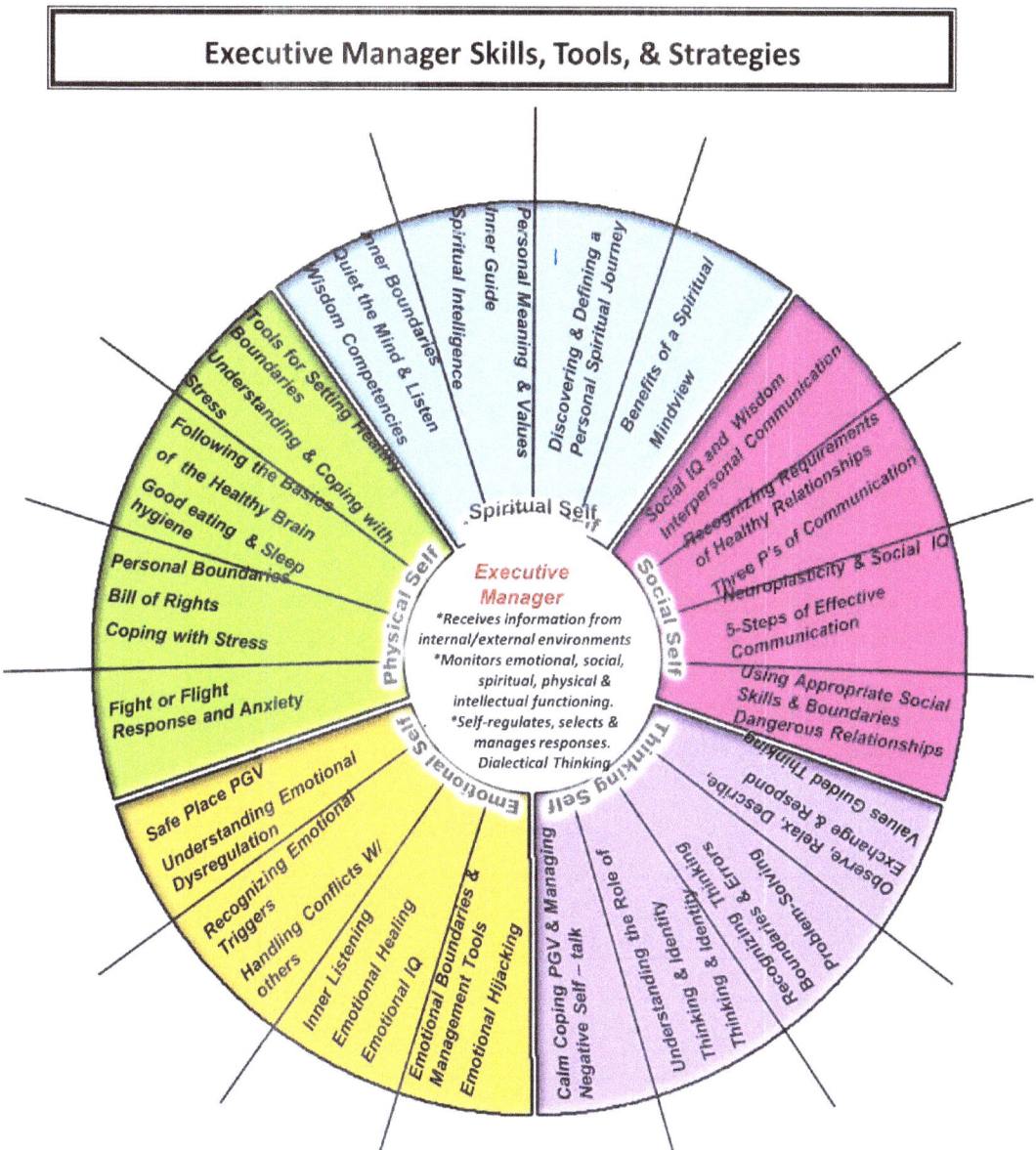

Guided Meditation for Self-Acceptance and Inner Balance

This guided meditation is designed to help you connect with and affirm your core self. Our Observer Manager plays a key role in how we perceive ourselves in relation to others. We often observe others and speculate about their thoughts and feelings. Since people rarely disclose their inner thoughts, we tend to create our own narratives and subsequently form ideas about ourselves based on these assumptions. Questions like, "What do they think of me?" or "Am I meeting their expectations?" stem from this process, which begins as early as infancy and is our initial way of navigating our social and emotional world.

The brain, constantly seeking information, uses this data to ensure our intellectual, emotional, physical, and spiritual safety. It's always looking for signs of danger, remaining vigilant even in peaceful times. The Observer Manager also guides the other MindViews to align our behavior with our social context, such as observing social etiquette at formal events or choosing age-appropriate conversation topics.

However, if we were raised in chaotic environments insensitive to our emotional needs, or to the emotional needs of others. Our Observer Manager might have adopted similar insensitivity, often manifesting as internal criticism. This can lead to an overactive Inner Critic, feelings of inadequacy, low self-esteem, and possibly anxiety or depression.

The purpose of this next meditation is to recalibrate this internal signaling system. It's about recognizing that being a good, loving, and deserving person doesn't equate to being flawless. We learn and grow through our experiences and mistakes. This meditation focuses on acknowledging yourself as a complete individual capable of growth. The sense of being "good enough" doesn't stem from perfection but from embracing our entirety, including our imperfections. We are all works in progress, imperfect yet evolving. Journeying through life with these imperfections need not be a burden; it's not indicative of your worth any more than the moon phases reflect its true nature. You are a marvel of intelligence with a remarkable capacity for growth and learning. You are already sufficient, and your abilities simply enable you to better express your true self at the core.

Journal Lines

_____
_____
_____
_____
_____
_____
_____
_____
_____
_____
_____
_____
_____

GM Journaling: Ch.12~I Am Enough

ᛉ How might the process of realizing and believing that you are enough as you are, help you to heal the painful memories in your life? _____

_____

ᛉ Did you notice yourself struggling to accept who you are at the core?

_____

ᛉ By the end of the guided meditation were you able to come to a place of self-acceptance and self-love? What was that like? _____

_____

ᛉ Each time you practice this guided meditation jot down how it felt, and how your experience with it changed.

Guided Meditation: Chapter 12 ~ Guided Meditation: Inner Healing

Settle into a comfortable position and begin to unwind. Focus on relaxing your body and take a moment to tune into your breathing. Let your mind clear of all thoughts for now, and allow your body to gradually release any stress, tension, or worry. Breathe deeply and naturally, observing the rise and fall of your abdomen with each breath. Let each breath find its natural rhythm and simply accept it as it comes. If your mind drifts, gently guide your focus back to your breathing. Sink deeper into a state of relaxation, feeling peaceful, calm, and serene. Let everything go.

Visualize the oxygen you breathe entering your body through the soles of your feet and exiting through the crown of your head. With each inhalation, imagine this oxygen flowing up from your toes, ankles, calves, knees, and thighs, infusing every muscle, bone, and tendon with energy. Feel the breath moving up through your hips, lower back, and abdomen, easing discomfort. Let this breath continue its journey up through your chest and shoulders, down your arms to your fingertips, releasing and relaxing more with each cycle. Breathe in this pure, cleansing oxygen through your feet and release it from the top of your head. Feel completely relaxed and at ease.

Reflect on a time in your life when you felt truly happy and self-confident. Picture yourself in that moment. What were you doing? Where were you? What aspects of yourself did you appreciate most during that time?

Now, envision a beautiful, ornate staircase and invite your Inner Guide to meet you at its base. Feel the smooth, polished wood of the railing beneath your hand. As you ascend the staircase, allow each step to take you deeper into relaxation. Step one is feeling more relaxed. Step two, each step brings you closer to a time of happiness and peace. Now step three, and step leads you into a small room filled with a positive, significant memory that helps you understand who you are.

Let your Inner Guide take you through a memory that fills you with peace. Continue ascending – step five might bring another memory or insight from your Inner Guide, filled with wisdom, warmth, and care. Step six – remember, each person's journey is unique. Embrace who you are and feel the safety and support around you. Step seven – feel the protection of your Inner Guide, absorbing only loving, nurturing information. Step eight opens to another meaningful, positive memory, reinforcing that you are remarkable and capable.

Now, proceed up the stairs with your guide. Step nine surrounds you with healing light and tranquility. On step ten, the staircase leads you to a personal sanctuary where you receive a special gift. This gift could be emotional or intellectual, a new understanding, or wisdom. Maybe it's the resilient part of you that has always been there, guiding you through challenges. Be present in this moment and accept whatever comes to you, knowing you've never been alone. Your guidance and strength have always come from within, from a higher self that has navigated you through every obstacle.

Allow the encompassing light to permeate through you, bringing its healing touch. It shines through, alleviating pain, regret, guilt, and past shames. This light is a balm for all wounds, comforting your fears and anxieties, and mending any damage to your body, mind, and spirit. It revitalizes you, restoring the vitality, confidence, courage, hope, and trust you once held in your youth. Your entire being – body, mind, and spirit, across past, present, and future – now radiates with this magnificent, healing energy. See yourself as whole and complete. Recognize your strength, your brilliance, your miraculous nature. You are exactly as you should be. You are sufficient. Nothing you have done or will do can alter this truth. Let go of the self-doubt that obscures your purpose. Take a moment to sit with this new awareness.

Now, it's time to return. Move towards the staircase, feel the familiar texture of the wooden handrail under your palm, and begin your descent with your guide. Step 10: The radiant, healing *light continues to envelop you, and you feel lighter and more liberated in mind and body. <u>Step 9</u>: Notice the ease of your breath, the sensation of healing pervading your entire body. <u>Step 8</u>: Pause to express gratitude for the lessons and experiences of this journey, knowing you can return at any time. <u>Step 7</u>: Feel a renewed connection with your past, present, and future. <u>Step 6</u>: Experience unity with yourself, embracing your learnings and the knowledge yet to come. <u>Step 5</u>: Let go of any lingering hurts, reconnecting with your higher self. <u>Step 4</u>: Embrace peace, knowing you are loved and capable of love. <u>Step 3</u>: A sense of peace and light continues to surround you. <u>Step 2</u>: Gently bring yourself back to the present moment. And on <u>Step 1</u>, refocus on your breathing. Feel the rise and fall of your abdomen with each deep, rejuvenating breath, filling you down to your toes.*

Through this meditation, you've discovered that feelings of inadequacy only persist if you allow them space in your thoughts. You've learned that your brain, like a detective, gathers information to protect you and guide you. Your life experiences have built a reservoir of knowledge, strength, and wisdom. Trust in these resources. Remember, there's a deeper, wiser part of you, always ready to offer guidance and bring tranquility to your thoughts, emotions, and body.

Before you fully return to the present, take this message with you: whenever doubts about your self-worth arise, remind yourself that mistakes are essential for learning. Embrace this new perspective of self-appreciation. As you continue this practice, the painful feelings of inadequacy will gradually diminish. Each day, you'll become more attuned to the strength and wisdom within you. The inner courage that has sustained you will become increasingly evident. Rely on this inner guidance rather than external influences. The light that envelops your core will be a continuous source of healing and empowerment. Let it illuminate and heal all wounds, soothe your fears, and restore vitality, confidence, and hope in your life. Embrace the peace, strength, and wellness that radiates from your being. You are precisely as you should be - a miracle of existence, intelligence, and light. Be at peace with yourself.

Now, take a deep, revitalizing breath and refocus your attention on your surroundings. I will count from five to one, and with each number, you will become more alert and energized. Five, feel yourself reconnecting with your body and conscious mind. Four, begin to reorient yourself to this space, Three, taking deep, rejuvenating breaths. Hold onto the insights and imagery provided by your deeper, wiser self from this experience. Two, feel the energy returning to your body.

<u>And now step 1</u>. Open your eyes, fully awake, feeling rested, and rejuvenated, ready to embrace your day with a renewed sense of self and purpose.

Chapter 13 ~ Cultivating Inner Well-Being and Equanimity

"A compassionate heart still feels anger, greed, jealousy, and other such emotions. But it accepts them for what they are with equanimity, and cultivates the strength of mind to let them arise and pass without identifying with or acting upon them." ~Stephen Batchelor

As we near the conclusion of this workbook, we would like to briefly review a couple of the main ideas we have covered and then discuss several we haven't: equanimity, resilience, sense of coherence, and Ikigai, which we discuss below. First, let's pause to reflect on a subtle yet important hurdle in cultivating a fulfilling life: self-awareness. Throughout our journey we've tackled identity, problem-solving, and communication. Ask yourself, if you understand yourself better since beginning this workbook? Can you better articulate who you are to someone else? If you're struggling to answer these questions, it might be worth revisiting previous chapters to review some of the things you've written.

In Chapter Six, we discussed the importance of mindful self-observation. Our choices, talents, and skills shape our identity and reflect our deepest values. Our values shape the choices we make throughout our lives. Think about what you've discovered regarding your aspirations and how your sense of self may have evolved since starting this workbook. You might take a moment to journal about the changes you've noticed in yourself, your growth, and your reflections on this journey. We've also included another copy of the Psychological Well-Being Scale by Diener and Biswas-Diener (2009). Comparing these results to the one in Chapter Two might help you to gauge your progress and areas that need further attention. Revisiting the most impactful parts of this workbook can deepen your understanding – rarely do we grasp all we need from a single read.

Just to give you an idea of what the score means, the maximum number of points available on this scale is 56. A score of 42-56 would put you in the top 25% ~ which is a great score. A score below 28 would probably mean you have more areas to work on. Your life would be greatly enriched by practicing the tools and skills you have learned in this program. Also, it is important to know that this is just a general reflection of how you perceive your personal well-being. It can change dramatically on a daily basis depending upon how you interpret your life experiences. Use it with great flexibility and caution as it has not been empirically validated for this presentation.

^Pause & Reflect ~ Psychological Well-Being Scale^

Copyright by Ed Diener and Robert Biswas-Diener, 2009

> 1) I lead a purposeful and meaningful life.
>   Disagree ─O─────O─────O─────O─────O─────O─────O── Agree
> 2) My social relationships are supportive and rewarding.
>   Disagree ─O─────O─────O─────O─────O─────O─────O── Agree
> 3) I am engaged and interested in my daily activities.
>   Disagree ─O─────O─────O─────O─────O─────O─────O── Agree
> 4) I actively contribute to the happiness and well-being of others.
>   Disagree ─O─────O─────O─────O─────O─────O─────O── Agree
> 5) I am competent and capable in the activities that are important to me.
>   Disagree ─O─────O─────O─────O─────O─────O─────O── Agree
> 6) I am a good person and live a good life.
>   Disagree ─O─────O─────O─────O─────O─────O─────O── Agree
> 7) I am optimistic about my future.
>   Disagree ─O─────O─────O─────O─────O─────O─────O── Agree
> 8) People respect me.
>   Disagree ─O─────O─────O─────O─────O─────O─────O── Agree

Cultivating Inner Stability in Our MindView Systems

Equanimity. Equanimity is defined as mental calmness, composure, and evenness of temper, especially in a difficult situation. Embracing wiser choices and behaviors leads to the development of equanimity and inner peace. Individuals who grasp this concept tend to transcend reactive patterns, flowing harmoniously with life's rhythms. They tap into their intuitive understanding and grow more attuned to their surroundings. This heightened awareness allows them to foresee potential challenges and unearth solutions that might not be immediately apparent to others.

Life inevitably brings its share of pain and frustrations. Sometimes these arise from unforeseen obstacles or simply because we haven't yet mastered the necessary strategies to tackle them. This is precisely why we need to develop skills for problem-solving, communication, relationships, etc. We can turn pain or adversity into wisdom. This wisdom, born of our struggles, can significantly alleviate – or even eradicate – future suffering. Thus, challenges and contentment are interlinked aspects of our journey toward well-being ~ as long as we learn from our experiences. Every strategy you have learned and mastered from Well-being: The Artfully Lived Life Program will increase your ability to handle your life with equanimity.

Acknowledging that emotions such as peace, joy, happiness, sadness, and suffering are fleeting is a powerful act of self-compassion. It embodies the concept of equanimity. Although equanimity is a principle deeply rooted in Buddhist traditions, it holds universal, secular values. The equilibrium that defines resilience protects μs from losing our inner and outer sense of balance and poise during life's trials or helps us to swiftly restore it in a crisis. Imagine navigating through life's ups and downs with this level of steadiness! Think, for example, about two people who are engaged in a heated exchange, and rather than continuing the conflict through impulsive, argumentative, comments that further perpetuates the conflict, one person decides to step back and to adopt a more balanced perspective that considers both points of view. Which approach is more likely to result in a positive resolution? That individual may still feel uncomfortable or angry but those feelings need not overwhelm their expertise in managing or resolving the contention.

Resilience is similar to equanimity in that it refers to the ability to recover from or adjust easily to misfortune or change. Resilience is comprised of three qualities, 1) the ability to manage one's energy, 2) the ability to shift one's focus, and 3) the ability to return to one's inner sense of purpose of personal meaning. In the above example, resilience is the quality that allows one to readjust their behavior and to adopt a response that is more in line with their values and goals. In life, this ability is the rescue we need for situations in which our emotions pull us in directions that are not in our best interest.

A diagram toward the end of this chapter summarizes the concepts, skills, and qualities within each MindView that we have addressed in this workbook. With resilience at the center, divided into the five MindView Domains, we can see how they contribute to the maintenance of resilience, as well as growth and stability.

Navigating the Path to Wellness

The study of emotional wellness suggests that excess emotion, regardless of its nature, can be counterproductive, leading to overstimulation and stress on our endocrine systems. Social wellness, meanwhile, emphasizes the value of effective communication, interpersonal skills like assertiveness, problem-solving, and pro-social behaviors – essentially, the ability to interact harmoniously even with challenging individuals.

Wellness isn't a passive state; it's a dynamic quality of life shaped by reactions to thoughts, emotions, and the choices we make. This underscores the importance of understanding what wellness personally means to us. Without this understanding, we might not act in ways that promote our well-being.

True wellness is a deliberate choice, not a random occurrence. We can all learn to define and actively pursue in our lives. The key components in building a life marked by success, inner peace, and well-being include:

1. **Consistency:** Regularity in actions and behaviors is fundamental. Consistency forms the bedrock of habits that foster wellness.
2. **Making Appropriate Choices:** The ability to make decisions that align with personal and ethical standards is critical for maintaining wellness.
3. **Commitment to Core Values and Beliefs:** Adhering to a set of fundamental values and beliefs about the world guides us in making choices that resonate with our true selves.
4. **Self-Identity and Self-Regulation:** Understanding who we are and effectively managing our responses to various situations is vital for emotional balance and well-being.

5. Personal Meaning in Life: Discovering and embracing what genuinely matters to us provides direction and purpose, enhancing our sense of fulfillment and wellness.

6. Social and emotional intelligence concepts: By being self-aware of our responses, we empower ourselves to rely on, and utilize tools and strategies that will meet our needs as well as the needs of those around us, as we interact with our environment.

By focusing on and practicing these skills and behaviors, we can actively cultivate a lifestyle that not only nurtures our well-being but also enriches our life experiences.

Cultivating and Maintaining Equanimity in Reactive Situations

In our pursuit of well-being, we might encounter situations that unexpectedly stress us or provoke a strong reaction. One vital insight we share with our clients is recognizing the body's role as a first responder. Often, physical signs like tension, accelerated heart rate, or rapid breathing precede emotional or cognitive awareness of a stressful trigger. Being attuned to these bodily changes is crucial for realizing when you're entering an alert state. Once you detect this shift, focus on physical awareness and breathe deeply, aiming to remain present and composed.

Tapping into your Spiritual MindView can be immensely beneficial during such times. Reciting a peace mantra, a practice you might have cultivated during meditation, can engage your vagus nerve and parasympathetic nervous system, both instrumental in calming you down. Activities like singing, humming, and chanting stimulate the vagus nerve, promoting relaxation. Though it might not always be feasible to chant or sing, by adjusting your breathing to be slower, deeper, and evener, you can similarly activate the vagus nerve's calming effect. As you access your Thinking MindView to problem solve and to identify the best solution, your Social and Emotional MindView skills will guide you in ways to broaden and enrich your relationships and to create a sound support system.

Although you may have specific goals for yourself, Well-Being: The Artfully Lived Life Program is also a journey of personal growth. Having progressed this far suggests a deep commitment to self-improvement. Human nature often shows a pattern of initial enthusiasm for new goals, which can wane under life's pressures. To keep the concepts that guide you towards your life's Masterpiece at the forefront, consider creating physical reminders. For instance, placing key values, goals, and actions from your Journey Map in strategic locations can help maintain focus. While some goals may evolve, core values usually endure and merit regular reflection.

Rediscovering Your Core Identity

Revisiting your initial inquiry, "Who are you at your very essence?" Given your work and progress, the answer should be more accessible. The essence of your identity is that of an artist. Each day presents an opportunity to craft and refine your being, utilizing the array of tools at your disposal. As you master one tool, you transition to exploring another, ensuring a continuous journey of self-discovery and growth. This process symbolizes an unending progression, where even in times of challenge, there is movement forward because the artist's work within you is perpetual. There will always be new realms to explore and internal aspirations striving for expression.

Imagine yourself as both the sculptor and the sculpture in Michelangelo's vision. You are the artist tirelessly shaping the marble, and simultaneously, you are the masterpiece emerging from within the stone. This masterpiece, ever evolving and delicately detailed is aptly named, "Me!" Your journey is about continuously unveiling the layers of your identity, revealing the intricate masterpiece that resides within.

Understanding and Cultivating a Sense of Coherence

Another researcher, by the name of Aaron Antonovsky (1987, 1993) developed a theory he called a **Sense of Coherence** (SOC), which delves into why some people maintain health under stress while others do not. Sense Of Coherence is essentially a blend of optimism and a sense of control over life's events:

1. Comprehensibility: This is the ability to cognitively understand and make sense of life events. It involves seeing the broader context of a situation, which can motivate us to adapt and overcome challenges instead of avoiding them.

2. Manageability: This aspect relates to the belief in one's capability to handle life's challenges. It's about having confidence in your abilities and resources to tackle problems effectively.

3. Meaningfulness: This component is the recognition that life events, even difficult ones, have significance in shaping our experiences. It involves seeing challenges as worthy of our effort and commitment, understanding that they can be leveraged for personal growth.

Throughout this workbook, we have addressed each of these three components. As you utilize the tools and strategies you have learned, you will find effective ways of making sense of your world. Even in the face of adversity, we can enhance our well-being by seeking understanding, finding meaning, and refocusing on our core values.

Living a Long and Meaningful Life

People who live in what has become known as Blue Zones (areas of the world such as Okinawa, Japan, and several others) tend to be active into or beyond their 90s. Interestingly; they typically don't think much about living a long and meaningful life, they just do it. Nevertheless, physicians and scientists who have interviewed them and studied their lifestyles report a few consistent habits and behaviors. Some of these you may have heard recommended by your primary care doctor and some of them you may not have considered. These healthy lifestyle choices include lowering your stress levels, exercising that might be as simple as moving, stretching, and walking every day, considering what and how much you eat, how long and how well you sleep, having strong social connections, and having a sense of purpose in your life. These lifestyle behaviors have been shown not only to extend one's life but, they can also improve their health and well-being. Developing the motivation and commitment to follow these lifestyle habits may be a bit challenging for many of us. However, there are a few ideas that can make adopting some of these behavioral changes easier. As suggested by Dr. Lien Vuu (a regenerative medicine physician), rather than starting a new habit from scratch, it is helpful to "stack" a new habit onto an existing part of your routine. For example, one might add a short mindfulness meditation or deep breathing activity to their morning coffee or green tea.

You might have noticed that you have been learning and practicing many of these behaviors during your journey toward an Artfully Lived Life. For example, in a previous Chapter we discussed managing your stress levels by establishing a Mindfulness practice as well as using The Artists Tools (Acceptance, Forgiveness, Self-Compassion, Commitment, and Gratitude).

Another of the behavioral characteristics of those that live in Blue Zones is daily movement. Although high intensity exercise such as running and resistance training can tone muscles and increase endurance, simply walking, bending and stretching has been shown to increase life span as well as physical and psychological well-being.

If you struggle with getting a good night's sleep, recall the sleep hygiene recommendations in Chapter 7. Some of these include maintaining a consistent sleep schedule, avoid screen time 1 hour before bed, no caffeine 4 hours before bed, no napping after 3:00 pm and keep your sleeping room dark and free of distractions.

Concerning diet, there are hundreds of books, blogs, and plans available for losing or maintaining a healthy weight. A recent study conducted at Harvard compared four diets such as the Mediterranean diet considered to be healthy and suggested that diets that include primarily whole grains, fruits, vegetables, nuts, and legumes resulted in reduced mortality rates. These are common dietary features reported by those living in Blue Zones, which, in addition to eating a variety of fruits and vegetables including beans (which are a good source of protein), a moderate amount of meat and fish and smaller amounts, if any of sugar. The amount of food consumed typically follows the "80% rule" that is when you feel 80% full stop eating.

Another characteristic of the residents of the Blue Zone is they have close social connections both within and outside of their families. This is also an important concept in building your artfully lived life. In Chapter 5, you constructed your Journey Map and included those in your community as a means of help and support. The people you listed represent your community, and those close to you. Recall these are the people that you wish to have with you when you reach your goals. People in your community also help to keep you grounded because they are likely to share similar goals, values, and personal qualities. Members of a healthy community provide support, inspiration, compassion, and encouragement for one another as they journey together. Maintaining and protecting the community you belong to is one of the most important keys to your success and happiness.

Another characteristic of Blue Zone residents in Okinawa, as suggested by Ken Mogi in "The Little Book of Ikigai, live a happy and long life the Japanese way", is having a purpose or a reason to get up every morning. Mogi further provides the translation of "iki" (to live, pronounced ee-kee) and "gai" (meaning reason, pronounced guy), which literally means the reason to live. Mogi goes on to outline the 5 pillars of Ikigai. These are:

1. **Start Small:** Consider incremental progress in your goals and aspirations.
2. **Release Yourself-Accept Yourself as You Are:** seek to <u>find</u> who you are rather than trying to <u>change</u> who you are.
3. **Harmony and Sustainability:** Build a connection with your community, your social and natural environment.
4. **The Joy of Little Things:** Look for your joy and passion wherever you find it: hobbies, family, etc.
5. **Being in the Here and Now:** Move past your regrets of the past and worries for the future by focusing on the here and now.

In Well-Being: The Artfully Lived Life process, you have been working with the concepts in each pillar. For example, in your Journey Map, you will have considered small action steps and larger goals. Although you have chosen several goals you have recorded in your journey map, creating your artfully lived life is a continuing process in developing values-directed thinking and behaviors.

With respect to discovering who you are, recall the story of the golden Buddha and the work you have done to discover your true self. You have been discovering and observing thinking and behaviors resulting from stories others have been telling you about yourself and that you may have started to believe. These sometimes result in defense mechanisms or other behaviors that are not helpful in your present life.

In the chapter focused on the Social MindView you worked on improving your relational skills and community connections. The relationships you currently have or those you build in the future are an invaluable part of your sharing and support community.

Finding and appreciating small and meaningful things in life becomes a reality by practicing some of The Artists Tools (Self-compassion, Gratitude, Acceptance, Forgiveness and Commitment). I have often heard the statement that you find what you are looking for. When we allow ourselves the time to find and pursue our passions or simply pay attention to the things that make us smile, these things contribute to our Artfully Lived Life.

Finally, striving to stay in the here and now is one of the concepts that you may be working at during your mindfulness practice. Present moment awareness can add a vitality to our senses (what we hear, what we touch, what we smell, what we taste, and what we see) that we often just ignore.

So, essentially, the work that you have been accomplishing toward your Artfully Lived Life is also helpful in enjoying a longer life by finding your Ikigai. Nevertheless, finding one's Ikigai has greater implications than just increasing your years of life. Finding your Ikigai can also increase your well-being and improve your mental health. Okuzono et al. (2022), reported that in a Japanese population, having a higher degree of "Ikigai was associated with decreased depression symptoms and hopelessness as well as higher happiness and life satisfaction…" But what about the Western population? Using an English translation of an Ikigai questionnaire, Wilkes et al. (2022), reported that a higher degree of Ikigai positively predicted well-being and negatively predicted depression. A copy of Wilkes and Fido's questionnaire is shown below. These are not yes or no questions but rather can be answered on a scale from "this applies to me a lot to this does not apply to me". This is presented here simply for you to ponder as you progress toward your Artfully Lived Life.

^Pause & Reflect ~ Ikigai Philosophy^

I believe that I have some impact on someone.
My life is mentally rich and fulfilled.
I am interested in many things.
I feel that I am contributing to someone or society.
I would like to develop myself.
I often feel that I am happy.
I think that my existence is needed by something or someone.
I would like to learn something new or start something.
I have room in my mind.

Wilkes et al. (2022)

A Letter to My Core Self and a Summary of What We Have Learned

A Letter to My Core Self. Imagine that you could go back in time and deliver a letter to yourself before life's difficulties started getting in the way. What advice would you give to your core self? What encouragements would you share? As you prepare to do the last guided imagery in this workbook, imagine that you are accepting that same advice and encouragement here and now. What would you most want to hear?

Remember The Tools for the Artist Within (Acceptance, Forgiveness, Self-compassion, Commitment, and Gratitude.) How would you convey the importance of these tools to your core self? Coming back to what you have learned from Well-Being: The Artfully Lived Life ~ which of the principles would you most like to take away with you? What would be most helpful to remember?

Because our conscious thinking mind is so engaged with our day-to-day activities, we often forget that we have a deeper wiser mind that can be participating in every aspect of our lives as well. If you could remember to include this deeper part of you in your everyday world, how might you feel differently about your life as you know it to be? Do you think you might do things differently than you have?

Take some time here to write a letter to your deeper, wiser self – your core- self. Share what you would like that part of you to know and invite your core self to respond in kind. There are many benefits to a close relationship between you and your deeper, wiser self. How might this relationship enhance your life right now? Take some time to write that letter to yourself right now. And close your letter, Lovingly ~

and your name. Re-write this letter to yourself at least every two weeks. This will encourage continued progress on your goals and remind you to keep working on them.

^Pause & Reflect ~ A Letter to My Core Self^

The purpose of this exercise is to write a <u>Letter to My Core Self.</u> It is not to be given to anyone. It is addressed only to you! Follow the outline provided below. Please make it as long as you need and use as much paper as will help. While you are writing this <u>Letter to My Core Self</u>, imagine yourself reading it with the greatest of respect and care, for it is a letter that is offered deeply and caringly to yourself to help you remember the ideas and principles you have taken to heart and wish to exemplify in your life. When you finish with the letter, read it out loud to yourself – two or more times. Then, do the following guided meditation. This is your chance to say all of the things you would like to say to help heal your deeper self and to create a peaceful and safe space within yourself.

A Letter To My Core Self

1) Start your letter with "Dear _____, I believe in myself because _____.
   No one and nothing can take that away. No one knows you better than you know yourself.
2) Think about what you most need right now for your well-being? Is it time, energy, encouragement, confidence, support, or gratitude? What do you need right now? Can you take the time to receive that right now? Answer, "I need _____."
3) Consider The Tools for the Artist Within, which of them need your attention for enhancing your self-esteem? Is it Compassion, Acceptance, Forgiveness, Commitment, or Gratitude? Can you bring that forward in your mind for the next few minutes? "I need _____."
4) And what you know about yourself is that "_____."
5) When you feel _____ it is hard to remember that you are worthy of all things. Can you say that to yourself right now?
   _____
6) Can you also say, "I am loved and valued by the universe. Therefore, I can love and value myself."
7) Difficult events and feelings are a part of all life. Even plants and animals experience these. In those times I have many resources for making myself feel better. Can you say, "I have many resources for making myself feel better. They are_____"
   All people have the Resource of self-care, such as, the tools for the Artfully Lived Life, community, family, friends, hopes and dreams. Especially, we all have an Inner Guide that wants the very best for us.
8) Reach for your Inner Guide now. What advice is there for you, can you ask for encouragement, love, hope, and companionship?
9) Now imagine you have a beautiful golden box within you. Can you store all that you have experienced in the last few moments within that golden box, and keep it with you always?
10) Finally, can you take the hurts, worries, fears, anger, regrets, and insecurities, and store them in this box, where your deeper core self of love, forgiveness, and compassion can heal them?
11) Now surround yourself with beautiful golden light that warms you, encourages you, and strengthens you, from the top of your head, to the bottom of your feet, and store it in your mind.
12) And finally, say goodbye for now. Remember you can visit your deeper core self anytime you need.

A Quick Reference and Summary of What We Have Learned. The tools of the Artist Within are timeless principles, refined over millennia. Maintaining these practices is essential for navigating life's journey. The table below summarizes each chapter's main content, providing a quick reference for areas where you've grown and areas that might still need attention. Bookmarking this table can serve as a handy resource for future challenges and opportunities for growth.

\	Summary of Information and Skills by Chapter
Chapter One: Getting Started with a NewMind View	Scientific studies suggest our knowledge of the brain expands every day. We introduced the MindView Counsel (Emotional, Social, Physical, Thinking, Spiritual, and Observer Manager MindViews) and how it can bring a sense of balance to your life.
Chapter Two: Tools for the Artist Within	*We explored The Tools for the Artist Within: Acceptance, Forgiveness, Self-Compassion, Commitment and Gratitude *We discussed the words we use to describe ourselves, which are important to our core identity.
Chapter Three: Well-Being and our New MindView	*We introduced Acceptance and Commitment Therapy and Mindfulness. *We introduced the Guiding Principles for Well-Being: The Artfully Lived Life. *We included a Pause & Reflect for each member of the MindView Counsel.
Chapter Four: Where We Get Stuck and How We Move On	*We talked about self-esteem, and how to repair it. *We introduced the Inner Critic, how it helps and how it hurts. *We learned seven steps for moving past the difficult moments
Chapter Five: Mapping My Journey	*You completed a Journey Map summarizing your values, goals, and action steps. *You also defined your Action Steps and your pitfalls of impulse and swamps of habit.
Chapter Six: Discovering the Artist Within	*We began to discover an identity and Self-Definition. *We develop awareness & sensitivity as we begin to listen inward. *Feeling "not good enough" can interfere with knowing who we are & where we belong
Chapter Seven: Life Strategies for the Brain & Body	*Stress can turn into distress when it happens too much, too often, and it's too persistent. *Unmanaged stress affects us in every way. *We learned about dysregulation and how to release it using the body scan.

Chapter Eight: Emotional MindView Skills	*Emotional IQ summarizes important components for healthy emotional reasoning. *We learned about emotional boundaries, how to set them, and how to protect them. *We learned several strategies for creating inner safety through visualization.
Chapter Nine: Thinking MindView Skills	*Thinking errors are mistakes people make when evaluating a problem. *ERAC and OLIVE are two main strategies for managing and solving problems. *Boundaries of thought are violated when we resort to manipulation, dependency, etc., to be well.
Chapter Ten: Social MindView Skills	*Social IQ skills improve empathic understanding and social/emotional synchrony between people. *Assertiveness and Active Listening skills help with communicating, caring, and respect in relationships.
Chapter Eleven: Spiritual MindView Skills	*We can reach our Inner Guide if we quiet the mind, listen inwardly, and ask for clarity. *A Spiritual Journey is individually chosen and defined by goals, values, guiding principles, and actions. *Spiritual boundaries are a personal stewardship for reaching our higher potential.
Chapter Twelve: The Observer Manager	*Our Observer-Manager watches over the five MindView Domains. *The Observer-Manager and the MindView Counsel can form a powerful Synergy *Integrating our skills and experiences, we maximize our potential for embracing courage, forgiveness, acceptance, and gratitude.
Chapter Thirteen: Living the Artfully Lived Life	*Practicing what we have learned is critical to our Personal Masterpiece. *We completed the Letter to My Core Self. This helped to clarify personal goals for change.

This workbook has ventured to define and motivate action, some of the most important well-being principles in the literature. We have strived to present this information in the most positive fashion with hope and excitement for the future as you create your very best life. A main theme throughout this book has been the idea that seemingly negative experiences, and positive experiences, can contribute to positive aspects of human transformation, particularly when we are equipped with the necessary tools and skills for coping with difficult life experiences.

Many scholars have argued that self-acceptance, and self-compassion are key factors in psychological well-being. Our relationship with ourselves and learning to accept ourselves in spite of our weaknesses or deficiencies is key to a sense of well-being. A person with self-acceptance does not regard themselves as more than others, or less. Rather self-acceptance means that an individual aims to be the best possible version of themselves, out of self-love and self-care. Researchers have described psychological well-being as thriving in the face of the challenges in life by pursuing meaningful goals, growing and developing as an individual, and creating positive and healthy relationships with others. This implies that an individual striving for psychological well-being is living a life that is meaningful and purposeful, is developing the capacity to manage one's life, and is doing so through a sense of personal autonomy and responsibility. A result of these goals is to create opportunities for experiencing events or activities that foster personal growth and a sense of purpose. In this way, the pursuit of well-being is circular: Psychological well-being promotes strength-based experiences, which fosters increased psychological well-being. McQuaide & Ehrenreich, 1997, defined "strengths" as: "the capacity to cope with difficulties, to maintain functioning in the face of stress, to bounce back in the face of significant trauma, to use external challenges as a stimulus for growth, and to use social supports as a source of resilience. The characteristics that allow humans to effectively cope with their life experiences have been the central theme throughout these chapters, offering you, the reader, the opportunity to begin to live a life of well-being.

ON YOUR OWN ACTIVITIES

The following table is a list of "On Your Own" exercises that you could do to help you to continue to learn and incorporate the principles from "The Artfully Lived Life" into your daily experience. They are listed by chapter. There is also space with each activity to journal about the activities and what you learned. You can also find journaling pages, and a summary of the skills and tools we have presented, in the appendices. Use these as daily meditations to help you to continue your journey toward Well-Being: The Artfully Lived Life. This activity is intended for you to select areas you may wish to further explore.

On Your Own Activities for Each Chapter

Chapter	Activity	Response/Journaling
Ch. 1 – Getting Started	*Take a quiet moment to think back on your experience with the guided meditation (GM). What message stood out to you? *Think of a person that you love. If you saw this person suffering, how would you try to help him or her? Would you do that for yourself? *Go to the dictionary and spend 15 min. looking for positive words. Come up with at least 25. Then, for 5 minutes every hour for 2 days, review the list. What did you notice?	
Ch. 2 – Tools for the Artist Within	*The Artist's Tools will enrich your life with greater peace, and a more positive attitude. Meditate on these tools for 5 min. Each day and you will notice a change in how you feel within yourself and in your world.	
Ch. 3 – Well-being and the NewMind View	*How many ideas can you generate for improving wellness in your life? *What strengths do you have right now for working toward wellness, and how can you implement them? *What is holding you back from being well and discovering the Masterpiece you have within you?	

Ch. 4 – Where We Get Stuck & How We Move On	*Spend some time thinking about what you have learned from your life experiences and how they have made you better. *How is your life better for your experiences? *Are there ways that the wisdom you have gained from your experiences can benefit others that are important to you in your life?	
Ch. 5 – Mapping My Journey	*Think about someone in your life whose values & qualities you have admired. Now, imagine yourself possessing those values and qualities. How would your life be different? *Think about the journey map you created. Hang it on your wall where you can see it every day. Notice the difference it made in how you think about your goals.	
Ch. 6 – Discovering the Artist Within	*Think about a time you did something important and meaningful to you. Imagine where you were and what you were doing. *Remember the feeling you had and visualize the joy that you experienced. *Take a mental snapshot of that moment. What can you do each day to recreate your feeling at that moment?	
Ch. 7 – Life Strategies for Well-being~Brain & Body	*Now that you know that you have personal rights in your life, how will it change how you see yourself and how you conduct your relationships? *Think about ways that you can begin to protect your personal rights without violating the rights of others. *How might the concepts of acceptance, forgiveness, self-compassion, commitment, & gratitude make a difference in your life?	

Ch. 8 – Emotional MindView Skills	*Consider a recent experience when your emotions seemed to be "over the top." What were the circumstances? *Can you identify a trigger for this emotion? *What actions did you take to calm down? *It isn't always easy to prepare ourselves for a strong emotional response. It isn't easy to anticipate emotional reactions. *With this in mind, how might you manage an unexpectedly strong emotion? *What environments trigger these emotions?	
Ch. 9 – Thinking MindView Skills	*In this chapter, we identified four personality subtypes for the expression of negative self-talk. (The Worrier, The Critic, The Victim, and The Perfectionist). Do you recognize any of these self-talk styles in your everyday thinking? *Can you recognize that these thoughts are not true, and can you choose a positive strength that moves you toward achieving your goals?	
Ch. 10 – Social MindView Skills	*In this chapter we mentioned an approach for solving a problem, called the 3-P Process: the first P is the Problem, the second P is what you Prefer, and the third P is what you propose. *Think of a problem that has come up and try out this formula. Remember to keep the emotion out of it, and to incorporate the other person's feelings into the suggestion you propose. *How did it go?	

Ch. 11 – Spiritual MindView Skills	*Can you think of any areas that might benefit from a gentler, kinder, and perhaps more spiritual approach to your decision-making or behavior? *Make a commitment to yourself to practice the Inner Guide guided meditation on a daily basis for one week. Journal your experience.	
Ch. 12 – The Observer & the Manager	*Think about a decision that you made recently that required that you choose between two possible solutions. *How did you go about making the decision? *What inner resources did you draw on to help you make it? How did it work out? *What could you have done differently?	
Ch. 13 – Living The Artfully Lived Life	*Thinking about the Ikigai Philosophy, how close do you think you come to being in the "Blue Zone?" *What is it that gives your life meaning & Purpose? *How do you demonstrate it in your life?	

References

Adams, G.R. (1996). A developmental social psychology of identity: Understanding the person-in-context. *Journal of Adolescence,* 19, 429-442, P. 69.

Amen, D. G. (1998). *Change your brain, change your life: The breakthrough program for conquering anxiety, depression, obsessiveness, anger, and impulsiveness.* New York: Three Rivers Press.

Amen, D. G. (2005). *Making a good brain great.* New York: Three Rivers Press.

Antonietti, et al. (2019). The role of spirituality and religiosity in subjective well-being of individuals with different religious status. Frontiers of Psychology. Vol. 10 doi 103389/fpsyg 2019.01525.

Antonovsky, A. (1987). *Unraveling the mystery of health: How people manage stress and stay well.* San Francisco: Jossey-Bass Publishers.

Antonovsky, A. (1993). The structure and properties of the sense of coherence scale. *Social Science and Medicine,* 36, 725-733.

Black, J. & Enns, G. (1997). *Better boundaries: Owning and treasuring your life.* Oakland, California: New Harbinger Publications, Inc.

Boudreaux, E. D., O'Hea, E., & Chasuk, R. (2002). Spiritual role in healing: An alternative way of thinking. *Primary Care,* 29, 439.

Bourne, E. J. (2010). *The anxiety and phobia workbook.* Oakland, California: New Harbinger Publications, Inc.

Canfield, J., Switzer, J. (2015). *The Success Principles*, How to get from where you are to where you want to be. New York: Harper Collins Publishers.

Canfield, J., & Hansen, M. V. (1993). *Chicken soup for the soul.* Deerfield Beach, Florida: Health Communications, Inc.

Cloud, H., & Townsend, J. (1992). *Boundaries: When to say yes, when to say no, to take control of your life.* Rapid City, Michigan: Zondervan.

Diamond, A. (2014). Understanding executive functions. www.research gate.net Publication 267509815

Diener, E., Wirtz, D., Tov, W., Kim-Prieto, C., Choi, D., Oishi, S. & Biswas-Diener, R. (2009). *New measures of well-being: Flourishing and positive and negative feelings.* Social Indicators Research, 39, 247-266.

Emmons, R. A. & Crumpler, C. A. (2002). Gratitude as a human strength: Appraising the evidence. *Journal of Social and Clinical Psychology*, 19, 15-69.

Enright, R. (2001). *Forgiveness is a choice: A step-by-step process for resolving anger and restoring hope.* Washington DC, APA Life Tools.

Fotuhi, M. (2003). *The memory cure: how to protect your brain against memory loss and Alzheimer's Disease.* New York: McGraw-Hill.

Frankl, V. E. (2006). *Man's search for meaning.* Boston, Massachusetts: Beacon Press.

Goldscheider, L. (1986). *Michelangelo Paintings, Sculpture, Architecture*. Phaidon Press: London.

Goleman, D. (1995). *Emotional intelligence.* New York: Bantam Books.

Goleman, D. (2006). *Social intelligence: The science of human relationships.* New York: Bantam Books.

Jeste, D. V., Ardelt, M., Blazer, D., Kramer, H. C., Vaillant, G. & Meeks, T. W. (2010). Expert consensus of characteristics of wisdom: A Delphi method study. *The Gerontologist*, 50, 668-680.

Kabat-Zinn, 1990. Mindfulness Based Stress Reduction, p. 27.

Kabat-Zinn, J. (1994). *Wherever you go, there you are: Mindfulness meditation in everyday life.* New York: Hyperion.

Kashdan, T. B., Ciarrochi, J. (Eds.). (2013). *Mindfulness, acceptance and positive psychology: the seven foundations of well-being.* Oakland, CA: New Harbinger Publications, Inc.

Keyes, C. L. M. (2002). The mental health continuum: From languishing to flourishing in life. *Journal of Health and Social Behavior*, 43, 207-222.

Keyes, C. L.M. (2010). The next steps in promotion and protection of positive mental health. *Canadian Journal of Nursing Research*, 42, 17-28.

Linehan, M. M. (1993). *Cognitive-behavioral treatment of borderline personality disorder.* New York: Guilford Press.

McQuaide, S., Ehrenreich, J., (1977) Assessing client strengths. www.semanticscholar.org., p.175.

National Sleep Foundation (www.sleepfoundation.org). p.85.

Nelson, N. (1997). *Dangerous relationships: How to identify and respond to seven warning signs of a troubled relationship.* Cambridge, Massachusetts: Perseus Publishing.

Norris, F. H. & Stevens, S. P. (2007). Community, resilience, and the principles of mass trauma intervention. *Psychiatry – Interpersonal and Biological Process*, 70, 320-328.

Okuzono, S.S., Kim, E.S., Shirai, K., Kondo, N., Fujiwara, T., Kondo, K., Lomas, T.,Trudel-Fitzgerald, C., Kawachi, I., andvVanderWeele, T. J., (2022). Ikigai and subsequent health and wellbeing among Japanese older adults: Longitudinal outcome-wide analysis. www.thelancet, 21, 1-14.

Park, S. H., & Sonty, N. (2010). Positive affect mediates the relationship between pain-related coping efficacy and influence in social functioning. *Journal of Pain,* 11, 1267-1273.

Payman, V., George, K., & Ryburn, B. (2008). Religiosity of depressed elderly in-patients. *International Journal of Geriatric Psychiatry,* 23, 16-21.

Rogers, C. R. (1961). *On becoming a person: A therapist's view of psychotherapy.* New York: Houghton Mifflin Co.

Rogers, D. R. B., Ei, S., Rogers, K. R., & Cross, C. L. (2007). Multi-component approach to cognitive-behavioral therapy using guided meditations, vibroacoustic therapy and cranial electrotherapy stimulation. *Complementary Therapy in Clinical Practice,* 13, 95-101.

Rogers, K. R., Hertlein, K., Rogers, D., & Cross, C. L. (2012). Guided visualization interventions on perceived stress, dyadic satisfaction, and psychological symptoms in highly stressed couples. *Complementary Therapy in Clinical Practice,* 18, 106-113.

Ryff, C. D., & Singer, B. D. (2001). Integrating emotions into the study of social relationships and health. In: C. D., Ryff & Singer, B. D. (Eds.), *Emotional, Social Relationships and Health.* New York: Oxford University Press.

Selye, H. (1978). *The stress of life.* New York: McGraw Hill.

Southwich, S. M. & Charney, D. S. (2012). *Resilience: The Science of Mastering Life's Greatest Challenges.* New York: Cambridge University Press.

Thomas, M. L., Bangen, K. J., Palmer, B. W., Martin, A. S., Avanzino, J. A., Depp, C. A., Glorioso, D., Daly, R. E. & Jeste, D. V. (2019). A new scale for assessing wisdom based on common domains and a neurobiological model: The San Diego Wisdom Scale (SD-Wise). *Journal of Psychiatry Research,* 108, 40-47.

Thomas, M. L., Palmer, B. N., Lee, L E. E., Daly, R., Tu, X. M., and Jeste, D. V., Abbreviated San Diego Wisdom Scale (SD-WISE-7). *Int. Psychogeriatrics*, 37, 617-626.

Wen, C. P., Wai, J. P. M., Tsai, M. K., Yang, Y. C., Chen, T. Y. D., Lee, M-C., Chan, H. T., Tsao, C. K., Tsai, S. P., & Wu, X. (2011). Minimum amount of physical activity for reduced mortality and extended life expectancy: A prospective cohort study. *The Lancet,* 378, 1244-1253.

Wigglesworth, C. (2014). *SQ21: The Twenty-One Skills of Spiritual Intelligence*. New York, Select Books.

Wilkes, I., Garip. G., Kotera, Y., and Fido, D. (2022). Can Ikigai predict anxiety, depression, and well-being? *International Journal of Mental Health and Addiction.* Doi.org/10.1007/s11469-022-00764-7.

Zohar, D. & Marshall I. (2004). *Spiritual Capital: Wealth We Can Live By*. New York: Berrett-Koeler Publishers, Inc.

Well-Being: The Artfully Lived Life ~ Journal Pages

Well-Being: The Artfully Lived Life ~ Journal Pages

Well-Being: The Artfully Lived Life ~ Journal Pages

Well-Being: The Artfully Lived Life ~ Journal Pages

Well-Being: The Artfully Lived Life ~ Journal Pages

Well-Being: The Artfully Lived Life ~ Journal Pages

About the Authors

Dr. Donna Rogers is a clinical psychologist and trained marriage and family therapist who has been working in the clinical field since 1986, or for the last approximately 35 years. She uses a holistic approach to treatment that includes Acceptance and Commitment Therapy, Mindfulness, Biofeedback, Vibroacoustic, and Binaural Sound Frequency-Enhanced Guided Meditation. The workbook, The Artfully Lived Life, was initially intended as a workbook to accompany therapeutic work for individuals who had experienced trauma and were suffering from Posttraumatic Stress Disorder.

Along with individual, couples, and family therapy, Dr. Rogers conducts wellness groups using this workbook's tried and true material. She has also written, recorded, and mastered over 40 guided meditations using a cognitive, behavioral, and acceptance and commitment therapy approach to address some of the more common issues, such as phobias, anxiety, low self-esteem, and negative self-talk. Her clients can take these exercises home and practice them between sessions. Dr. Rogers has published the findings of this work in a peer-reviewed publication: <u>Complementary Therapies in Clinical Practice</u>, Volume 13, pgs. 95-101.

Dr. Rogers is the founder of the Sound for Healing Institute. She is also one of the first psychologists to develop a multi-strategy program for treating the cognitive and emotional symptoms of anxiety, depression, trauma, and many other disorders by using the newest research in guided meditation, vibroacoustic technology, and binaural sound frequencies. She has worked extensively with the founder of Biopulsonics, who developed the sound technology she uses in her work.

Dr. Kim Rogers is a licensed Marriage and Family Therapist working with clients for the past 15 years. He is also a biochemist and neurotoxicologist. He is also a biochemist and neurotoxicologist.

He has published over 90 scientific papers and edited three books in the areas of membrane chemistry, biosensors, and, more recently, alternative therapies for stress management. His approach to therapy includes Acceptance and Commitment Therapy, Mindfulness, Biofeedback, Vibroacoustic, and Binaural Sound Frequency-Enhanced Guided Meditation. Dr. Rogers' approach to therapy focuses on presenting issues and the clients' pathway to well-being and greater life satisfaction. The Artfully lived Life Program encompasses this approach.

About the Author of the Foreword

    Dr. Maya McNeilly is a licensed clinical and health psychologist with 30+ years of clinical practice in integrative and mindfulness-based psychotherapy, along with research and teaching at Duke University Medical Center, Departments of Psychiatry and Integrative Medicine. She has published in the Journal of American Medical Association (JAMA), the Journal of Clinical and Consulting Psychology, Psychophysiology, and many other peer-reviewed scientific journals. She is currently an instructor at the Duke Integrative Medicine Mindfulness Based Stress Reduction Program, where she teaches and conducts research. She has also co-facilitated the Mindfulness training for Professionals at Duke with Dr. Jeffrey Brantley, founder of the Mindfulness-Based Stress Reduction Program at Duke University.

About the Artist

We have always been admirers of the art of Jeanine Downing, not only because she is my mother (KRR), but rather because we find it to transform the beautiful into the inspirational and the ordinary into the extraordinary. We are appreciative that she has graciously allowed us to include some of our favorite pieces in our book.

Jeanine was born and raised in Ogden, Utah. Her work is hanging in collections in such far away places as Denmark and Tasmania, as well as Maryland, Texas, Idaho, and the areas where she has lived (Utah, California, and Washington). Her work has won acclaim in the Sydney Art Gallery in Washington, the San Bernadino County Museum, and various invitational shows in Southern California.

In the artist's words, "I believe that art can uplift and inspire. It can amplify the beauty in life and find beauty in the ordinary. I wish for my art to be a reverent statement about the innocence of children, the elegance of flowers and the never-ending varieties of color and light. If someone wishes to own one of my paintings, I am ecstatic! I feel I have been able to share some of the beauty I see. That is why I paint."

"In telling you about my art, I could list teachers, awards, and honors, I doubt that you would be too interested. I could tell you about my own art students, some of whom have become fine artists themselves. I'll resist. I will let you know that my greatest reward is your enjoyment. If someone sees or feels beauty in my work, I am elated."

www.ingramcontent.com/pod-product-compliance
Lightning Source LLC
Chambersburg PA
CBHW060311240426
43661CB00059B/2730